Group Therapy:

A Behavioral Approach

Group Therapy:
A Behavioral Approach

SHELDON D. ROSE

University of Wisconsin

Prentice-Hall, Inc., Englewood Cliffs, New Jersey 07632

Library of Congress Cataloging in Publication Data

ROSE, SHELDON D
  Group therapy.

  Bibliography: p.
  Includes index.
  1. Group psychotherapy. 2. Behavior therapy.
I. Title.
RC488.R65   616.8'915   76-27689
ISBN 0-13-365239-4

© 1977 by Prentice-Hall, Inc., Englewood Cliffs, New Jersey 07632

Printed in the United States of America

10 9 8 7 6 5 4 3 2 1

Prentice-Hall International, Inc., *London*
Prentice-Hall of Australia Pty. Limited, *Sydney*
Prentice-Hall of Canada, Ltd., *Toronto*
Prentice-Hall of India Private Limited, *New Delhi*
Prentice-Hall of Japan, Inc., *Tokyo*
Prentice-Hall of Southeast Asia Pte. Ltd., *Singapore*
Whitehall Books Limited, Wellington, *New Zealand*

Contents

Preface

Therapy in groups has a long and respected history. Until recently groups have been used solely in the context of therapies with psychodynamic orientations. A new literature is presently emerging in which leaders, utilizing behavioral as well as small group principles, have demonstrated themselves to be highly effective group therapists. Although there has been a profusion of research and theoretical articles on various aspects of behavior therapy in groups, few books have emerged which set forward a comprehensive set of operational principles for the treatment of clients in groups. To fill the gap, this book has been written.

This volume is further designed to serve both as an introductory text to group therapy with a behavioral perspective *and* as a resource book for trained behavioral practitioners who have limited experience with groups. It will also be of use to group therapists with a psychodynamic orientation who wish to explore the possibilities of the behavioral approach as a supplement to their own.

As part of the behavioral tradition the author has limited the discussion to groups in which the target of intervention is the behavior of the clients. In most cases clients are taught within the group to generate new and more effective behaviors in situations where they had previously experienced stress or inadequacy. They are taught to discriminate among situations calling for different types of behavior.

As a part of the small group therapy tradition in the approach presented in this book the group is considered both the context and vehicle of individual behavior change. The author describes how the group attraction, interaction, and group norms are all incorporated into treatment plans in order to maximize this change.

As a part of the empirical tradition the author has given high priority to the integration of theory and research findings from behavioral and small group research into the practice model presented in this book. A wide variety of empirically tested procedures are presented which have been demonstrated to be useful under small group conditions. In order to develop a data based set of practice principles, it has been necessary to extrapolate from a wide variety of experiments both in therapy and in the laboratory. In some cases where no research could be found, we have been forced to draw on our extensive clinical experience as a guide to practice. Whenever possible, clinical experience should be merely a first step in the way to more systematic research as an improved basis for decision making.

The approach described here is applicable in wide variety of settings and with different presenting problems. The therapists tend to come from a variety of professional backgrounds. The book does limit itself to group therapy with adults. For examples and an analysis of behavior therapy in groups with children, the reader is referred to an earlier work of the author (Rose, 1972).

This book is divided into two parts. Part I, *Principles and Procedures,* presents the various steps a group therapist must take in order to assess problems of the clients, to monitor the problems, to design and implement a treatment plan, to utilize the group process, to effect the transfer and maintenance of behavioral change achieved in the group, and to evaluate the effectiveness of the treatment program. Although most of the procedures and concepts may be familiar to the experienced behavior therapists, the examples and principles of application are drawn primarily from the unique conditions of the small group.

Part II, Applications and Results, consists of the description of a series of clinical case studies on groups of parents, unassertive clients, institutionalized patients, overweight clients, couples and professionals. Each of these chapters describes the general approach as it is specifically applied to each of the given populations and problems involved in carrying out the program. In each chapter in Part II, descriptive and outcome data are also provided as a basis of comparison for group therapists working with similar groups.

As with most books, this volume would not have been written without the cooperation, encouragement, and assistance of many people. Although only some of them can be named, all played a significant part in the development of this book, and to all of them the author expresses his profound appreciation:

To Drs. Steven Schinke and Stanley Witkin, each of whom coauthored with me several of the chapters of this volume and who provided the research on which these chapters were based.

To Drs. Raymond Munts and Martin Loeb, former directors of the School of Social Work of the University of Wisconsin, who made the facilities of the School available and provided personal interest and encouragement.

To Dr. Barbara Brockway, my colleague at the School of Social Work and director of the Wisconsin Research and Therapy Institute, who made the laboratory facilities of her institute available and, of greater importance, provided me with her creative ideas and critical thinking.

To Ms. Patricia Estevez, who provided much of the editing in the development of the manuscript.

To Mary Jane Hamilton, Teresa Mayfield, and Jay Cayner, who helped me with the exacting task of putting the final touches and corrections on the manuscript.

To the entire secretarial staff of the School of Social Work, who provided many hours, often overtime, in typing and editing of the several manuscripts this book has undergone.

And finally, to my wife Cynthia Rose, who served as therapist for several of the groups, as trainer of the therapists of other groups, and, of far more importance, who provided me with the encouragement to persevere throughout the several years in which this book was evolving.

Although without any part of this assistance this book would never have been completed, it is I alone who must take the responsibility for its final content.

:

Part One
PRINCIPLES AND PROCEDURES

1 Behavior Therapy in Groups:

Introduction

Five men and four women, all in their twenties and thirties, are just completing relaxation exercises led by two therapists. Several of the group are now making themselves comfortable on the couch and chairs; others sit on the floor. Jane, one of the therapists, indicates that the group is ready to review the behavior of each member during the past week, so they take out the notes and charts they have been keeping.

Pete, who comes to the group because he has been unable to express his opinion when it differs from others, explains how he told his landlady that he could not accept a rent increase and that if she still demands it, he will leave. The members warmly praise him. Grinning with pride in response to their enthusiasm, he shows a chart of the daily estimates of his anxiety level. It has gone down this week, a breakthrough because it remained level the first few weeks he attended the group.

The group members continue to discuss the various happenings in their lives since they last met. Every time Mary contributes to the group conversation, a small green light goes on; an observer sitting behind a one-way mirror gathers data on her group participation. Mary's chart indicates that although her participation in the group is increasing, there has been little increase in the other situations. The group spends some time discussing Mary's in-group progress, and then another person speaks.

After each person explains what he or she has been doing about his or her problem during the week, the members pair off in a "buddy system" to develop treatment contracts. The contracts are written plans that state what each person intends to do during the following week. Each "buddy" serves as a consultant to his or her partner; every member reports to the group the plan he or she intends to follow.

Frank has a job interview lined up for the next week, so several members demonstrate how they think he should perform. He then role-plays what he might do in several circumstances, with Pete playing the role of the employer. Now Frank says he is less apprehensive of what lies ahead—he has had some good practice in the role-playing session and he knows the group is pulling for him.

Eileen, who joined the group because she can not complete or even work on her thesis, agrees to outline four pages of text before the next meeting. Several members recommend that if she fails to complete the outline, she pay each member one dollar. Eileen agrees, laughing about the loan she may have to float.

And so the session continues. The group discusses, and adjusts, each plan. When this is completed, they evaluate in writing this week's session; then each member makes an appointment to see or call his or her partner during the week. Most help themselves to coffee and cookies, and chat with each other before departing.

BEHAVIOR THERAPY

This is a book about behavior therapy of adults in small groups. Behavior therapy is the process of changing behavior with a set of therapeutic methods based on experimentally established principles of learning (Franks, 1969). Although its basic roots lie in experimental psychology, it also derives knowledge from a wide variety of other empirical disciplines. As you have observed in the above example, behavior therapy aims at changing specific behaviors. Behaviorally oriented group therapy commonly deals with behavioral problems that involve interaction with others. Examples include approaching others, developing conversation skills, establishing friendships, reducing social anxiety, increasing certain kinds of affectual responses while reducing others, and increasing refusal responses when appropriate. But almost all problems amenable to individual therapy also can be dealt with in a group since the majority of such problems have social interactive components. Most fears, for example, are at least partly maintained by social events, such as the attention of others. Individual behaviors such as smoking, excessive eating, or drug addiction often occur under the control of or at least in the presence of other persons.

By concentrating on specific behaviors as the targets of change, the behavior therapist de-emphasizes the relevance of early life histories. The therapist places less emphasis on subjective experience, insight, and general attitude than does the psychotherapist, and gives no attention to dreams.

The behavior therapist regards those behaviors about which the client expresses concern as *the* problem; they are not symptomatic *of* the problem. Successful resolution of the problematic behaviors resolves the problem; it does not, the therapist assumes, automatically lead to a new array of problems. Moreover, he or she assumes that the problematic way of behaving has been learned according to laws of learning and that new, more effective behaviors can be learned following the same laws. The therapist primarily draws upon intervention derived from learning theory, such as reinforcement, shaping, modeling, rehearsal, relaxation training, and desensitization. But he or she also may intervene with procedures derived from other theoretical frameworks as long as their effectiveness is evaluated in terms of attaining change goals. For this reason the behaviorist closely follows the progress of the client prior to, during, and following all interventions. This provides data to evaluate the effectiveness of treatment, and it supplies both therapist and client with continuous feedback about their progress. The behavior therapist is both a clinician and a scientist who constantly provides data for testing the efficacy of his or her procedures, while continually drawing upon the best available research to select those procedures.

In Small Groups

Not all therapy can or should occur in the context of the therapist-client dyad. Often there are definite advantages to using the group: it not only is the situation in which change occurs; at the same time it also may be the means of effecting those changes. Because most problems are social-interactional in nature, the presence of other clients provides an opportunity for practicing new social-interactional skills with peers in a protected setting. The group more nearly simulates the real world of most clients. The situation consisting solely of a high status therapist and a low status client does not reflect the reality of the client's everyday life. As such, the group provides the client an intermediate step between performing a newly learned behavior in a therapy setting and transferring that performance to the community.

The group gives the client an opportunity to learn and practice many behaviors as he or she responds to the constantly changing group demands. The client must learn to deal with the idiosyncracies of other individuals. He or she must learn to offer other clients feedback and advice, as a result, developing important skills for leadership. By helping others, the client usually learns to help him- or herself more effectively than when he or she is the sole recipient of therapy.

In group interaction, powerful norms arise that serve to control the behavior of individual members. If these norms (informal agreements among members as to preferred modes of action and interaction in the group) are introduced and effectively maintained by the therapist, they serve as efficient therapeutic tools (see Lawrence and Sundel, 1972, for examples of how such norms are used in behavioral group therapy). The group pressures deviant members to conform to such norms as attending regularly, reinforcing peers who do well, analyzing problems systematically and specifically, and assisting peers with their problems. Of course, if the therapist is not careful, anti-therapeutic norms also can be generated. In some groups, norms indicated by such behaviors as erratic attendance, noncompletion of agreed-upon assignments, and constant criticism of therapists work against the attainment of therapeutic goals.

To guard against such problems, the therapist can call upon a vast body of experimentally derived knowledge about norms and other group phenomena in which individual behavior both influences and is influenced by the various attributes of the group (see Cartwright and Zander, 1968, for an extensive summary). In addition to modifying the norms of the group, the therapist can facilitate the attainment of both individual and group treatment goals by such procedures as modifying the cohesiveness of the group, the status pattern, or the communication structure in the group. Much of the power of group therapy is lost if negative group attributes remain unbridled.

Another characteristic of behavior therapy unique to groups is the opportunity for peer reinforcement. Each person is given the chance to learn or to improve his or her ability to mediate rewards for others in social interactive situations (with spouse, family, friendship groups, work group). The therapist can construct a situation in which each person has frequent opportunity, instructions, and even rewards for reinforcing others in the group. Reinforcement is a highly valued skill in our society; there is good reason to believe that as a person learns to reinforce others, he or she is reciprocally reinforced by others, and mutual liking also increases (see Lott and Lott, 1962).

More accurate assessment can be another major contribution of group therapy. Lazarus (1966) points out "that many facets of a problem which elude the scrutiny of even the most perspicacious therapist often become clearly delineated during or after an intensive group discussion." The group provides the client with a major source of feedback about what in his or her behavior is annoying to others, and what makes him or her attractive. This is helpful especially when clients cannot pinpoint their own problems. A very important fringe benefit: the group provides a natural laboratory for learning discussion skills that are essential to good social relationships.

In addition to facilitating assessment, the group allows the therapist to use an abundance of therapeutic procedures that are either unavailable or less efficacious in the therapeutic dyad. Among these procedures is the use of group reinforcement, which is somewhat more powerful than individual reinforcement (see Wodarski, and others 1971). Other advantages of the group include an abundance of models, role-players for behavioral rehearsal, manpower for monitoring, and partners for use in a "buddy system."

Since the group supplies so many of its own therapeutic needs and gives simultaneous treatment to a number of people, this type of therapy appears to be less costly than individual treatment in terms of staff and money. However, this is an empirical question for which little data exist. Of course, the criterion of cost should be evaluated in terms of successful outcomes maintained over time.

Finally, the group serves as a control on the therapist's value imposition. Clients in groups appear to be less accepting of the arbitrary values imposed by therapist action than patients in dyads. A group of people can more easily disagree with the therapist than can the individual. The group therapist is constantly forced by group members to make his or her values explicit.

CLIENTS, STAFF, AND CLINICAL SETTINGS

The types of groups reported on in this book include assertive training or social skills workshops, parent training, communication training in multicouples groups, weight control groups, institutional groups, and group supervision and/or staff-training groups. There is no difference in the general format between the training groups and the more therapy oriented groups. In the latter case, the focus is on the client's learning behaviors to cope more effectively with his or her social and physical environment. In the former groups, the trainees learn behaviors to deal more effectively with their children or their clients. In both cases, the laws of learning are the same. The differences lie in the specific behavioral targets; even in this area, there is often overlapping (for example, learning to be more reinforcing with other people).

The clients or group members come from all walks of life. They range in age from 17 to 65, and their education is from less than eighth grade to Ph.D.s and M.D.s. The assertive training groups in the author's experience have worked with people on welfare, housewives, students, blue collar workers, unemployed, secretarial staffs, and professionals. In the parent training group, the clients have similar employment categories, as do the obesity control groups. In the communication training for couples, almost everyone was middle class. In the institutional setting, the members primarily were from the lower economic classes, although some were from the middle class. And in the supervisory groups, most of the members were professional social workers.

This book is limited to a discussion of the application of behavior therapy and training in and with groups of adults, drawing primarily from experience and research concerning adults. Although the principles of learning are the same for children as for adults, some of the engineering problems are unique. For example, the lack of availability of external controls on self-reporting and self-monitoring is often a greater problem with adults than with children, whose parents, teachers, siblings, or classmates often serve as monitors. Discovering what is reinforcing to adults is often more difficult than with children. In the literature, some procedures such as systematic desensitization and thought stopping seem to be more frequently utilized with adults than with children, whereas others such as group reinforcement are used almost solely with children. Moreover, in an earlier book by the author (Rose, 1972), the focus was on the application of the principles of behavior therapy to groups of children.

The examples and results of groups reported in this book have been organized under the Group Therapy and Research Project of the School of Social Work of the University of Wisconsin. The project staff works in cooperation with the Wisconsin Behavior Research and Training Institute of the University of Wisconsin. Although many groups were recruited through and conducted directly in the School of Social Work, most were organized and carried out in settings outside of the university. Among those settings cooperating with the project were two family service agencies, a mental health clinic, the county department of social services, a private medical clinic, an association for mental retardation, a colony for the retarded, a nursing home for the elderly, and a state hospital for the mentally ill.

The therapists of the groups either have been staff of the agency or advanced graduate students placed in the given agency for field work in social work, residency in psychiatry, or psychology internship. Their participation in the project was on the basis of having received or receiving concurrently behavioral supervision concerning their leadership of a treatment group. All the therapists had received training in behavior modification prior to their work with a group and were receiving a more specific course in behavior modification in groups.

Therapist Activities

The first section of this book is organized around the activities of the therapist. At least nine major categories of therapist activities universally found in behaviorally oriented group therapy can be identified. Although there is some degree of overlapping, each category is different enough to describe separately. These categories include organizing the group, orienting the members to the group, establishing group attraction, assessing the problem and possibilities for resolving it, monitoring the behaviors determined as problematic, evaluating the progress of treatment, planning for and implementing specific change procedures, modifying group attributes, and establishing transfer and maintenance programs for behavior changes occurring in the group. Obviously, each category consists of a series of still more specific activities, some of which will be described in the following sections.

BEGINNING THE GROUP

In the beginning the therapist focuses on three major activities: organizing the group, orienting the clients, and building group attraction. Organizational activities involve decision-making about type of group, size and duration of group, length of meetings, number of therapists, location of meetings, nature of fees and/or deposits, and similar structural concerns. During the pregroup interview and in the first session, the group members may be involved in some of these decisions, such as when and where the group is to meet and the length of meetings. They also may help to decide whether new members should be added. In the pregroup interview each client decides whether the therapist's description of the group's focus adequately meets what he or she perceives to be his or her needs.

Orientation refers to those activities in which the therapist informs the client of the group's purposes and content, and the responsibilities of the clients to themselves and to the others. It also involves the process of negotiating the content of the general treatment contract. In the process of orientation, the therapist is the major contributer. He or she provides information and case studies as examples. As seen in Table 1.1, the major therapist activities of the pretreatment interview and the first session are concerned with orientation. Building group attraction focuses on increasing the attraction of the group members to each other, to the therapist, and to the content of the program. It involves using methods such as introduction games, specially designed communication exercises, and activities such as role-playing, which also are used for assessment or orientation as well as other purposes. Assessment, monitoring, and evaluation are also a part of beginning the group, but because these activities continue throughout treatment and are so central to the approach to this type of therapy, these are discussed under a separate section.

Assessment, Monitoring, and Evaluation

Assessment is the group activity concerned with determining the problem to be modified and the resources of the individual and his or her environment that will facilitate remediation of the problem. Although assessment begins at the very first meeting, it is constantly refined and added to throughout treatment. In the pregroup interview and early in treatment, members are encouraged to present the reasons they have come to the group. Clients are taught to define their problems in terms of directly observed behaviors. Feelings or attitudes of a problem may be inferred from directly observed behavior or verbal descriptions of these inner states. The group members are taught how to help each other to specify the behavioral content and the conditions impinging on it in each problem. They also learn to identify with each other the behavioral, social, physical, institutional, and economic assets they can use to resolve their problems.

Behaviors, once defined, are systematically observed and measured in some way by the client and by others, if possible, prior to the application of any explicit change procedure. The data collected at this time are called "baselines." Group members often help each other in establishing them. The process of data collection is carried out throughout treatment and is concluded only at the follow-up interview. The design of data collection instruments and the process of data collection are refered to as "monitoring."

The therapist uses the data as it is collected to evaluate the effectiveness of specific treatment procedures, meetings, and the course of therapy. Effectiveness is determined on the basis of whether the goals of a given technique, a given meeting, or a given therapy have, indeed, been achieved. If it is discovered that the format of a given meeting has been partially or totally unsuccessful (because of the high frequency of critical comments on the session's evaluation, low participation in the meeting, and failure of most members to complete their weekly assignments), the format can be changed. Changes thus are brought about by a review of data, not unsubstantial hunches. Because of the abundance of data and the regularity of feedback, change procedure can be initiated as soon as the problem occurs and is identified.

The therapist also evaluates whether the group treatment is correlated with the achievement of individual treatment goals. By keeping a record the therapist and others with whom he or she shares the data can ascertain what kind of clients can best use the procedures commonly found in various models of group therapy. Each therapist can expand the knowledge base further if he or she establishes research controls. In behavior therapy, if all treatment steps are followed and explicated, the total treatment of each group and each client can be viewed as an experiment in which the client and group are observed before, during, and after treatment. Variations of this time series model without a control group have been suggested by a number of authors (Sidman, 1960; Campbell and Stanley, 1963) to strengthen the conclusion of a causal connection between treatment and outcome. Such designs as the multiple-baseline, the ABAB model, and other time series designs (see Leitenberg, 1973) are especially suited to small samples. In some instances, agencies also have found ways to use contrast or control groups in the more classical before-after with control group design (Selltiz and others, 1959), in spite of the difficulties involved in random assignment of clients to two or more conditions.

Treatment Planning and Implementation

Treatment planning involves choosing from a number of highly specific procedures that have been demonstrated to be related to achieving behavioral change goals. Most procedures are derived from operant and respondent conditioning and modeling theories. Reinforcement, shaping, extinction, and time out from reinforcement are examples of operantly derived procedures commonly used in group treatment. Most of these are used with group as well as with individual behavior. Systematic desensitization, used either with individuals in the group or with the whole group, is an example of a commonly used respondent conditioning procedure. The presentation of high status models, the reinforcement of models in the presence of the imitator, and the use of role-played model presentations are examples of procedures used in group treatment that are derived from modeling theory. These procedures lend themselves especially well to the group treatment situation because of the need for extra role-players and models who receive reinforcement in the treatment situation.

Procedures derived from other theoretical or technical points of view also are used, primarily in determining the problem or achieving behavioral change. From the group dynamics technology, role-playing for purposes of determining the problem, recapitulation, brainstorming, subgrouping, buzz sessions, the fishbowl, and a wide variety of other group discussion techniques often are used in behavioral group treatment. A therapist may use a number of didactic procedures, such as lectures, quizzes, and exercises, as a means of presenting information or the experiences of others to the group members and monitoring whether it has been learned. Cognitive procedures such as relabeling and systematic problem-solving are important tools for the behavioral therapist.

The therapist uses weekly behavioral contracts as a means of making clear what the expectations are for each client during the week. This is an important technique, since the major part of treatment activity occurs outside of the group. To facilitate this "homework" still further, each client works with at least one other client as mutual observer, reinforcer, or in some other designated role calling for the buddy system.

By midpoint in its meeting schedule, the group is focusing on reaching agreement on the following week's activities, preparing to carry out those activities, and monitoring at the beginning of the meeting the degree to which assignments have been completed. In preparation for the assignment, extensive use is made of role-playing demonstrations, social reinforcement, behavioral rehearsal, contingency contracts, and many of the other procedures already mentioned.

The therapist is concerned not only with achieving individual treatment goals, but he or she also is engaged in activities that promulgate the attainment of group goals. Those activities are referred to as "modifying group attributes." In treating clients in groups, the therapist will note that group attributes affect the process of attaining treatment goals whether the therapist wants them to or not. For this reason the group therapist must take steps to create those group conditions that facilitate rather than hinder goal achievement. Procedures derived from both operant and small group theory are used to improve interpersonal relationships among the members, to create therapeutic norms that will facilitate broad participation by all members, to improve the rank of low status members, and to decrease domination by an overly assertive subgroup. It is these activities that most clearly distinguish group therapy from individual therapy.

Transfer and Maintenance of Behavioral Change

Transfer of change includes those interventions designed to facilitate the transfer of learning occurring in the treatment situation to the real world of the client. There are two major types of procedure for transfer of change. The first is such intragroup procedures as the rehearsal, which simulates the real world and represents a step toward performance outside the group and the behavioral assignment in which the client tries out the rehearsed behavior in the community. Other extragroup techniques, such as meeting in the homes of the clients and using the buddy system outside of the group, represent examples of the second type of procedure to facilitate transfer.

Maintenance of change refers to activities oriented toward maintaining the goal level of behavior achieved during the course of treatment. Several techniques are used. Among them are the gradual fading of the treatment procedures, thinning of the reinforcement schedule, and overlearning the new behavior.

In preparing for termination, the attraction of the group is reduced relative to other groups. Members are encouraged to join nontherapeutic groups; greater reliance is placed on the decisions of the clients; and members perform the major leadership tasks. The role of the therapist shifts from direct leader to consultant. These activities not only serve to make termination easier on the client, but they teach him or her to function independently of a therapist. And this independence is necessary for the maintenance of changes occurring in the group and ease in dealing with new problems should and when they happen. It should be noted that preparation for the transfer and maintenance of change is found throughout treatment. As early as the fourth meeting in the following example, partners are working with each other outside of the group, rehearsal is occurring within the group, and behavioral assignments are given to practice the desired behavior outside of the group.

Treatment Phase and Therapist Activity

The members of an assertive training group were seen individually by the therapist in a pregroup interview; then they met in 10 consecutive weekly group meetings and in one follow-up meeting three months after the weekly

Table 1.1   Therapist Activities in an Assertive Training Group.
(X = Occurrence in a Given Meeting of the Activity Indicated Below.)

Session	Organization	Orientation	Attraction	Assessment	Monitoring	Evaluation	Treatment	Group	Maintenance
Pregroup	X	X		X					
1	X	X	X	X	X	X			
2		X	X	X	X	X			
3			X	X	X	X		X	
4				X	X	X	X	X	
5				X	X	X	X	X	
6					X	X	X	X	X
7					X	X	X	X	X
8				X	X	X	X	X	X
9					X	X	X		X
10					X	X			X
Follow-up					X	X			X

sessions. The relation of therapist activity to phase can be seen in a content analysis of the agendas of those meetings in terms of the nine categories suggested earlier.

Although monitoring and evaluation are activities performed in every group meeting, sufficient variation is found among the remaining activities from one period to the next to suggest several phases of treatment. In the first phase the focus is on orientation, organization, building the attraction (cohesiveness) of the group, and assessment. In the middle sessions the focus is on treatment activities and modifying group attributes. The final sessions are devoted to planning for the transfer and maintenance of change. Even among these activities there is considerable overlapping from phase to phase. Nevertheless, this general format appears to be found commonly in all the groups described in this project, and it forms a natural way of organizing this book. Let us now look at the first three categories—organizing the group, orienting the clients, and building group attraction—included under the chapter heading "Beginning the Group."

2 Beginning the Group

The Eagle River mental health clinic is offering a social skills workshop each Tuesday, 8 to 10 P.M., for ten weeks. The group, consisting of no more than eight members, will be led by William Right and Sandy Hall. The focus of the group will be on helping persons:

> to talk up in groups,
> to make friends more easily,
> to enjoy social contacts,
> to say "no" when they should,
> to express feelings when appropriate,
> to date,
> and to deal with similar social situations.

ORGANIZATION

Before the above advertisement can be submitted to the agency clientele, the therapists involved must decide on a number of organizational details. Before treatment can begin, questions must be answered as to the size of the group, the frequency and length of meetings, the degree of similarity of members, the number of therapists, and the comparative merit of group and dyadic treatment for each client. Additional concerns include the type of group to be organized, recruiting policies, physical attributes of meetings, and organizational restraints to organizing a group. Although there is little data to guide these decisions, the therapist can rely on clinical experience and on principles extrapolated from research on optimal conditions of learning.

Group Size

How many clients should participate in a behavior therapy group? Several questions must be considered in making this decision. The first is the skill and experience of the therapist. The new and inexperienced therapist should work with a relatively small group (5 to 6 members); it is usually difficult for the new therapist to keep track of too many aspects of treatment simultaneously. The second question pertains to the complexity of treatment procedures to be used. When one treatment procedure, such as desensitization, is employed, a relatively large group of 10 to 12 members can be treated at one time. Greater diversity in presenting problems requires more individualized treatment plans. Under these conditions, it is necessary for even the experienced therapist to work with fewer members. A third question to consider is the number of therapists. Although a larger group obviously can be handled with two therapists, the author's preference is to split the group of 12 to 14 persons and have each therapist lead an independent subgroup.

The intake of the clinic where the group is being organized may also influence group size. For example, there may be no more than three clients at a given time available for treatment; it is imperative that the therapist consider the problems created by working with a group this small. One problem is cost, either to the client or the community. In addition, very small groups can cause special burdens for their members. If one or two people are absent, group interaction suffers a dampening effect. Moreover, the smaller the group the greater the pressure on each member to participate. Thus, small groups (for example, 2 to 3 members) should be avoided by clients with extremely high levels of social anxiety. (When there are too few clients to form a workable group, it is best to wait until more members are available.)

On the basis of six years experience with assertive training groups, Lazarus (1966) advises that 8 to 10 members is the ideal number. He states that a group with fewer than six members tends to become sluggish because of insufficiently diversified opinion, and groups exceeding 10 in number tend to be rather cumbersome. Most other authors working in the area of anxiety management seem to agree (see, for example, Lewinsohn and others, 1970; Brinkman and others, 1973).

The anxiety management groups in the author's experience usually have ranged from 4 to 8 members. Weight loss and other self-control groups have included from 5 to 10 clients. And parent training groups ranged from 3 to 11, with the average close to 7 members per group.

In summary, although no particular number of members is ideal for all groups, a decision readily can be made if the therapist considers the homogeneity of the presenting problem, the participation of a coleader, the experience of the leaders, and the agency intake practices. In most cases, the best range appears to be between 6 and 9 persons per group.

As we said earlier, another decision in setting up a group concerns the number of therapists. Even in the absence of research indicating that two therapists are better than one, most groups have two. Each therapist can act as a control on the behavior of the other, reducing the tendency to stray to pet subjects that are not entirely relevant. With two therapists, a proclivity toward unsystematic reinforcement can be offset, and preparation is usually more stringent. However, on occasion power struggles do occur between co-therapists. Sometimes each therapist tends to add constantly to the statements of his or her cotherapist; such back-to-back talking reduces the opportunity, as well as the zeal, of the members to participate. For this reason, when there are two therapists, one is usually assigned the major role, and the second becomes the cotherapist. This provides excellent training for a relatively inexperienced cotherapist. However, since two therapists increase the cost of treatment, experienced group therapists eventually should consider working alone.

Number, Frequency, and Length of Sessions

Little has been written about the appropriate number of group sessions. Most of the parent groups in the Group Research and Training Project at the University of Wisconsin varied in length from 6 to 18 sessions. Just as in the case of group size, frequency of meetings is determined by a number of factors. The first is the education of the clients. In the parent training groups, the college-educated participants seemed to learn the basic skills more quickly than did parents with high school educations or less (Rose, 1974a). However, in the treatment of phobias and other anxiety-related problems, no differences appeared to exist as a result of education. Another factor that played a role was the clarity of the presenting problem. When parents had highly specific complaints, they needed relatively short treatment periods (7 to 8 sessions) to attain the "goal." With highly anxious clients, more time is required to attain treatment goals. For the anxiety management groups in the author's experience, 12 sessions were not enough. Brinkman and others, (1973) required 25 sessions to treat a heterogeneous group of highly anxious clients. Lazarus reports treating similar patients in about 18 sessions. Beyond that, he claims, the meetings become dull and repetitious (an observation with which the author agrees).

In self-control groups such as those concerning weight loss or smoking, although substantial improvement occurs in as few as six sessions, original eating and smoking habits tend to return quite quickly unless there is a long follow-up treatment period. It would seem, at least for weight control groups, that following the initial 6 to 8 weekly meetings, monthly or bimonthly sessions for another six months may be necessary to maintain the quick achievement of the first sessions.

In treating more complex sets of problems, the trend is toward an increased number of meetings. Some therapists are allowing the achievement of goals to dictate the number of meetings for each person. As a client achieves the goals he or she sets and designs a plan for the maintenance of the behaviors that have been learned, he or she leaves the group. In this type of open group, new members are introduced as old members leave. The advantages of this particular structure are that experienced models always are available to the new members and the length of treatment is individualized. However, it is the author's observation that goals tend to be achieved in the time allotted to them. And in an open group, the tendency is for clients to remain longer than necessary, increasing the cost of treatment. Another disadvantage is the complexity of treating six or more persons who are in different phases of treatment. In summary, each therapist after reviewing the complexity of the problems, the homogeneity of the group, the specificity of the complaint, and his or her own experience then determines the appropriate number of meetings. In most cases, it will be between 10 and 18 sessions.

Other questions of importance pertain to the frequency of group meetings and their length. Most groups meet weekly for the convenience of the therapists and sometimes the clients. However, meeting twice a week for the first two or three weeks, then weekly for another three or four sessions seems ideal. This schedule gradually fades to once every two weeks, once a month, and then a follow-up session six months after the last.

The reason for frequent meetings in the beginning is to facilitate monitoring of the behavioral assignments. Because of the inexperience of the clients, a week without therapeutic contact usually results in a predictable pattern: compliance to the self-imposed assignments at the beginning of the week; increasing failure toward the end. This can be dealt with partly by contacting clients during the week by telephone, but in the initial meetings assignments for a shorter duration more likely would be completed. As the clients gain skills in carrying out assignments, longer time periods can be used. Two-week and one-month assignments gradually facilitate independent functioning, an important step in learning to deal with problems long after treatment has ended.

Length of meetings varies from one to three hours; most groups meet for two hours, with a 10-minute break between each hour. Larger groups tend to use more time than do small groups, although this is not always the case. But no matter how much time is allotted, it rarely appears to be enough unless the leader holds tightly to the agenda.

Group Composition

How varied in education and socioeconomic class can the members of the group be and still function as a group? Best results, according to Lazarus (1968), who bases his judgment on his extensive experience, are achieved when group members are of the same sex and not too diversified in other areas, such as educational and social backgrounds. The author's own experience, however, does not bear this out. Mothers on welfare successfully modified more behaviors when working in groups of both welfare and middle-class mothers than when working only with other welfare mothers. And there was no cost in the tempo of learning to the middle-class mothers (Rose, 1974a). Diversity in education also appeared to be no barrier to attaining training goals in groups consisting solely of middle-class parents. In some groups the education ranged from as low as tenth grade to as high as a Ph.D. and M.D. without creating group problems or impediments to learning.

Subgroups of persons who knew each other prior to treatment have presented problems. On occasion they have formed cliques that have excluded those with no previous connection. This problem, however, readily has been resolved by discussing it with the group members in terms of its relevance for achieving group goals. (See Chapter 10 for a discussion on how to alter goal-hindering subgroups.)

Homogeneously composed groups have members with the same or similar problems. Heterogeneously composed groups are those whose members have diverse problems. The composition of most groups lies somewhere between the two. For example, in a group with all members deficient in assertive responses in social situations, one client may need to learn grooming skills, another self-control in respect to eating, another control of depressions, and so on. For this reason, one rarely, if ever, observes a group homogeneous in all respects or even in respect to the presenting problem.

Groups composed of persons with similar problems offer the advantage of one common treatment procedure, resulting in a clear savings of time. The most frequent example has been the use of group desensitization to reduce the fear and avoidance responses to common objects or situations. Paul (1966) treated the fear of public speaking in groups by desensitizing all the members at the same time, and Ihli and Garlington (1969) desensitized test anxiety in small groups in the same way. He discovered that desensitization was as effective with groups as it was with individuals, but groups provided a large savings in therapist time.

In addition to the treatment of common phobias in groups, some authors report the successful use of the group in the treatment of smokers (Marrone, Merksamer, and Salzberg, 1970), of excessive eaters (Wollersheim, 1970), of alcoholics (Miller and Nawas, 1970), of depressives (Killian, 1970, and Lewinsohn, Weinstein, and Alper, 1970), and of hysterics (Kass, Silver, and Abroms,

1972). A number of authors report on the successful treatment in groups of clients who were deficient in assertive responses (see, for example, Rathus, 1972, 1973a; Brockway, Brown, McCormick, and Resneck, 1972; Hedquist and Weinhold, 1970; and Rose, 1975). In most of these groups, a large number of diverse procedures were required because of the complexity of the problems.

Homogeneously composed groups can offer some major disadvantages, however. First, the therapist is restricted to dealing primarily with the behaviors around which the group was organized. More serious problems unearthed after therapy begins may not be treated in the absence of available time, agreement with other clients, or structure for such treatment. Moreover, because there is usually a self-selection based on the acknowledgement by the client that he or she has a problem in a given area, assessment is quite limited. Although this, too, represents a savings in time to the therapist, it may result in the treatment of a less relevant problem.

The heterogeneously composed group exposes each member to a number of people who do not have his or her problem and others who may have overcome a similar difficulty. Thus, the member is provided with diverse points of view and recommendations for treatment from which he or she can choose. Alternately, most members also are provided with an opportunity to give help to someone else, stepping occasionally from the role of client to that of therapist. And perhaps most important, the member of the heterogeneous group is confronted with procedures for solving a broad range of problems. No matter how effective therapy may be, new problems eventually will occur. Because the client has observed the treatment of many problems (albeit of other clients), he or she is able more readily to generalize that learning to the new problem situation as it develops. (See Chapter 11 for a further discussion of this principle.) There is at least one reported study in which certain advantages of the heterogeneously composed group has been demonstrated. In treating groups of adults on a psychiatric ward, Fairweather (1964) discovered that on the basis of the chronicity of their problems, patients in the heterogeneously composed groups were both more productive and problem-focused in their discussion than were patients in the homogeneously composed groups.

Most of the models discussed in this book are composed of clients who have similar problems, such as shyness, obesity, professional behavioral deficits, and lack of certain parental skills. When one assists them to spell out the specific behavior under these common rubrics, one finds that there is great diversity in the concrete presenting problem. Thus, the models presented here tend to find a balance between heterogeneity and homogeneity of the presenting problem.

Group Versus Dyadic Treatment

Prior to composing the group, the therapist must decide whether group therapy is preferable to individual treatment for each potential member. One way to determine this is by asking the applicant in the assessment interview about his or her previous group experiences in therapy and in social-recreational groups. Clients with histories of persistent failure in groups are less likely to make effective use of this type of therapy. Equally important, of course, is the preference of the client. Whenever possible, the client should be allowed to choose the context of therapy. If within a given agency or clinic no choice is available, the therapist should be aware of individual therapy possibilities in other agencies or from private practitioners.

Observing group treatment or talking about it with other clients before commitment is a comfortable first step for some clients. If an ongoing group is available for observation, it will demonstrate to the client the characteristics as well as the openness of the method. For these reasons, it is recommended that this opportunity be made available to *all* clients.

Following the prospective client's observation of a session, he or she should feel free to ask the participants about the group. This also is helpful to the ongoing participants in reaffirming their own treatment and group goals. It also saves time in therapy since many problems of orientation are solved early in treatment. If the client elects to forego the group therapy, the therapist should guide him or her to other available means of treatment.

Recruitment

Once it has been ascertained that a number of clients may be available for group treatment, the therapist normally determines the type of group he or she is going to organize. This usually centers around the problems about which incoming patients are complaining. For those agencies whose intake is limited, a broadly heterogeneous group might result. For this reason, groups also are organized around problems in which the agency or therapist is interested, has adequate skills, and for which there is a documented community need. Agency staff and referring sources are then informed that such groups dealing with problems of self-control, unassertiveness, and a deficit of parenting skills are available.

To assure adequate intake, groups can be organized around themes being publicized in local newspapers. When there is a rash of articles concerning a specific problem, such as being overweight or the dangers of smoking, people throng to treatment facilities. More innovative organizers have encouraged the media to publicize those topics for which agency interest and staff competence existed. For example, by contacting a special feature writer, DeLange's (1977) Assertive Training for Women project was covered in the local paper. (Since advertising for participants for groups is sponsored by nonprofit organizations, and since these groups charge no fee and the program also provides training and research possibilities, no breach of current psychological ethics is involved.) Following the article, DeLange received numerous applicants.

Thoreson and Potter (1973) advise the behavioral group counselor actively to recruit members. On college campuses, they suggest that the counselors visit classes and dormitories, explaining the group to students. They also recommend putting announcements in the campus paper. The following ad produced over 50 calls in three days for them.

"Lonely? Trouble making friends? Group starting soon. Call ————." All of the researchers in comparative group studies in the Group Research and Training Project utilized both posters and advertisements. Many of the other assertive training and parent groups in the project were organized in the same way. To Thoreson and Potter's list might be added the activity of visiting agencies that serve other populations but do not provide the specific skill training offered by behavioral groups. For example, the author has spoken to staff of a family service agency, a protective services program, a court services program, to groups of pediatricians and general practitioners, and to parent-teacher groups about the values and possiblities of parent groups. After each talk, one or more parent groups were formed. The agencies often cooperated with the group treatment project by providing the space and the intake for the groups. In some cases the agencies organized groups led by their own staff. And two agencies recruited recent graduates as staff members to organize and lead such groups in the agency or clinic.

Another approach is simply to ascertain the problems most common in the population one is serving and to organize groups around these central themes. In the university clinic, dating groups, test anxiety groups, study skills groups, sexual counseling in groups, and weight loss and smoking groups probably would fill up very quickly. In a family service clinic, parent training groups, multicouple or multifamily groups, sexual counseling, divorce counseling, and anxiety management groups would do likewise.

Location and Physical Attributes of Meetings

Most meetings take place at the sponsoring agency or, if there is a distinction, the referring agency. However, we are beginning to increase the use of settings that serve as more natural laboratories for the behaviors we are trying to teach. For example, some meetings of a dating group were held at a dance, others at a bar. The adolescent delinquents spent part of their meetings wandering around department stores where they previously had shoplifted. Alcoholics spent one meeting at a bar sipping soft drinks while talking to those who drank harder beverages. Residents of treatment homes who were in a transitional group spent group meetings shopping and participating in a wide number of recreational and self-maintenance activites. Weight-loss groups spent several meetings eating out together.

Most therapists advocate that initial conditions should be as attractive and comfortable as possible to attract and keep members. But as the group progresses, one would gradually do away with the comfortable meeting room and simulate as nearly as possible the type of social situations in which the clients will find themselves following their treatment. These include the living rooms of homes, community center meeting rooms, restaurants, bowling alleys. Liberman (1970, p. 158), however, found no differences in group interaction between bleak, ascetic rooms and warm, comfortable ones.

Organizational Restraints

Groups are not organized in a vacuum. They are usually part of a larger institutional or clinic structure. If the clinic has a history of both small group and behavior therapy, the organization of new groups rarely presents a problem. In most clinics, however, either or both of these approaches are new. And in the case with many innovations, they often result in disinterest, lack of cooperation, and/or excessive criticism among those staff members whose status is based on their skills in other approaches. A common strategy is to introduce the innovation as an experiment and incorporate other staff members into its planning. If possible, include a comparative group in which the prevailing mode of treatment is carried out. This step provides a firm basis for evaluating the usefulness of the program to the agency.

There may be particular agency policies that restrict the practices of the behavior therapy group. In some behavior therapy groups, we sometimes use a partial fee rebate as an incentive to complete group assignments and to attend regularly. In many agencies, the fee collection practices do not allow for such rebates. Even the use of deposits may not be permitted. The agency may have rules about contact among clients outside of the agency. This would restrict the use of the buddy system. Some agencies require that all meetings be held in the agency, a condition that would delimit the transfer of change (see Chapter 13). None of these rules is so restrictive as to render a group program inoperable. Usually after an initial demonstration project, it is possible to lobby for more flexible rulings in the areas that restrain the behavior group therapist.

Groups readily lend themselves to observation either through a one-way mirror or by observers sitting in the room. As a result colleagues and supervisors can be invited to observe meetings and to review data of demonstration projects as a means of incorporating them into agency practice. Observation also can be used for staff training.

Once the group is organized, the therapist(s) must take two important steps to get the group started. The first is orienting the clients; the second is building group attraction, or cohesiveness.

ORIENTATION

The prospective client usually knows very little about behavioral programs. For the most part he or she has heard about psychotherapies only in the media, in novels, and from friends. For this reason each potential client must be informed fully about what he or she can expect in the way of treatment. The client must be helped to decide on the basis of his or her own expectation whether behavior therapy in groups is what he or she wants. Both in a pretreatment interview and in a first group meeting, the purposes of group therapy and its program and procedures are clearly delineated.

To further this explication, in the first meeting previous members of similar groups may be invited to explain what they did as group members and what the results were. The new members are encouraged to ask questions of the former clients. Of course, care must be taken in both the selection and preparation of the model. The model must have some skill in organizing ideas and presenting them, and must be able to answer questions. As part of his or her preparation, the therapist may role-play a group meeting with the model; this serves both as practice and check to make sure that the model can handle the assignment. Where skilled models are not readily accessible, written case studies may be shared with the clients and discussed in the group as a means of providing more personalized information.

In giving clients an abundance of information, the therapist must be careful not to overwhelm them with details. This form of information satiation is avoided by means of successive structuring of the information given in each subsequent contact. In the initial sessions, the general approach and basic assumptions described, and a few specific case examples, are given. In subsequent sessions, successively more detail is given until the client can clearly describe what he or she can expect from others and can expect to perform him- or herself. Sharing of information thus is a continuous process moving from general to specific description.

In both the interview and the first meeting, the therapist explores the interests, concerns, and expectations of the group members to facilitate the decision whether or not to join the group. Once a decision has been made, a treatment contract is presented to the clients. This written document specifies what the client can expect from the therapist and agency, and what the agency can expect from the client in the course of therapy. This contract is renegotiable by mutual agreement. The contract serves as clarification of mutual expectations. Below is an example of a treatment contract used several times in assertive training.

The contract is a major tool in orientation. But it has implication for the cohesiveness of the group as well. In groups in which expectations for members are clearly stated, cohesiveness tends to increase (see Chapter 10). However, this is neither the only nor even the major step in increasing cohesiveness. As described in the following section, an elaborate program is developed to increase (and later decrease) the attractiveness of the group for its members.

TREATMENT CONTRACT

I. Each group member agrees to:

A. Pay a deposit of $25 for 10 meetings.

B. Attend each session. In return he/she will receive $1 per class attended ($10).

C. Arrive for each class on time (4:00 P.M.). In return he/she will receive 25¢ per on-time arrival, as evidenced by the door to the group room being open (total possible $2.50 per individual).

D. Show evidence of assignment completion. In return, he/she will receive a) $1 for 100 percent completion (total possible $10 per individual). In addition, persons completing part of their assignments will receive that percentage of $1 for each part completed. b) Priority to work on their problems during the group meeting.

E. Allow data accumulated during the group to be used for research and/or educational purposes, with protection of confidentiality assured; and to allow the group leaders or a representative of the Agency to contact him/her in the future, by mail or phone, for follow-up. In return each person will receive a lifetime membership in the Assertive Training Alumni Program (ATAP), which qualifies them to assist (if desired) in future groups.

II. The group leaders agree to:

A. Begin and end each session on time.

B. Help members clarify their problems in such a way that something can be done about them.

C. Help members identify their personal and other resources, and make use of them in dealing with their problems.

D. Provide members with the procedures that offer the best chance of an effective and efficient resolution of the problem.

E. Respect confidentiality of members' communication.

F. Provide refunds and awards under conditions outlined above.

_____   _____

      Group Member   Date

_____   _____

      Group Leader   Date

BUILDING GROUP COHESIVENESS

. . . we then asked the members to introduce themselves to their neighbors and describe one major personal characteristic and one major interest. Each member then introduced his or her neighbor and his or her neighbor's characteristics to the group. At the break, coffee, cake, and soft drinks were served. The members were asked to get to know two other persons during the break. One of the therapists, by way of example, explained that he was attempting to reduce his high frequency of advice-giving behavior. The second therapist interviewed him in a role-played situation much to the amusement of the members. They in turn interviewed each other using the similar questions. When Mr. S. said that he was glad to be in a group that dealt with concrete problems, one of the therapists responded that she was pleased that Mr. S. found this orientation useful and wondered what others thought. In planning for the next session, members volunteered to take care of refreshments. Ms. T offered to bake a pie, and Mr. K said he would provide the liquids (at which everyone laughed).

For treatment to succeed, members must attend regularly. They should be subject to the influence of the other group members and participate in the process of changing. For these activities to occur, the group must have reinforcing qualities for the members. The source of this reinforcement may be the other members, the therapist, or the activities of the group. In the early sessions a great deal of effort is placed on creating in the group a reinforcing set of conditions to facilitate the attainment of treatment goals.

One might define group cohesiveness as the degree to which the members, therapist, and group activities have reinforcing value for the members. Staats and Staats (1963) have argued that when individuals have reinforcing properties for each other, they are more likely to cluster together since they are being intermittently reinforced. It is this clustering effect that is sought after by the group therapist.

In the above example, several types of procedures were used to increase the attractiveness of the group. First, the therapists attempted to reduce the initial anxiety characteristic of members in first meetings with unfamiliar people in unfamiliar surroundings. The procedures they used were the subgroup introductions, which seem to be less threatening than introductions in the total group. They also reduced anxiety by modeling what was expected of the members in the given meeting. Role-playing, regardless of its purpose, is usually greatly enjoyed by the members. Another common practice at first meetings is to teach relaxation, which seems to diminish initial anxiety.

Food in the first meeting and the promise of food in subsequent meetings were used to make attending the group more reinforcing. Members generally become much more relaxed in initial meetings around food, even if it is not much more elaborate than a cup of coffee. Involving the members in bringing and serving the food adds to its attractiveness (and quality).

Interaction of the members was increased through subgroup interactions, which required that everyone talk but gave them the structure that suggested content for speaking. Describing characteristics of the others in the larger group appears to be easier for clients than describing their own characteristics.

In the above example, the therapist reinforced a positive evaluative statement by one of the members by acknowledging it and having the rest of the group comment on it. Reinforcement of such statements should result in their increase. In studies, the author has noted that a high frequency of positive verbal evaluative statements enhances the group's evaluation by its members (as indicated by the answer to a question about how well they like the group).

The investigations of Myers (1962) and Julian, Bishop, and Fiedler (1966) conclude that intergroup competition results in increased cohesiveness. An actual or implied threat from external sources also should draw the members closer together. Although a procedure such as competition with other groups is rarely used in adult therapy, it may be worth considering. For example, the rate of behavioral change or completion of behavioral assignments could be compared between two groups. Or the presence of another group as observers at a given meeting might increase both the attractiveness of the group and the quality of the interaction. Having a meeting videotaped to be shown in a class or on television might work in the same way.

Although cohesiveness is, indeed, a vague concept, the lack of attention to this important area results in dull meetings and poor attendance. However, an overconcern with cohesiveness also can result in failure to maintain a task orientation and ultimately to achieve treatment goals. Many therapies that are quite effective in increasing group cohesiveness fail to consider the work to be done. The ultimate goal is not a high level of cohesiveness; it is only a means to the end. In fact, in the last phase of treatment, steps usually are taken to decrease therapy group cohesiveness as a means of facilitating the transfer of changes learned in the group. Thus, in addition to building group cohesiveness, the therapist must provide the members with goal-oriented work.

In the early meetings, the work assigned to the clients is twofold: to become familiar with the structure of therapy and to define one's problem in such a way that it can be corrected. In the next chapter we will discuss what this process is and how it can be carried out in groups.

3 Assessment in Groups

Linda: My problem is simply that I'm much too shy. Even saying this to all of you is difficult for me.

Group Therapist: On the basis of what we have learned about describing a problem, maybe we can suggest ways to Linda for spelling out her shyness so that we all can see exactly how it appears to others; that is, in concrete, observable terms.

Roger: Perhaps you could describe a recent situation to us in which you were shy; that would be a good starting point.

Linda: Oh, that's easy. Just last night at a party I was so uncomfortable I scarcely said a word. And when I did speak, it was so softly that people usually asked me to repeat myself.

Roger: Even softer than you're speaking now?

Linda: Oh, yes. I'm much more comfortable with you.

Therapist: So you hardly ever speak and when you do, you speak too softly? I wonder if shyness is anything else to you?

Linda: I guess it also means this terrible anxiety I feel with people and also a sense of shame.

Tom: Are you this way with everyone?

Linda: No, not with my family or a few close friends. And lately I feel much less shy in this group.

Tom: That suggests to me that you can learn to become less shy with others as well.

Walter: I was wondering how people you feel comfortable with react to you when you do speak?

Linda: Well, if they hear me, I think they respond to me. But I guess you people can tell me more about that than I can.

Walter: I don't know what the others think, but I find your ideas for others interesting, and your self-description is quite lucid and useful, at least, when I hear them.

Others: (Nod agreement.)

Linda is presenting her problem to the group. The members and the therapist are in the process of helping Linda to define the complaint in such highly specific terms that something can be done about it. This is part of the assessment process, or functional analysis,[1] of Linda's problem. The purpose of this chapter is to summarize the major principles involved in the assessment process that are common to both individual and group treatment, and to point out procedures for carrying out assessment within the context of the group.

Behavioral assessment is based on the assumption that there are lawful relationships between the behavior and the immediate environment within which it occurs. For this reason the focus of assessment is on identifying the problematic behavior and determining the environmental and other conditions controlling or otherwise impinging upon it. Thus, the major variables to be considered in such an analysis are the problematic behavior, the conditions preceding or concurrent with its occurrence, the consequences of that behavior or the events immediately following its occurrence, and the contingency or pattern with which the consequences are delivered.

PROBLEMATIC BEHAVIOR

Most clients come to treatment with extremely general complaints, such as Linda's shyness, discussed above, or Frank's depression, in the following example.

Group Therapist: Well, we've examined Linda's problem and the situation in which it occurs. Does anyone else have a similar problem?

Frank: (slowly) Well, I don't speak much either; it's not because I'm shy though. I'm just down a lot of the time.

G.T.: Can anyone help Frank to spell that out in a way similar to what we did with Linda?

Linda: I guess I should be the one to try. Frank, what do you do when you're down?

[1]To a large degree, the first part of this chapter is based on the work of Kanfer and Saslow (1969), to whom the reader is referred for a more detailed analysis of the assessment process.

Frank: Well, I don't do much of anything. I sleep a lot; that's about all. Oh yeah, I watch TV, but I don't really enjoy it.

Roger: What do you think you should be doing? Or what would you like to be doing?

Frank: I don't eat much when I'm depressed. I guess I should eat more. I stay in my room most of the time. Maybe I should go out more, although I really don't want to. I do want to study, though, but somehow I can't even do that.

The initial task of the therapist is to analyze general complaints such as these in terms of specific behaviors that can be observed directly or indirectly. A general problem or complaint thus is translated into a set of problematic behaviors in a specific situation. (For the purposes of analysis, the problematic behavior here has been separated from the situation in which it occurs. In a following section we shall examine the behavior in interaction with the situation.)

A problematic behavior prevents an individual from attaining personal goals or causes him or her extreme or continuous personal discomfort. In most cases, it results in undesirable consequences for other persons who are significant to the given individual. Thus, there are two definers of the problematic behavior; the individual who experiences personal discomfort and failure in attaining goals, and the significant persons in his or her life, who suffer the undesirable or aversive consequences of that behavior. However, in the case of adults and most children, the person who comes to therapy has the ultimate responsibility of defining his or her own problem.

For purposes of analysis, two major categories of problematic behaviors can be identified. The first, behavioral excesses, is considered problematic because the frequency, intensity, and duration are too high or the situation in which they occur is inappropriate. Since Frank's sleeping is of too long a duration, it falls into this category. The second category is behavioral deficits. These are behaviors that fail to occur with sufficient frequency, with adequate intensity, with sufficient duration, in the appropriate form, and/or under the appropriate conditions necessary to attain personal goals or avoid intense personal discomfort. Linda's infrequent speaking in groups and Frank's failure to eat, go out of his room, and study are examples of this category.

Often behaviors may be defined either as excesses or deficits. For example, in a couples group Mr. T admits that he spends most of his time complaining to his wife about his job and their low standard of living. There is an excess of complaining behavior, but there is also a deficit of friendly, affectionate physical and verbal responses. Frank's problem could be defined as a deficit of going out of his room or an excess of remaining in it. One could analyze the problem from either point of view or both. However, it is essential that at least the deficit be identified, since the procedures (positive reinforcement, modeling, and so on) used in increasing low frequency deficit behaviors seem to have fewer negative side effects than the procedures used to decrease or eliminate behavioral excesses (aversive conditioning, response cost, stimulus satiation).

Both behavioral excesses and deficits may be described in terms of overt motoric or verbal behavior, or covert emotional or cognitive responses.

The most common type of behaviors dealt with in the behavioral approach are overt motoric behaviors and verbal statements. Examples of motoric behavior in the previous examples are Frank's eating and sleeping excessively. Mr. T's complaining and his affectionate statements are examples of verbal behaviors. However, clients also may complain of such indirectly observed phenomena as anxiety, embarrassment, and other emotional states and/or their inability to express anger or affection. These, too, are amenable to behavioral analysis and treatment. However, treatment of overt behavioral phenomena associated with the emotional responses may result in elimination or lessening of the latter. For example, anxiety in relation to test-taking is related to a lack of studying skills in some individuals. If this is the case, when the client has learned the necessary skills, the panic experienced previously is significantly reduced. Teaching people with low esteem to make more positive self-references seems to improve their general self-perception. Thus, both motoric and emotional concomitants of behavior problems must be analyzed.

Another category of covert behaviors, cognitions, or thoughts also may be considered legitimate targets of change. Cognitive problems include pervasive thinking, inability to make decisions, choice conflicts, distorted information, or perception about a given subject. Most of these also lend themselves to behavioral analysis and eventually behavioral treatment.

Whether or not the client complains about this area, problem-solving skills frequently are examined with each person. Problem-solving refers to the ability to deal with a problem systematically. Since groups inevitably must solve problems, the role of each individual in that process can be scrutinized to ascertain his or her relative skill in this area. Moreover, the therapist uses group exercises in problem-solving, first for assessment and later as a form of training.

Inappropriate cognitions also are intricately related to motoric, verbal, and emotional behavior. For example, pervasive thoughts may be accompanied by high anxiety, avoidance of certain situations that seem to elicit these thoughts, sleeplessness, and constantly complaining to friends about the problem. All must be analyzed separately, and their components identified.

Cognitive distortions may be a function of faulty or inadequate information. Often sexual problems can be alleviated, or at least improved, by providing corrective information. Wolpe (1973, Chapter 4) discusses in detail how general misconceptions about one's self or therapy can be corrected. A common misconception discussed by Wolpe is that in light of his or her complaints, the client may feel that he or she is going insane. Often the simple reassurance,

plus information on the wide distribution of the behavioral disorder, is sufficient to dispel the notion (Wolpe, 1973, p. 56). Because of their importance
to therapy, such cognitive distortions and misconceptions must be explored
early in treatment. In a group, a questionnaire often is handed out to members
on subjects of concern, and they are asked to respond to a number of questions
concerning their knowledge in crucial areas.

Most of the examples, thus far, have been of simple isolated behavior. But
the client comes to treatment most often with general complaints that also are
quite complex. Often each problem area is defined in terms of a set of interrelated problematic behaviors that may stand in some kind of relation to one
another. If possible, it is desirable to identify the characteristics of the interrelationship. In the following example, the problems stand in a sequential relation; that is, some problem behaviors must be resolved before others can be
dealt with.

Another member of Linda's group, Roger T, complains of low self-esteem,
which the group has helped him to identify as low frequency of positive
self-references, a high frequency of negative self-references, a deficit in social
interactive skills such as meeting other people and carrying on social conversations, and grooming that is inappropriate for the social group to which he
desires membership. It first may be necessary for Roger to learn to approach
others before he can carry on conversations with them; and it may be necessary
for him to learn to groom himself in a way that is acceptable to the people he
wishes to approach, if this is one of the major impediments to their accepting
his initial approaches (he also may choose to learn to find an alternative group
whose values about grooming are similar to his own). As in this example,
complex problems are not avoided; they are broken down into logical component parts to make them more amenable to treatment.

Nonbehavioral Complaints

Nonbehavioral complaints also may surface in the analysis of problems.
These include economic, health, intellectual, legal, and social problems. Many
can be dealt with directly in the group; others may need referral to other social
agencies for treatment. Often the group members have had more experience
than the therapist in resolving these kinds of problems. Regardless of where
they are treated appropriately, these categories of potential problems must be
considered in determining the focus of treatment. Often they are either more
important than the behavioral problems or they strongly influence the outcome
of treatment of problematic behavior.

In therapy with economically deprived persons, many problems may be—
at least in part—a function of inadequate economic resources. In such cases,
before therapy has any meaning it is necessary to facilitate the client's search
for adequate material resources. For example, one client failed to attend

groups meetings because he had no money to pay a baby sitter or for gas for transportation. In another case, a client's assertiveness as measured by the Rathus inventory (Rathus, 1973b) was radically reduced following the loss of a job and economic security. A couple in therapy complained that they were arguing constantly over the distribution of an extremely meager income. The wife's procurement of a part-time job alone resulted in more satisfying interaction. Of course, many of these economic problems have behavioral concomitants that can be dealt with readily in the group. Azrin, Flores, and Kaplan (1975) organized a job finding club to train people in the necessary skills to look for and interview for a job. These groups showed a significant improvement in economic status of the trainees as opposed to that of a control group.

Health problems may give rise to the illusion of behavioral problems. For example, in one group a man was treated as a phobic because he claimed he was afraid of falling from ladders or high staircases. When treatment failed, it was learned that the client had very poor peripheral vision. Glasses corrected the "psychological" disturbance. Most problems, but especially complaints such as depression, insomnia, obesity, or nervous tension, require a physical examination by a physician prior to treatment. Even if the problematic behaviors are not related to a physical ailment, the individual's good health should be considered a personal asset that might be drawn upon in treatment.

Intellectual capabilities also should be considered in a functional analysis. Although we have found that people with a wide range of education can use behavioral procedures, the pace may be somewhat slower and the language needs adjusted for the more poorly educated (Rose, 1974a). In most cases, training tends to upgrade the performance level of clients, but there appear to be biological limits beyond which training cannot go. Although the limits for each client may not be clear, some estimate of the range of intellectual functioning is useful to facilitate the statement of achieveable treatment goals.

Since the social groups one belongs to strongly influence one's values as well as one's behavior, it is relevant to examine the client's membership in the family, work group, friendship groups, and subcultural groups. This analysis includes a discussion of the expectation of other group members for his or her behavior, the degree to which he or she values membership in these groups, his or her centrality in that group, and the degree to which members in these groups might participate in the client's treatment. In this analysis, problems of relationship often can be noted along with social resources for furthering treatment.

Behavior in a Situation

As pointed out earlier, problematic behavior occurs in a material and social environment. It is this environment that constitutes the target of later intervention. Those events in the immediate environment that occcur prior to or concurrent with the problematic behavior often are referred to as "antecedent conditions" or " discriminative stimuli." Only when Roger was in the presence of persons he knew intimately was he inclined to make negative self-referent statements. Only when Linda was with people she did not know intimately did she speak so softly that she could not be heard. In both these cases, the antecedent events were the necessary—although not sufficient—conditions for the given behaviors to be emitted.

Frank was depressed especially in the evenings and on weekends and when alone. In this case, the antecedent conditions of time and person, although neither necessary nor sufficient, were highly likely to be linked with depressive responses.

Antecedent conditions refer to the interaction of such dimensions as time, place, material attributes of the situation, persons present, behavior and personal characteristics of those individuals, and relation of those individuals to the given client. Not all of these may be equally relevant. Some problems are highly restricted as to the conditions under which they occur. A particular exhibitionist, for example, exhibited only at twilight on the edge of a park in the presence of any young woman who was walking alone. Other behaviors occur under almost all conditions, such as the case of the client who bit his nails even in his sleep. In most cases, however, certain limited number of identifiable conditions seems to be necessary for the given behavior to be emitted. To determine the most appropriate course of treatment, these conditions must be identified clearly. In the author's experience, groups become quite expert in eliciting these conditions from fellow members.

In some instances, the initial conditions seem to elicit the behavior rather than merely to provide the conditions for its performance. If a person has a rat phobia, the sight of a rat, the word "rat," or the thought of a rat elicits an anxiety response. This type of connection between behavior and its antecedent conditions is called a "respondent relation" and is usually treated with respondent procedures (for example, desensitization).

Often the treatment focus will be at least in part changing the antecedent conditions. The obese client will be taught to create a world about him or her where high calorie foods are not readily available. A cigarette addict will cue him- or herself with written signs as reminders not to smoke.

More often the client will learn procedures for modifying the consequences of behavior in such a way as to bring about change in behavior. For this reason an analysis of the events immediately following the performance of the target behavior also must be ascertained carefully. In addition, assessment involves an analysis of all events that might be used as potential reinforcers for increasing the frequency, intensity, or duration of behavioral deficits. To this end, all group members prior to treatment fill in a Reinforcement Survey Schedule similar to the one developed by Cautela and Kastenbaum (1967). And these reinforcers are discussed in the group. The particular survey often used in this project is on pp. 96–97.

Since the schedule of reinforcement has implications for the speed of learning and the maintenance of learning after treatment ends, information about existing schedules definitely should be included in a behavioral analysis (see Rimm and Masters, 1974, pp. 185–187, for a more detailed analysis of schedules of reinforcement and their implication for clinical practice).

One particular task closely related to the exploration for potential reinforcers is exploring the client's area of competence and nonproblematic behaviors (behavioral assets). The analysis of these areas provides the therapist and other group members the opportunity early in treatment to talk positively about each member. The client has the chance to talk positively about him- or herself. Dwelling solely on deficits and excesses creates a highly self-punishing phase of treatment and may result in a lowering of the attraction of the group. In fact, the assessment process in groups usually begins with a discussion of assets rather than problems.

Also important in the analysis of behavioral assets is the opportunity to discover additional client resources that may be incorporated into treatment. For example, when Linda revealed that she has some skill in painting, the group encouraged her to bring her paintings to the group meeting. And later Linda developed a treatment plan making painting contingent on her interacting in a clear and loud voice with a certain number of unfamiliar persons in the course of the week. Without a careful analysis of her assets, this plan might not have been developed.

At the end of a behavioral analysis, the therapist should be able to devise a treatment plan using the reinforcing as well as antecedent conditions related to the problematic behavior. Knowledge of the biological and social factors should help to determine resources and limitations of certain approaches and certains goals. How this data is incorporated into a treatment plan is discussed in Chapter 6.

Selection of an Initial Problem

The tasks of selecting and analyzing an initial target behavior to work on are connected inseparably. A problem must be selected to be analyzed, but once the analysis has begun the relevance of the selection may be questioned, and changes may occur. Selection normally begins after the introduction and as a part of the training in behavioral theory.

Where there is one problem and its boundaries are clearly differentiated, the task is a simple one. Most clients, however, have a number of problems differing in relevance, clarity, and level of difficulty. In such cases, selection of an initial problem can be a highly difficult and even an aversive event for the client because he or she alone is responsible for the ultimate results. The client can be given models, demonstrations, and suggestions, but the actual selection is his or her first major responsibility. The client may be mistaken in the choice, but the therapist, in interpreting the problem, is *more* likely to be mistaken.

A client may not be willing to reveal immediately what he or she feels to be the central problem, but it is not necessary to deal with the core problem right away. The therapist can make certain criteria of selection available to the group. For one, it is essential that the problem chosen be relevant to the patient. Only if it is relevant, will the patient be willing to commit him- or herself to a certain amount of daily work on the problem (monitoring, reading about it, consulting others, reinforcing him- or herself).

For example, many parents in training groups choose "picking up toys" as the initial behavior they want their child to change. As they rapidly solve this problem, they are better prepared to deal with more relevant behavioral problems such as destructive combat among siblings. Moreover, in the early phase of treatment, members learn a vocabulary and a conceptual system for formulating their more complex problems, making them amenable to treatment. This cannot always occur in the first few sessions of the group.

Another criterion for the selection of a target problem is that it must be one the person is willing to talk about in the group. If a man's experimentation in homosexuality is such a private concern to him that he is not willing to talk about it with others, it has to be left until such revelation is possible, even though other evidence suggests the problem. On hearing the problems of others, clients are willing increasingly to disclose materials about which they initially remained silent.

METHODS IN ASSESSMENT

It has been stated that before data can be collected, group members must be able to describe their problems in highly specific terms. Often this is a difficult task; most clients are accustomed to describing themselves and others in highly general categories. Certainly the popular literature and previous therapies the patients have undergone may contribute to the value placed on the use of such categories. Because of the difficulty usually experienced in the important skill of problem description, a number of procedures have been used in the group to facilitate assessment. These procedures involve the use of questionnaires, behavioral checklists, feedback procedures, role-playing, model description or vignettes, exercises in the group, and group discussion.

Pretreatment Questionnaires, Checklists, and
Interviews

Each client is given a questionnaire to fill out prior to the intake interview or first meeting. In addition to clinical data about the nature and severity of the client's problems, questions are asked concerning personal characteristics, physical health, recent physical examinations, previous treatment history, interests and hobbies, occupational data, family data, and marital history (see Kanfer and Phillips, 1970, for more detail). In groups concerned primarily with one particular problem, such as assertiveness, anxiety management, weight loss, or reduction of phobic responses, specific questions as to the onset and the scope of the given problem also are added. In addition to the questionnaire, clients complete behavior checklists. Highly specific descriptions of various problems are checked in terms of their relative frequency. These initial checklists also provide the client with a vocabulary and a model for describing his or her problem. (How these checklists are developed and other uses are described in more detail on p. 54.) The members are asked to read to the group their most problematic items on the checklist. For example, Mr. K read, "On the checklist I have indicated that I very seldom go out of the house in the evenings, that I very often watch television, that I rarely talk to anyone in the course of the weekend, that I usually eat irregularly, and that I usually sleep whenever I get the chance." In reading the problems aloud, he gets practice in speaking in highly specific terms.

Often the therapist will have either a brief or an extended interview with the client before admitting him or her to the group. Such an interview serves several purposes. It provides the client with an opportunity to discover what the group is all about and to have his or her questions answered. It sometimes serves to clarify what is expected of the client. Moreover, it helps the applicant decide whether to enter the group at all. For purposes of assessment, it provides the therapist with an opportunity to collect data that help him or her to decide whether the group is the correct context of therapy for the clients. He or she also has the chance to gather individualized data that the patient may not want to share with other group members. This is the time to explore further the results of the questionnaires and checklists and to explain the reasons for these problems.

Although such an interview may add to the cost of treatment, most therapists find it saves considerable group time. Some therapists claim that the intake interview establishes a norm for the client to rely on the therapist rather than the group. Moreover, the client, once knowing the path to the therapist's office, may be inclined under the slightest frustration in the group to run there rather than using the group. In spite of these objections, pregroup individual interviews were used without apparent negative side effects in about half of the author's project groups.

One variation of the pregroup assessment interview is the use of experienced clients as "buddies" to interview the applicants to the group. When a new member enters an already existing group, some therapists use the group meeting as if it were an assessment interview for the entering client. Both of these methods provide leadership opportunities for the members, which should enhance the stabilization and transfer of changes obtained in the group. (See p. 162 for a more detailed discussion of this principle.)

Another variation is to have the assessment interview after the first or second meeting. Therapists using this method assume that the clients now know the vocabulary and criteria for assessment. A common practice is for the therapist following a formal course in behavior modification for the clients to hold an intake interview to see whether group members know what behavior modification is all about. This interview reveals whether they can identify problems, and if they would like to continue in the course with a new focus on changing problem behaviors.

Vignettes and Exercises

The checklist is only a first step in training the client in the principles of behavioral specificity. After clients have read the relevant items on their checklists, they are presented with a highly specific description or vignette of a client with problems similar to their own. The principles of behavioral description are pointed out to them. In addition to specificity, the description should be of a behavior accessible to therapy. The behavior should be relevant to the client and one that can be dealt with in some way. The last criterion may be difficult for the client to consider, since he or she is not yet familiar with the treatment procedures. The group members then are given several new vignettes to discuss either in subgroups or in the large group; they decide if the criteria have been met. They are asked to modify the descriptions to conform with the criteria. The vignettes are then discussed in the larger group. Since skill in defining problems in terms of specific behavior is one of the intermediate goals (or facilitating goals) of treatment, a vignette usually is given to each participant for problem analysis prior to entering the group and again following the fourth session. This allows the therapist to evaluate whether the appropriate formulations have been learned. An example of a vignette and accompanying questions follow.

Martin T, age 22, stock clerk, came to the group because he is lonely. He avoids contact with the men and women he works with. He has no friends or family. He goes home immediately after work and watches television. He spends his weekends alone at the movies or sitting and thinking. He would like to meet women, but he claims he is afraid to address them. He likes to eat well and to cook, but lately he has done very little of either.

Which of these statements are sufficiently specific that they can be observed? Which are too general? What are the long-range consequences if this behavior pattern were to persist? What events might serve as reinforcement for Martin?

Following discussion of the vignette, clients are asked either as teams or as individuals to develop personal vignettes to be discussed at the following meetings. If a person is not yet ready to describe his or her own behavior as evidenced by work in the group, he or she may be asked to describe the behavior of someone else or even a fictional character from a book.

Another procedure often used in the group is the presentation of a number of general statements, with members inventing specifics. They are asked to imagine someone with some general problematic characteristic and then to describe the person according to the newly learned criteria. Some of the general characteristics used are assertive personality, overly friendly person, depressive reaction, passive-aggressive personality, dominating person, effeminate male, masculine female.

It may seem to the reader that a great deal of effort and time is spent on what appears to be a rather simple problem. But one of the major reasons for treatment failure often is that too little time is spent on training for correct problem formulation. As a consequence, inadequate formulations result in inadequate treatment plans.

Keeping a Diary

Early in the assessment process each client may be requested to keep a diary recording all problematic behaviors and the surrounding circumstances. In the case of behavioral deficits, he or she may describe those situations in which the client thought desired behaviors should have occurred; then he or she also notes whether they actually did occur. The client also records the level of anxiety experienced on a scale from 0 to 100, and his or her satisfaction with what he or she did on a similar scale. The diary comments are evaluated, if possible, by his or her partner or by the group members in terms of specificity and revelevance to the above criteria. Each subsequent meeting should result in subsequently more concrete observation, until the client is ready to use more precise measurement instruments. Even after the client begins to note or count behavior, he or she may be asked to continue the diary. It is a means of ferreting out other problems and provides additional training in behavior specificity.

Keeping a diary requires special skills not always found in the clients' repertoire. Even those who have these skills may find writing too tedious. It may be preferable to advise such clients initially to keep extremely brief notes or cue words. The notes are used as a basis of their contribution to a group discussion during the predominantly assessment phase.

Feedback Procedures in Assessment

A number of group procedures can be useful to identify a problem for the client who admits to no problem at all or who finds it difficult to pinpoint the problem. One procedure is the systematic use of feedback; each member responds to all of the others about each person's behavior. This is a similar procedure used in encounter groups except that patients in behavior therapy groups are required to identify the specific behavior to which they are responding. Moreover, they are encouraged to identify behaviors they judge to be attractive or useful or in other ways functional within the group.

Since this particular procedure can produce high anxiety, several rules are established to protect the individual. He or she can ask the other members at any time to stop their comments. He or she can choose not to undergo criticism, but if the client does avoid criticism, he or she is to refrain from evaluating others. Patients rarely use these safety valves, but they claim it is comforting to know they are available.

Another technique currently being used in groups is videotape feedback (Robinson and Jacobs, 1970). Although there is mixed evidence of the effectiveness of this procedure for changing behavior, it appears to be an excellent device for confronting the individual with his or her behavior in groups. When reviewing the tapes, parents became aware of such behaviors as "put downs," teasing, and verbal aggression, which they later worked on with other methods. With multifamily groups, the showing of tapes was sufficiently attractive to be used as a reward for task-oriented behavior.

Role-Playing Procedures in Assessment

Role-playing is another procedure commonly used in assessment. Clients demonstrate to the group how they would handle a given stress situation, such as a request for a loan from an unsympathetic relative or an interview situation. If the individual is unable to play his or her own role, he or she can direct a therapist to play the role as the client would do it. Following is an example of this process and how it is used in assessing the behaviors of the patients in a group.

A therapist in a group meeting discusses a problem with Mrs. Browne, one of the six group members.

Mr. H (a group member): It's still not clear to me exactly what happens, Mrs. Browne, just before these anxiety attacks occur.

Mrs. B: Oh, I don't know, I just get anxious, that's all. Sometimes my son just won't do what I say or my husband doesn't listen to me.

G.T.: I wonder if we couldn't take that situation with your son you were telling us about earlier and role-play it; that is, act it out as nearly as it actually happened. I'll play the son; you be you. If I make any mistakes, you let me know. But first, tell us what happened again.

(Mrs. B. reviews the situation with the group.)

G.T.: O.K. I think I've got it now. What about the rest of you?

(Group members nod agreement.)

G.T. (in role of son): Listen, Mom, I've got to go with the guys to the quarry. It's not dangerous. No one's ever been hurt there yet.

Mrs. B: There's got to be a first time, and with your luck it's bound to be you. You know how I worry.

G.T. (in role of son): I'm going. I don't care what you say. (G.T. moves out the door.)

(Mrs. B begins to become anxious.)

G.T. (in own role): Okay, okay. We're just acting, Mrs. B. But we certainly have a clearer picture of what happens.

Since Mrs. B's anxiety subsided immediately, the therapist asked if she felt comfortable enough to play a similar situation with her husband. The therapist asked for a volunteer to play the role of the husband. A similar pattern evolved. The therapist then asked the other group members if they could identify the antecedent conditions to the anxiety. It was quite clear to the group members that the antecedent conditions in both cases was not merely noncompliance with her wishes but also the threat to have an attack. Once the threat was made, the attack inevitably occurred. In exploring this with Mrs. B, the therapist and group members found that the husband usually conformed before the threat was made.

A behavioral approach primarily involves determining the sequence of events with the client. Once the sequence is clear, that part over which the client has the most control—in this case, the verbal threat of having an attack —can be modified. Even though Mrs. B could have been told by the group therapist that the "threat" was the crucial antecedent condition, it was made real to her by the role-playing and group discussion that followed.

When the purpose of role-playing is behavioral assessment as in the above examples, the client will play his or her own role and the therapist and/or other members in the group will play the parts of the "significant others." As demonstrated in Mrs. Browne's case, it usually is best to role-play several related situations to discover what they have in common in the way of antecedent conditions and problematic behavior. In the therapeutic group situation, this form of role-playing has the further advantage of training the nonplaying members in the observational skills necessary for assessing their own behaviors.

Another role-playing technique used to train group members in the skills of assessment is one in which the group therapist plays the role of a fictional client. A group member or several group members interview the therapist (in his or her role as client), trying to obtain as much information about the problem and the impinging conditions as necessary to determine the nature of treatment. Following each role-play, the group discusses what further information would be useful to obtain a clearer picture of the problem. This process usually is repeated with two or three new fictional patients being portrayed. If the resumes have been written in some detail, a group member also may play one of the fictional patients.

After a series of role-plays, the members discuss their own problems. The role-plays function to give the group members practice in assessment skills in a nonthreatening situation.

Assessment of individual problems is not complete when a problem has been selected to work on, and even when it is sufficiently well formulated that it can be measured. It is only when the initial measurement procedures have been designed and carried out that the assessment of any given problem is complete. Measurement, of course, is not limited to assessment. It goes beyond the treatment phase to record in summary form the entire history of the process and outcome of therapy. In the following chapter, we will discuss the principles and procedures in the process of observation and measurement commonly used in group therapy.

4 Monitoring Group and Individual Behavior

Andy has completed 40 percent of his behavioral assignments this week, Arlene 75 percent, Ann and Edward all of them. The group's average for this week is 10 percent higher than the previous week.

Ann shows the group her chart containing the number of situations when speaking up in a class or other group was possible, the number of times that she did speak, and the estimated level of anxiety that she experienced in each situation.

During the meeting the observer counts the number of times that each member and the therapist make either an opinion or advice-giving statement. At the end of the meeting these data are presented to the group.

Ralph and Edward show their graphs indicating the number of telephone calls they made for purely social purposes. They also indicate the total number of minutes spent each day on these calls.

Andy reports how many times his roommates made requests to borrow his clothes and the number of times he refused. He is careful to point out that no one made a request on the weekend because he was staying at his cousin's house.

Arlene had asked her roommates to count the number of times that they had observed her complaining, since they had suggested that this was something she should work on. She reports that only one of them had cooperated with her request.

In each of these examples the behavior of the clients is being counted either in the group or as part of the members' extragroup assignments. Once the target problem has been selected and a preliminary assessment made, the clients must learn to monitor or to teach someone else to monitor the specific behaviors. Monitoring is the process of observing and measuring, that is, assigning numerical values to the frequency, intensity, duration, or appropriateness of the target behavior. The client and the group keep track of the course of behavior through monitoring. Measurement has many purposes; it is a major concept in behavior therapy.

Measurement serves as a check on the adequacy of the assessment process. If a given behavior cannot be measured, the original formulation must be revised. For example, Jonathon first described his problem as "inability to express his anger with people who put me down." The initial attempt to record the frequency and duration of such events failed because of the vagueness of the complaint. With the help of the group members, Jonathan revised the formulation to read that in interaction with others, he neither disagreed nor revealed his annoyance when they criticized him or gave him unsolicited advice. This formulation was successful insofar as it pointed to readily countable units of behavior.

When measurement is repeated throughout treatment, it provides each client and the group as a whole ongoing feedback on their short-range successes and failures. As a result, minor adjustments can be made readily; therefore, ongoing measurement is often a change procedure in its own right. Additional change procedures usually are required, but in simple problems, measurement occasionally is a sufficient cause of change.

Measurement also provides a summary description of the progress and outcome of each case. This enhances the systematic accumulation, summarization, and reporting of data back to the therapeutic community, which in turn facilitates the treatment of other cases. In group therapy, these summary data make it possible for each client to describe succinctly and briefly his or her progress to others at each meeting. This makes it possible to work on many categories or aspects of problems in each group meeting. For these reasons, this chapter is devoted to the explication of measurement procedures that are relatively easy to apply. And they are especially relevant to group therapy insofar as group clinicians have had successful experiences using them.

The two most frequent measurement procedures are counting discrete units of behavior and the units of time involved in performing them and rating (usually on an ordinal scale) the intensity or frequency of a given behavior. Counting usually is used for overt behaviors such as the number of arguments or minutes spent in arguments. Rating usually is used to assess the intensity of covert behaviors, such as the degree of anxiety.

In the next section of this chapter, we will discuss the uses of counting procedures and time measurement in the service of treatment. In the following section, rating scales and other measurement will be discussed.

COUNTING

Counting is the major means of collecting data in behavioral treatment. Discrete behavioral units, units of time or products of behavioral activity are counted. When units of time are counted, one measures either the number of time units in which a given discrete behavioral unit does or does not occur, or one measures the length of time the client participates in a given behavior. The response latency (the length of time between the discriminative stimulus and the given behavioral response) also may be measured. Examples of counted behavioral units are the number of times a client approaches a given phobic object; the number of times a client praises other group members or husband or wife; the number of pages the client reads, and the number of problems he or she completes correctly. Examples of counting units of time are counting the number of five-minute periods in which emotional outbursts (crying, screaming, angry statements) did not occur; counting the number of hours in which at least one compliment occurred; measuring the length of time a person spent studying each day. An example of measurement of the response latency is the estimation of the time elapsing between a parent's request for a given action and the child's initiating the desired response.

Although one usually counts units of behavior or time, occasionally the product of behavior change is counted. For example, the number of pounds lost or gained is assumed to be the result of the quantity, intensity, and frequency of such behaviors as eating and exercising. Therefore, the weight record is used to validate the self-report of those behavioral performances. Other examples of the product rather than the behavior itself being recorded are the number of pages of notes typed as an indication of studying, or the number of items in the dirty clothes hamper as an indication of picking-up-clothes behavior. The number of feet that one moved in the direction of the phobic object may be counted as an indication of the strength of the approach behavior.

In each of these forms of counting, it is assumed that behaviors or time periods counted occur over a specified base time period. This may be per month, such as in the case of a client with several severe anxiety attacks during the period of a month; or per week, as in the case of the client who wets the bed once or twice a week; or per day as in the case of the patient who has several arguments a day with his or her spouse; or per hour as in the case of the client who writes about six pages per hour; or per minute as in the case of the client who manifests on the average 12 facial tics in that period.

Although one often speaks of the absolute number of a given behavior, in almost every case a rate—the frequency per given time unit—either is assumed or specifically stated. The denominator of the rate is the base time unit mentioned above.

One usually does not count all the occurrences of a given behavior unless it is extremely infrequent. It usually is preferable to observe sample periods and generalize from that time sample to longer periods. For example, the facial tic might be observed only for five minutes, four times a day for several days. The client or therapist would calculate the minute rate for each observation period by dividing the number of tics observed during the five-minute period by five. The assumption is that the average minute rate for the four time samples is representative for the given day. The higher the frequency of the behavior, the smaller the sample and the fewer the samples usually required to obtain a reliable estimate.

Reliability

Since data is being collected by an observer, it is desirable to know how accurate the observer is in assigning units of behavior to the defined categories. In behavior therapy the most common way of estimating such consistency or reliability is to have two or more independent observers make judgments of the frequency or time of a given behavior. The correlation between or among the judgments or the percentage of agreement are two ways of obtaining a rough estimate of the degree of reliability (see Selltiz and others, 1959, for a more thorough discussion).

There are many reasons for avoiding reliability checks. Not only do such checks add to the cost of therapy, but ready sources of reliability checks often are lacking. Most clients are not highly self-disciplined, nor do they come from a research background. They cannot be expected to place any value on reliability checking without strong reinforcement. Moreover, controls by others may be aversive to many clients and may be an imposition on their privacy. But even if we accept the assumption that clients are making the best possible judgment about their reported observations, the probability of error always is great. Without a reliability check, there is no way of estimating the size of that error. These checks have the added advantage of increasing reliability. Reid (1971) has discovered that observations of those who were aware that they were intermittently monitored were significantly more reliable than observations of those who were not aware of monitoring. For these reasons, practitioners, in spite of the difficulties, should seek reliability sources whenever possible. In the following sections, we will discuss means of obtaining additional observations on group members and the implication of these checks for treatment.

Reliability checks need not occur all the time. A small, preferably unpredictable, random check often gives a sufficient estimate of reliability and increases the degree of reliability of self-observations.

Prerequisites for Effective Counting

To insure adequate counting, the observer, who may be the client him- or herself, a "buddy" in the group, a friend or relative, should be provided with a set of clearly defined, written instructions. Ideally they should include a description of the conditions under which the observations should be recorded, the time sample when observations should occur, the location of the observer, the type of measuring and recording instruments to be used (for example, paper and pencil, stop watch, manual counter), and the location of these instruments. A well-defined description of the behavior to be observed, preferably with examples and a description of procedures for monitoring the counting, is of prime importance. At first glance this may seem a far too complicated list, but lack of concern for any one of these areas has contributed to failure in the counting procedure.

A client who complained about her lack of social contact serves as a good example of this process. The client decided that it was important to increase the number of her social contacts and the time spent in social contact with others. She defined social contact in terms of face-to-face interaction with others either during the lunch period at work, the breaks before and after work, and on weekends. To measure the frequency of social contacts, she used a counter that she carried in her purse. She pressed the button when she approached someone and conversation was initiated. If she left the situation and returned, the button was pressed again. As soon as she got dressed in the morning, changed clothes, or left the house, she checked to see that she had the counter with her. On returning home she recorded the time and the number on the counter and reset the counter to zero. At the end of the first three days, she called her partner in the group and indicated whether any problems in counting occurred. If there were any, the two of them would try to iron them out in a revised counting plan. If they were unsuccessful, they would wait until the next meeting for help from the group leader and other group members.

The client listed the following situations, noted in her previous week's diary, as units to be counted: the number of occasions she ate lunch with others and the number of times she addressed others at lunch. If she changed tables and went to another group under the same circumstances, it was recorded. If she returned to the original group, it was recorded once again.

In this example, all of these agreements and examples were written at the top of the sheet on which the daily total was noted. The client was instructed to reread the instructions each day for three days, until what she was to do was completely clear. If problems arose, such as categories that were difficult to classify, she was told to make a note of them and decide the solution with her partner.

Let us briefly examine problems that can occur if such detail is not available to the observer. (As in the above example, the observer was the client in the following cases). A client who found it difficult to study was instructed to record every day the amount of time he spent in studying. He ran into trouble the first day because he waited until the end of the day to record anything, and he could not recall accurately how long he had studied. The second day he had the additional problem of not knowing whether to classify writing behavior as studying. If he sat at his desk half thinking and half musing, was he to record it? On the third day he no longer remembered whether he was to record the number of times he studied or the amount of time. Then, he could not find his recording from the previous two days. So he decided to stop counting completely. The problems were resolved at the following meeting, but it cost him a week's delay in getting started. In addition, it was a highly frustrating initial experience.

At the group meeting, these or similar examples are given to the members. This may be followed by a role-played demonstration of correct descriptive procedures. Following a discussion of these procedures, the clients split into subgroups with their partners and designed their own recording instructions. (This may occur as a home assignment, with the further instruction of pretesting the instrument and the accompanying instructions.) The group members then review the instructions for each other and make alternate suggestions, which the member may or may not decide to incorporate into his or her set of instructions. After each person's plan has been reviewed by the group, a week of data is collected. Any problems that cannot be resolved with the partners are discussed at the subsequent meeting.

During this series of meetings, some members may be stuck at the level of establishing a measurable description and be unable to develop a monitoring plan. The therapist should point out that there is no reason for everyone to maintain the same tempo. When an individual requires more time to define a problem adequately, it should be made available, regardless of where the group is.

As suggested above, it is useful to include a short pretest of the counting instructions and other instruments. The pretest, in addition to ironing out the inevitable problems, serves to reduce the pressure on the client to develop, at first try, a perfect instrument. Usually the pretest period is kept quite short unless major problems arise. All minor problems can be adjusted readily by the client alone or in consultation with his or her partner. The pretest also provides the client with a brief training period in the use of his or her instrument. With complex behaviors, it may be necessary to provide more extensive training before the observer (client) is prepared to initiate counting procedures.

Who Monitors

In adult groups, the major (although not only) source of information is the client. He or she describes the problem both anecdotally to the group and in a diary. The client fills in scales about the relative frequency, importance, and other aspects of his or her problem behavior. Finally, as the target behavior is identified clearly and made amenable to counting, the client is asked to count units of the target behavior.

Self-monitoring as a source of information makes clients responsible for the data accumulated; therefore, they don't feel that something—in this case counting—is being done *to* them. Two disadvantages are that the counting procedure is subject to the moods of the client and his or her skill in self-observation. These problems can be offset by careful definitions, adequate training, and, if possible, occasional monitoring by someone else as a reliability check.

The group is one source of more reliable observers. Using buddies or others as monitors must be negotiated with the given client. In spite of the influence of awareness of observers on the client's behavior, this process of negotiation protects the rights of the client and increases his or her cooperation. Often it is easier for a peer to be invited to family or recreational situations than a staff member. The buddy can be introduced as a fellow member or, if true, a friend. It may be difficult for the buddy to make notations in such a situation, but the use of a small hand counter for high frequency behaviors and memory for low frequency ones usually works quite well. However, some practice in the treatment group is required first. Another advantage of using a buddy is that in other situations the monitoring role can be switched; such a reciprocal relationship increases the likelihood of cooperation.

The kinds of situations that buddies can observe most readily are those involving interaction with family or friends. For example, how often does the client initiate conversation, make sarcastic remarks, approach other persons, or assert him- or herself when justified?

Family members have been used as monitors by some therapists. There is danger in this, however, because the client is placed in a subordinate role, which may contribute to one of his or her existing problems. To offset this, the family member (like the buddy) might allow a relevant behavior of his or her own to be counted. Then, of course, it is better if the family members also attend at least several meetings, a form of multifamily therapy. Because of the difficulty in gaining this kind of cooperation, the family member only rarely is used as a collector of data for adult clients.

Group or case aides may be used to make observations outside of the group, although they too put the client into a subordinate position in his or her own milieu. Their advantage over family members is that they are professionally detached from the idiosyncracies of the client. They have the disadvantages of being an artificial stimulus in the home situation and adding to the cost of therapy. Even so, clients—especially alcoholics or drug addicts who live in boarding houses, hotels, or halfway houses—often make excellent use of the aide not only as monitor but later as an on-the-spot therapist.

Monitoring Group Data

Group data also is monitored in group therapy for several purposes. The first is to provide the clients a model for training in data collection procedures. Since trained observers usually are used to collect data, it is possible to demonstrate to the members the basic principles of developing a monitoring plan and procedures for carrying it out. The second purpose is to provide data about the cohesiveness of the group, the productivity of the group, and any problems in group communication that might occur. Cohesiveness is estimated from the subjective evaluations and attendance data, and productivity from the percentage of behavioral assignments completed. Problems in interaction are estimated from the observation of such categories as the direction of and frequency of communication, the number of positive and negative responses, and the number of off-task statements. Some of these categories are discussed below in more detail.

A third purpose of monitoring ingroup behavior is to provide a reliability check on extragroup self-observations. If, for example, a client is observing the frequency with which he or she gives an opinion in social situations, the observers could record similar behaviors within the group. If the rate in the group is different than that outside of treatment, some question can be raised either about the reliability of the extragroup observations or the success in obtaining transfer of change from the group to the outside world.

Only those motoric behaviors commonly occurring at meetings with a moderate or high frequency can be observed readily for any of the above purposes. Among motoric behaviors that have been observed in meetings are interruptions, irrelevant statements, eye contact, fidgeting, and postural symmetry (an apparent inverse correlate of relaxation). More often, however, verbal interaction is recorded.

Figure 4.1 presents several graphs in which data are summarized. Figure 4.1a is an example of directional data over seven sessions for all the group members. When compared with narrative data on these phenomena, the increase in member-to-member interaction indicates that no change in the degree of activity is required. Figure 4.1b is an example of two categories for all members over seven sessions. Both are desirable categories and both show positive increments. Figure 4.1c is the profile of the content of interaction for one meeting. We find too much data in the information-giving category, which

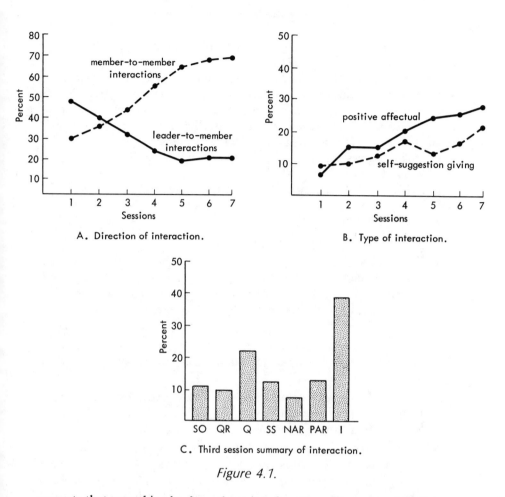

A. Direction of interaction.

B. Type of interaction.

C. Third session summary of interaction.

Figure 4.1.

suggests that something be done about it before the next session. All of these are but small samples of the data generated by the observation system for one interpersonal skill training group.

Linsk, Howe, and Pinkston (1975) have developed a similar observation coding system for group work with the elderly, which may be applicable to other types of groups. In this research, the group worker's questions, statements, positive comments, negative comments, listening, demonstration, and attending behavior were observed and coded. Similarly, group members' behaviors were observed and coded along the following categories: appropriate and inappropriate verbal; verbal behaviors related to environment; appropriate attention; and appropriate or inappropriate attention.

The two observers spend five seconds per minute observing and recording the behavior of each group member. Reliability was estimated by dividing the number of agreements by the sum of the number of agreements and disagreements. Linsk and others (1975) provide detailed definitions of their categories and coding forms (pp. 455–457).

To record content of interaction, a time interval observation system has been developed. In this system a signal is generated every seven seconds by a programmed tape recorder. At the signal the observer records who is interacting, the content of interaction, and the direction (to whom interaction is oriented). To ascertain reliability, two observers are used.

The following system for coding the content was used in a recent Group Therapy and Research Project. It was possible to train observers in 10 hours to achieve an index of agreement of .85 in this system.

CODE DEFINITIONS

SO *Suggestion-opinion giving response:* statement of at least one sentence in length made to another member, leader, or entire group regarding the content of the session, role-play performance, or assignments, such as "I think this session ought to be only an hour."

Q *Questions:* interrogative statement of at least one sentence in length made to another member, leader, or entire group regarding the content of the session, role-play performance, or assignments, such as "How can I improve on that?"

QR *Question response:* statement of at least one sentence in length made to another member, leader, or entire group that answers a previous question, such as "In response to your question, I think . . ."

SS *Self-suggestion giving response:* statement of at least one sentence in length made to another member, leader, or entire group regarding one's own performance in role-plays, completion of assignments, behavior in the natural environment, or past experiences, such as "I feel that I could have improved on eye contact."

NAR *Negative affectual response:* statement made to another member, leader, or entire group that expresses a personal dislike, irritation, or disagreement with another or other's verbal and/or nonverbal behavior, such as "I don't like it when you stare at me."

PAR *Positive affectual response:* statements made to another member, leader, or entire group indicating a personal liking for another or other's statements, character, or behavior, such as "I really like what you just said."

I *Information giving response:* statements made to another member enlarging or expanding on a previous topic or theme, such as "This is what I meant" or "Another example would be. . . ."

As in the following example, the data are recorded in four columns. The first is the number of the observation, the second for the communicator, the third for the content of the communication, and the final column for the recipient of the communication. Each member has a code number either as giver of communication or as recipient. The 0 is the code number for the entire group.

observation	who	what	to whom
1	1	Q	2
2	2	SO	0
3	5	NAR	3
.			
.			
.			
N			

In the above example, John (1) asks a question of Pete (2). Pete (2) gives his opinion to the group (0). At the third observation, Anna Marie (5) gives a negative affectual response to Liane (3).

Using this system, one can analyze the matrix of interaction, the content used by clients, the content used by leaders, and the degree of participation of each member. The data may be used to evaluate shifts in the leaders or members role.

Figure 4.1 is an example of data taken from the observations of one interpersonal skill training group.

RATING SCALES

Some behaviors such as anxiety are not easily accessible to an outside observer. Often the units for counting other behaviors are not adequately defined. Sometimes the instrumentation for counting is cumbersome and expensive. Under these conditions, rating scales may be used to assess the problem and later to estimate changes in the behavior. They also may be used as a means of preassessment to establish units that eventually can be counted.

There are many types of rating scales, but only those used in group treatment will be discussed in this chapter. The most common among these are self-rating scales for covert behaviors.

Griffiths and Joy (1971), in comparing Kelly's repertory grid technique (Bannister, 1963) with a 10-point rating scale and a paired comparison, forced-choice technique in the prediction of phobic behavior in a standardized avoidance situation, discovered that the rating scale and the paired comparison were significantly more accurate than the grid but did not differ from each other. The rating scale was by far the most economic in terms of time and effort necessary to construct and administer the instrument and to interpret its results. Their results are compatible with many other studies, indicating that simple and economic self-ratings can be more useful than sophisticated and time-consuming instruments (Mischel, 1968). For this reason, rating scales are recommended as one means of assessing changes in covert behavior, especially anxiety, which is the most pervasive complaint in adult groups.

Clients are asked to rate their anxiety on a scale of zero to 100. Zero is absolute calm, and 100 is the greatest anxiety the person has ever experienced (Wolpe, 1973, p. 120). There are several ways to use this scale. The most common instruction is to ask the client to record the degree of anxiety or subjective units disturbance (SUDs) experienced at specified intervals throughout the day. More specifically, in most anxiety management and assertive training groups, clients are instructed to record, at 8:00 A.M., 12:00 P.M., 4:00 P.M., 8:00 P.M., and before they go to bed, the SUDs level that each experiences. Another instruction commonly given to clients is to describe anxiety-provoking situations in a diary and indicate the level of anxiety each situation provokes. When desensitization is used, a SUDs level is assigned by the client to each item or situation on the fear hierarchy (see Wolpe, 1973, p. 120 for more details).

Sherman and Cormier (1972) also recommend the use of subjective scales for measuring interpersonal reactions. Specifically, they cite the experience of Sherman (1971) with a subjective unit of irritation (SUI) scale to measure the degree of irritation that students caused a teacher. The measure was used on repeated occasions to test the effectiveness of an intervention technique on improving the relationship between student and teacher. A decrease in SUI scores was interpreted as a measure of improved relationship. This was validated by SUI scores correlating highly with the overall rate of disruptive behaviors emitted by the students, the amount of attention given to inappropriate student behavior by the teacher, and the number of punitive statements made to target students by the teacher. The authors recommend additional scales, such as the subjective units of anger scale, which can be used to determine situations producing anger in a family or group situation, and a subjective unit of congeniality scale.

Likert Scales

Rathus (1973) uses a Likert-type scale (see Selltiz and others, 1959, for a description of these scales) to ascertain the degree of assertiveness of a client. On this scale each item is scored from +3 to –3, depending on the degree to which the client states the item is characteristic or descriptive of him or her. The scores of the 30 items are then added to obtain an assertiveness score. The following statements are the first five items of the Rathus Assertiveness Survey (RAS) scale.

RAS REACTION STUDY

_____1. Most people seem to be more aggressive and assertive than I am.

_____2. I have hesitated to make or accept dates because of "shyness."

_____3. When the food served at a restaurant is not done to my satisfaction, I complain about it to the waiter or waitress.

_____4. I am careful to avoid hurting other people's feelings, even when I feel that I have been injured.

_____5. If a salesman has gone to considerable trouble to show me merchandise which is not quite suitable, I have a difficult time in saying no.

The test was used by Rathus (1973) to demonstrate the effectiveness of assertive training in comparison with a nonbehavioral approach to group treatment. Rose (1975) discovered that the RAS distinguished significantly between the before and after conditions in assertive training groups. Shoemaker and Paulson (1976) demonstrated a difference on the RAS between mothers receiving assertive training in groups and a control group. Thus, the test was sufficiently sensitive to indicate changes in assertive behavior of group members and in two cases significant differences between different types of therapy. Unfortunately, it does not appear to differentiate between various dimensions of assertiveness.

An assertive training inventory that differentiates several dimensions but is designed solely for college students is the College Self-Expression Scale (Galassi and Galassi, 1974). It consists of 50 self-report items that tap three aspects of assertiveness: positive assertiveness, negative assertiveness, and self-denial in such contexts as in the family, with strangers, during business relations, in the presence of authority figures, and with members of the same, as well as the opposite sex.

The scale utilizes a five-point Likert-type format with 21 positively and 29 negatively worded items. Like the RAS, it is scored by adding the positively worded items and reverse scoring, then adding the negatively worded items. Low scores are indicative of a generalized nonassertive response pattern.

Two week test-retest reliability coefficients on two samples yielded coefficients of .89 and .90. Construct validity was suggested by positive correlation with Gough and Heilbrun (1965) Adjective Checklist Scales: number checked, defensiveness, favorable, self-confidence, achievement dominance, intraception, heterosexuality, exhibition, autonomy, and change. Negative correlations were obtained with unfavorable, succorance, abasement, deference, and counseling readiness scales. A correlation of .15 ($p<.04$) between supervision and self-ratings suggests concurrent validity. However, the correlation, although significant, is low.

As yet the test has not been used to measure changes over time. However, preliminary results suggest that the measure may be useful both for initial subject selection and as a posttest, and for identifying the specific type of situation requiring attention for each client.

The Gambrill-Richey (1975) Assertion Inventory provides similar data with a broader population; however, situations used for assessment on this scale are somewhat less specific. The strength of this instrument is that it allows the respondent the opportunity to rate anxiety or discomfort for each situation, along with response probability. Another value of using this instrument before and after treatment is that it also provides data on generalization since it measures the client's responses to situations not specifically handled in the training program.

Moreover, the 40-item test provides eight categories of assertive behavior: turning down requests; expressing personal limitations (that is, admitting ignorance in some areas); initiating social contacts; expressing positive feelings; handling criticism; differing with others; assertion in service situations; and giving negative feedback. The authors also provide reliability and validity data supporting the use of the instrument with a general population.

Behavior Checklists

Another kind of rating scale for overt behavior is the behavior checklist. It is used with almost all groups as a preliminary step to assessment (see p. 33) and as a means of deciding what eventually should be counted. Following is an excerpt from a checklist used in a supervisory group:

3 = high concern   To what degree are you concerned
2 = moderate concern   with the following behaviors as
1 = a little concern   potential targets of change?
0 = not concerned at all

0	having a clean desk
2	writing goals for therapy
2	using simulation procedures in treatment
3	setting clear-cut limits when required
1	increasing reinforcement for clients
	(etc.)

(Other examples of checklists for various types of groups are described in Part Two.)

Checklists are filled in either prior to or during the first meeting. Some leaders have experimented with giving them again at the third or fourth meeting, after the participants have learned a behavioral vocabulary and basic principles. Although checklists are not very sensitive instruments, they have been used on occasion for indications of behavior changes across a wide range of behaviors or as a test of changes on behaviors not treated. In that case the checklist is completed again at the end of treatment and/or during the follow-up interview. Unless other instruments are not available, the checklist is not recommended by the author except as a tool for assessment. However, for assessment purposes its use is recommended in all groups.

Rating Overt Behavior

It usually is preferable to *count* overt behavior. But often the difficulties of counting a large number of behaviors in a group is overwhelming, especially when a highly abbreviated time sample cannot be used, or observations on a large number of persons must be made. For this reason, rating scales sometimes may be used to assess and monitor behavioral frequencies of a group or individual clients. The most reliable type of scale is a two-point scale in which the observer judges whether a given behavior has been performed or not. An example of how such a rating scale was developed and utilized is described in the following example.

In a halfway house for retarded adults, Slavin (1972) reports on a rating scale that in itself was sufficient to accelerate desirable behavior. A survey was taken of the adaptive and maladative behaviors whose deficit or excess resulted either in loss of employment for the client or in causing difficulties for the house mother. From an initial list of 15 behaviors, 8 categories were selected: grooming, appropriate language, completion of assignment, neatness in own living area, getting along with others (not fighting), acceptable boy-girl behavior (no public petting), punctuality, and accepting correction. The 10 clients were rated on weekdays, usually at the end of the day, as to whether or not the given behavior occurred. The trainees were rated for three weeks without their knowledge. They were then rated for three months, and their rating sheet results were left on the dining room table for all to examine. After a two-week reversal, the program was reestablished. The mean daily rate for the baseline period, which was the sum of all 8 categories, was 1.8. The maximum attainable was 8. During the treatment phase, the mean daily rating was 4.1, an increase of 56.1 percent. During the reversal period, the rate dropped to 2.1 and increased to 4.6 when the ratings were again made public. The largest gain was in the category of getting along with others; the smallest for accepting correction.

This study demonstrates that public display of ratings of behaviors in a group of retarded adults can serve as an accelerator of the target behavior that is rated. Slavin recommends this procedure for programs low in funds and personnel, and hence unable to provide immediate concrete reinforcement. It is important to note that in spite of its demonstrated effectiveness, the presentation of the charts was not effective with all clients. Some seem to respond better than others to the charts as reinforcers. Slavin also suggests that instead of presenting the charts at the end of each meeting, more frequent presentation of the data may be still more effective with a larger number of people.

OBSERVER Smith   OBSERVED K. Jains   DATE 1/17

CONDITIONS OF OBSERVATION Group meeting

CHARACTERISTICS OF Assertive BEHAVIOR

(*Circle* the appropriate number in each category.)

1. Eye contact   1 2 3 4 5 6 7 8 ⑨ 10 No eye contact

2. Erect posture   1 2 3 4 5 6 ⑦ 8 9 10 Slouched posture

3. Speaks clearly   1 2 3 4 5 6 7 8 ⑨ 10 Mumbles

4. Speaks very slowly   1 ② 3 4 5 6 7 8 9 10 Speaks rapidly

5. Voice calm   1 2 3 4 5 6 7 ⑧ 9 10 Voice tense

6. Speaks affirmatively   1 2 3 4 5 6 7 8 ⑨ 10 Speaks unsurely

7. Relaxed facial   1 2 3 4 5 ⑥ 7 8 9 10 Facial tension
   expression

Rating Group Behavior

Another procedure commonly used to rate behaviors related to such characteristics as assertiveness or friendliness, as they occur in role-played situations, has three steps. First, the target area—for example, assertiveness—is selected. Second, all the observable characteristics of assertive behavior are identified, whether or not deficits exist in each of the identified behaviors. The group members are involved in the process of specification. Finally, the characteristics are listed on a set of rating scales as in the example below.

A prescribed situation involving the target client and another role-player is role-played for 5 to 10 minutes in the presence of the observers. Each observer in the group then rates the target role-player on the relative prominence of each of the behaviors. The data is presented to the target role-player, who can discuss briefly, if he or she chooses, the discrepancy between him or her and others or among the others. An example used in an assertive training group is as follows:

Sociometric Measures

One set of questions attempts to elicit responses from individuals in a small group concerning their positive, neutral, and negative evaluations of their relations with others in the group. These are called social-choice or sociometric measures. What is the significance of these measures for group therapy? First, they provide information about a purely social phenomenon not readily accessible by other means. They ferret out how each person feels about (subjectively evaluates) every other person in the group. Second, they provide data that correlates with such phenomena as group productivity, task orientation, attendance, participation in the group. Third, the response can be changed through a number of highly explicit interventions such as positive reinforcement, modeling, and role change (see p. 135). Fourth, they are relatively easy questions to formulate, to administer, to analyze, and to use. Because of the ease in administering, these questions do not incur the incomplete responses and other forms of errors common to other more lengthy tests.

Some specific questions that have been used in group therapy are: If you were to select a partner in therapy in the group, which member would you most prefer him/her to be? Least prefer?

Following termination of the group activities, with which persons would you *most* like to continue a friendship relationship? Least like to continue a friendship relationship?

Following termination, several members will be asked to serve as models in subsequent groups. Who do you feel is most qualified? Least qualified?

For research purposes, highly complex methods of data analysis are available, but for purposes of therapy, several rather simple uses can be made of the data. An index of acceptance can be calculated by the number of acceptances a client receives, divided by the number he or she could receive (N–1). Similarly, an index of rejection can be calculated. Some therapists have used an index of reciprocity as indicated by the number of mutual choices and other indices (see Lindsey and Byrne, 1968). In general, however, goals can be set for each person as to his or her level of acceptance or rejection in the group; after seeing which behaviors interfere with these levels, treatment plans can be established that should result in behavioral change, and hence sociometric status.

Simulation Tests

Several simulation tests have been developed to evaluate the effectiveness of certain interventions. According to the developers of these tests, the instruments have been demonstrated to attain a reasonable level of reliability and predictive validity. Although somewhat complex, they may be used by the clinician who deals with problems similar to assertiveness deficits. Simulation tests are used to evaluate the response to specific situations not readily available for observations. Therapist aides are used in standardized roles to place the patients under a set of standardized conditions. The patient usually is instructed to respond as he or she would normally to the role-played, simulated conditions.

McFall and Marston (1970) developed the Conflict Resolution Inventory (CRI). It consists of 16 role-play test situations, each lasting several minutes, which are tape recorded. Each of the situations requires assertive responses. The subjects are instructed to respond to each situation as if it were happening to them. Their responses are then tape recorded. McFall and Marston give the following examples: Friends are interrupting your studying; the laundry has lost your cleaning; the waiter brings you a steak that is too rare; your boss asks you to work overtime when you already have plans.

The format for the presentation of each stimulus situation is illustrated by the following excerpt from the script:

> *Narr:* In this scene, picture yourself standing in a ticket line outside of a theatre. You've been in line now for at least 10 minutes, and it's getting pretty close to show time. You're still pretty far from the beginning of the line, and you're starting to wonder if there will be enough tickets left. There you are, waiting patiently, when two people walk up to the person in front of you and begin talking. They're obviously all friends, and they're going to the same movie. You look quickly at your watch and notice that the show starts in just two minutes. Just then, one of the newcomers says to his friend in line:
>
> *Newc:* "Hey, the line's a mile long. How about if we cut in here with you?"

Person in line: "Sure, come on. A couple more won't make any difference."

In addition, the subjects rate each situation on two five-point scales: a) indicate how anxious you would be if you were in this situation; and b) indicate how satisfied you would feel with the response that you gave.

The McFall and Marston role-play test is primarily oriented toward students. More recently, similar tests have been developed for other populations along lines suggested by Goldfried and D'Zurilla (1969). Goldsmith and McFall (1975) developed a behavior role-play test for psychiatric inpatients. Freedman (1974) developed one for institutionalized delinquents. In the Group Therapy and Research Project, DeLange (1977) developed such a test for women; Schinke and Rose (1976) for a general outpatient population; Berger (1976) for the aged; and Rose, Edleson, and Cayner (1976) for social workers in professional situations.

One of the major limitations of these tests is that the client is aware that he or she is role-playing. How well this transfers to real life situations is not yet clear. To meet this objection, a number of tests have been created in which the client remains unaware that he or she is in a simulated situation. One such instrument, which was used for clients in a group, is the Simulated Dating Interaction Test (SDIT). The male subject is sitting in a waiting room when an attractive female confederate enters. She assumed the role of a freshman taking introductory psychology but enrolled in a different section from the subject. She is instructed to be friendly but to allow the subject to take the initiative. She also is told to initiate one compliment and one self-reflective statement during a four-minute period. Like the subject, she has ostensibly volunteered for the study but knows nothing about it. These sessions were audiotaped and rated by two female psychology students along four dimensions—appropriateness, anxiety, masculine assertiveness, and overall pleasantness. Immediately after hearing the tapes, the judges rated each individual on the basis of a comparison of pretreatment with posttreatment on each of the four dimensions so that a given individual was scored $++$ if both judges rated post better than pre, and $--$ if both judges rated pre better than post, and $+-$ or $-+$ if judges disagreed.

Such tests suffer, however, from too great a specificity. Unless, as one observes in the SDIT, all subjects have difficulty in a narrow range of approach responses, the test is not useful. A second, and more serious, problem for the clinician is the use of deception with clients. Unless the client participates in some form of informed consent to the general procedure, it may not be ethically responsible to use them. Yet such informed consent may defeat the purpose of the procedure.

Although the simulated tests have been used primarily as outcome measures in research projects, they do provide formats that clinicians also use to assess problem areas and to evaluate the effectiveness of treatment. Although it is extremely time-consuming to construct such instruments, several therapists have designed them to meet the particular problems of their clientele (for example, Witkin and Smits, 1974). For those group therapists who are working specifically with refusal responses, the CRI could be used in the form described above; for those working with dating behavior, the SDIT also might be applicable as is. Provided they have similar populations, therapists also may consider using the other role-play tests already developed for the elderly, delinquents, outpatients, inpatients, and women.

SESSION EVALUATION QUESTIONNAIRE

To obtain a subjective appraisal by the members, a questionnaire is submitted to them at the end of every session. It usually contains the following questions.

Which of the procedures used in today's session were the most useful?

Which of the procedures used in today's session were not useful or were in any way annoying?

What procedures used at previous meetings or in other groups would you like to have incorporated into today's session?

By circling the appropriate number, indicate on the following scale your desire to return to the next session.

By circling the appropriate number, indicate on the following scale your satisfaction with today's session.

Please give any other comments, suggestions, or criticism that you feel would improve the quality of the program.

It may not be clear always to the members what delineates a procedure. To help identify procedures, the therapist in the initial sessions will review the ones used at that given session. After two or three sessions, this is no longer necessary.

Initially, the author used only rating scales for session evaluation, but because of the general halo effect, very little variation was obtained. For this reason, open-ended type questions mainly were used. Rating scales for the desire to return were reserved as an indication of group attraction and of session satisfaction, since these variables tend to correlate with productivity and other group variables.

To get the most possible information from the open-ended questions, it is necessary to reserve at least five minutes to fill them out. If the questions are left until people are ready to leave, the clients will not have time to answer them thoughtfully. In the beginning, the therapist also reinforces the members for their valuable comments and then shows exactly how the information is used in evaluation and treatment planning. Failure to discuss the use of the client's contribution inevitably results in diminishing information in subsequent meetings.

Once data is obtained from the session—evaluations, self-monitoring, tabulations of the observers, self-rating scales, and so forth—they must be analyzed. In the following chapter, we will discuss how these data are organized and reviewed for the purposes of evaluating the effectiveness of techniques, sessions, and the entire course of therapy.

5 Evaluation and Research Design[1]

At the third meeting of a couples group, the therapist noted that all the couples were present, on time, and had completed the week's assignments. At the previous meeting, only 60 percent of the members had accomplished these goals. The third meeting was rated by everyone as either a 1 or 2 on a 7-point scale in which 1 was the most favorable position. This was slightly better than the previous week's ratings. Interaction this week increased from .9 to 1.5 per minute per person. On the evaluation everyone indicated approval of the rehearsals in communication training, but several requested that the contingency contracts be omitted in the future. On the basis of these data, the therapist concluded that the general direction the group was taking was a good one and that no radical change was necessary at this point. However, he did plan to discuss with all the members the relevance and usefulness of the contingency contracts at the next meeting.

The trainer in a dating workshop reviewed the same data following the fifth meeting. She discovered that the percentage of behavioral assignments completed had decreased from 85 percent to 65 percent. All the other data had remained constant and favorable. To increase the percentage of behavioral assignments, the therapist reviewed the problem with the clients. They pointed out that although they had accepted the assignments, they found them much too difficult. The therapist agreed that some incentive in the form of self-reward

[1]This chapter was coauthored by Sheldon Rose and Stanley Witkin.

62

presence of a problem was instrumental in beginning a series of changes in therapy procedures.

One of the major advantages of collecting data on various individual and group phenomena is that it facilitates ongoing evaluation and appropriate action. Data are used to evaluate the effectiveness of specific treatment procedures, an entire session, or the complete treatment package. The therapist constantly evaluates the above interventions to determine whether they should be maintained, adjusted, or eliminated and replaced by others. To evaluate the effectiveness of interventions, the therapist is able to systematically collect, organize, and review such variables as behavior change, group attraction, group productivity, interaction patterns, and subjective appraisal of each intervention procedure by the group members.

In the above examples, the therapist used the data to ascertain if changes were needed. He tested his hypotheses about changes by checking them out with the group members. Although one might come to the same conclusions intuitively, data provide more precise information as to the problems that should be dealt with and suggest areas that otherwise might not be considered.

When analyzing the data, the therapist needs a basis with which to compare his or her most current observations. The therapist may compare the current data to those collected in the same area in other groups or to the same type of data collected at earlier meetings of the present group. When such a basis of comparison exists, it is possible to determine if current observations indicate shifts in trend, pattern, frequency, or duration of the observed attribute. One particular basis of comparison is the baseline (Sidman, 1960).

BASELINE

A baseline refers to a series of sequential observations of behavior or of other individual or group attributes. These observations are made prior to the initiation of an intervention. In addition to providing a basis of comparison, the baseline gives the therapist information to be used in assessment. For example, the clinician may learn that the frequency of the target behavior prior to intervention is not at a problematic level. Therefore, contrary to original expectations, the target behavior requires no treatment. Or, the clinician may learn that the target behavior has such an extremely high or low frequency that immediate intervention is needed. In clinical contexts self-comparison often is more useful than comparison with other persons. There are two reasons for this: 1) in clinical practice random assignment of clients to comparison conditions often is not feasible, rendering the equivalence of individual or group comparisons questionable; and 2) even with randomization, there is no other person more like the client than himself or herself.

How long should a baseline be? To determine this, several principles should be considered. First, the less the variation among observations, the shorter the length of the baseline period and/or the fewer the observations required. For example, the rate of mutual reinforcement in an assertive training group was determined once every 10 minutes. Because the rate consistently remained between .07 and .10 per minute, 15 observations provided an adequate baseline. One member of the same group was recording his anxiety (SUDs) six times a day. Since the variation per day on a scale of 100, was as many as 30 SUDs, 84 observations (over two weeks) were required before a sufficiently stable pattern could be established; that is, a pattern from which one could discern even small shifts in trend, intensity, frequency, or duration.

Another consideration in determining the length of the baseline is whether it is sufficiently long to sample all relevant situations. If the therapist is interested in the behavior only as it occurs in the group context, then the baseline need cover only a sample of different situations during the group meeting. For example, group participation during alternate 10-minute segments might provide a baseline in two sessions. If, however, the client is interested in changing his or her response to the imposition of others, he or she must sample a wide range of conditions under which such imposition occurs. It may take three or four weeks before all the relevant conditions are sampled adequately.

Another consideration is the opportunity for observation. If group attraction as measured by the subjective perception of the members can be determined only once a meeting, then experience has shown us that at least four meetings are required to obtain an adequate baseline. Since the performance of leadership behaviors in the group allows the possibility of continuous observation throughout the meeting, a baseline could be established in one or two meetings.

Practical problems often impinge on deciding the length of a baseline. For example, if the attractiveness of the group is low as measured by the evaluation question (see p. 60) at the end of the first meeting, the therapist may not wait longer than one session to act on the basis of his or her data to prevent the group from deteriorating. In clinical practice the immediate clinical demands usually have priority over evaluation demands. In most situations, however, there is no conflict.

Ideally, the baseline period of observation must be distinguished clearly from the intervention period. To accomplish this during the baseline period clients are instructed to deal with the given problem just as they have been doing prior to entering treatment. They also are instructed to avoid the use of any new method they are currently being taught until the baseline period has been terminated. To add emphasis to this demand it is included as one condition of the treatment contract; occasionally a contingency is attached to premature initiation of treatment. Finally, care is taken *not* to teach the application of treatment methods in great detail prior to their use in treatment. Under these conditions, clients rarely will initiate the treatment of a first behavior prior to instruction from the therapist. The problem may occur more readily when collecting data for the baseline of subsequent behaviors, since the clients already have developed some intervention skills. However, even under these conditions instructions, contracts, and group pressure appear to delimit the frequency of premature initiation of treatment procedures by clients.

Ideally, to minimize the effects of observation on behavioral change, baseline data should be collected by relatively unobtrusive methods. When observations are made within the context of the group the use of independent observers can serve this purpose and is achieved readily. Our experience has indicated that group members are desensitized quickly to the presence of observers or recording equipment if they are used at every session. Often the therapist can increase the validity of his or her data by eliminating data from the first or second sessions. Moreover, group observations of verbal behavior can be recorded on tape and coded at leisure to obtain highly reliable judgments. Motoric behavior can be recorded on videotape or observed through a one-way screen and coded immediately.

However, most of the behaviors of concern to the client are those performed in the community. Although experimentation currently is being done with portable, automatic recording devices, most observations at present must be made by the client, occasionally by the client's family members or buddy from the group, and/or more rarely by other significant persons in the client's life. In each of these cases, the client usually is aware of the observations. As a result, mere collection of data can influence the target behavior. Usually it does not seem a factor sufficient to achieve goal-level performance; however, its exact effect is difficult to estimate. Nevertheless, self-monitoring may provide the best and only alternative for the collection of baseline data for some behaviors (for example, of obsessive thoughts).

Sometimes, when the pressure to begin intervention is high, or when self-report data is not adequate, data from an *ex post facto* baseline may be used. This is a baseline determined from data collected prior to the establishment of a monitoring plan. For example, a member of a weight loss group who wanted to begin a diet immediately used her doctor's records of her weight as an *ex post facto* baseline with which to compare the results of her subsequent efforts. In a group organized around improving study skills, the grade point average was used for all the members in spite of obvious limitations. This had the advantage of providing data that covered an extensive period of time. Several of the members requested their faculty members' previous records of their attendance as additional *ex post facto* data. In a group of chronically anxious clients, previous sick days taken from work were used as an *ex post facto* baseline.

The advantage of these and similar data are that they are for the most part nonreactive; that is, the client's behavior is not affected by the data collection process. A disadvantage is that nonreactive data alone may not correspond completely to the definition of the behavioral target of change. (For example, the number of cigarettes in the ashtray may be a useful but imperfect indicator of anxiety.) For this reason, Webb, Campbell, Schwartz, and Sechrest (1966), advocate the use of multiple measures of behavior.

Although people's memories of their previous behavior usually are notoriously unreliable, the memory of clients occasionally can be relied on to provide an *ex post facto* baseline when the baseline clearly is zero or 100 percent. An example of both was presented by a college student, who stated adamantly that during the past two months he had not talked to even one girl (thus, his weekly rate was zero); he added that every time he was required to make a class presentation, he became ill (thus his weekly rate was 100 percent). After a detailed interview, both series of self-observations were used as baselines.

Because of clinical demand, baselines used in treatment rarely meet all the ideal requirements of adequate length, nonreactivity, independence, and reliability. Nevertheless, the therapist uses the best available data to develop a baseline. When he or she compares the results of a subsequent intervention period, any deviations from the ideal are taken into account in the interpretation (for a more detailed discussion of baselines, see Sidman, 1960).

TIME SERIES DESIGNS

Once a baseline has been established for a given attribute, some form of intervention usually is initiated. Since data continue to be collected by the same procedures as during the baseline period, it may be possible to determine whether relevant changes occur following the onset of intervention. To ascertain whether these differences are relevant, a time series design is established. This is a research design in which successive observations are made throughout treatments. Time series designs serve several functions (Gottman, McFall, and Barnett, 1969, p. 299). First, they are descriptive. Since treatment usually covers an extended period, the time series data provide a continuous record of the dependent variables (behavior changes, productivity, attendance, cohesiveness, satisfaction with life, anxiety, and so on) over the entire course of treatment.

Second, the time series serves as an invaluable source of *post hoc* hypotheses regarding observed but unplanned changes in the dependent variables. Hypotheses can be developed by reviewing the interventions of therapists and scanning for shifts in the time series (Gottman, 1973, p. 99).

Third, planned introduction of interventions imbedded in the total program can result in a relatively powerful research design. The design must demonstrate that any major shifts in the pattern of data being collected are indeed the result of the interventions being applied. The major rival hypotheses that might also account for such changes must be rendered implausible. Three major designs that allow varying degrees of causal inference are AB design; the interrupted time series or ABAB design; and the multiple baseline design.

AB DESIGN

In the AB design, the baseline period (A) is followed by a period of intervention (B), during which data is collected just as it was during the baseline period (see Figure 5.1a).

Figure 5.1 provides several examples of group phenomena in which the therapist intervened at the sixth session after obtaining a baseline during the first five sessions. Each of these are AB designs.

One major threat to the conclusion that the intervention caused the increase is the possibility that an uncontrolled event occurring concomitantly with the intervention may have produced the change (Campbell and Stanley, 1963, refer to this as *threat to validity due to history*). In one group, for example, one of the members had a surprise promotion and salary increase; and her leadership behavior in the group increased at a dramatic rate. This increase was mistakenly attributed to the rehearsals that just had been initiated in treatment.

In spite of its inability to control for simultaneous events and other plausible rival hypotheses (see Campbell and Stanley, 1963), the AB design is most commonly used in behavioral group treatment. It always is available where continuous and careful data collection occurs. Even if the therapist and clients are not certain that the intervention was the sole cause of the changes, it still makes it possible to ascertain the degree to which goals are being achieved.

Not all time series results are as readily interpreted as in Figure 5.1a. The remaining graphs in Figure 5.1 allow for varying degrees of confidence in the assumption that the intervention contributed to change.

In Figure 5.1b, although the average of baseline for member to member interaction is lower than the average of intervention phase, causality cannot be attributed to the intervention because of the general upward trend in the baseline, which continues, uninterrupted, into the intervention period. This upward trend is typical in situations in which percentage of client participation is being recorded.

In contrast, Figure 5.1c shows a dramatic shift in the slope of member praise statements, suggesting a causal effect. In Figure 5.1d, there is a small difference in level between A and B and no difference in slope, making it difficult to determine whether the difference in leader-member interaction in the baseline and treatment phases is relevant. In Figure 5.1e, there appears to be a shift in direction of the slope following the introduction of intervention,

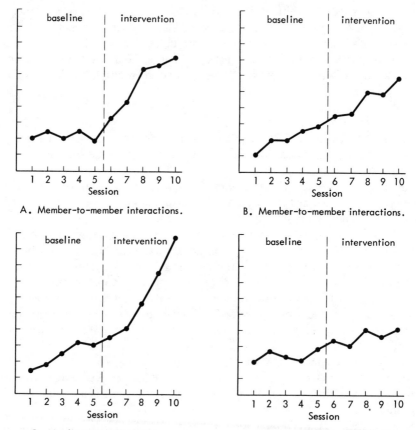

A. Member-to-member interactions.

B. Member-to-member interactions.

C. Member praise statements.

D. Leader-to-member interactions.

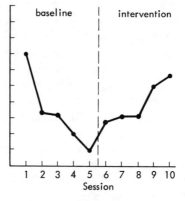

E. Leader suggestion-giving.

Figure 5.1.

which suggests the influence of the intervention in modifying leader's suggestion-giving behavior.

There are several ways of dealing with the alternative hypotheses that a simultaneous uncontrolled variable caused the shift. A similar outcome in the replication of the experiment with other persons within the group might increase confidence in the causality of intervention. A more common way is to use an interrupted time series (Campbell and Stanley, 1963), more commonly referred to as an ABAB or reversal design. In the ABAB design, baseline observations both precede and follow the introduction of an intervention. Figure 5.2, illustrates the use of this design with a group of divorced women.

In this example, since the predicted changes occurred contingent on treatment, the results strongly suggest that the intervention caused the shifts. Usually, in the reversal design it is necessary to keep the treatment period short to prevent irreversible learning from occurring. The return to baseline also is

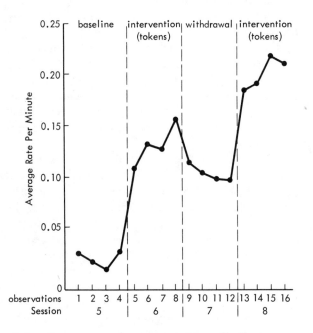

Figure 5.2.   Frequency of group positive affectual responses for members of an Assertive Training group. Data points represent 10-minute monitoring periods (four per session).

kept short so that the clients need not be deprived too long of their initial success.

In Figure 5.2, it should be noted that a general upward trend can be discerned. This is a common occurrence with the use of the ABAB design. It appears that with each reversal some irreversible learning often takes place.

According to many authors, the reversal design yields data that, when graphed, clearly points to significance or lack of it. Bandura (1969, pp. 241–244) demonstrates that at least in cases where the changes are not dramatic, the graphs alone may not be sufficient to estimate significance.

For most time series designs the correlation between successive observations makes the use of inferential techniques of data analysis problematic. A promising technique for estimating statistical significance, which takes dependency of data into account, is presented by Gottman (1973) and Glass, Willson, and Gottman (1975). This method of analysis is particularly useful in avoiding the interpretation of random shifts in the data as intervention effects.

MULTIPLE BASELINE DESIGN[2]

One of the reasons that the ABAB design is not used universally in analyzing time series data is that the learning that occurs during the initial treatment period often is not readily reversible—for example, learning to drive a car. Another objection to the use of the reversal procedure is the ethical problem in withdrawing treatment that seems to be working for previously long-suffering clients. Parents often have refused to withdraw what appeared to be a successful treatment even though they understood the rationale and knew that it was temporary. To deal with this problem, clinicians with increasing frequency háve begun to use multiple baseline design. These are characterized by the collection of data on two or more persons, behaviors, groups, settings, or treatments.

In Figure 5.3, the therapist compares the effects of treatment of three interactive behaviors in a group of four hospitalized, chronic schizophrenic patients. Although these behaviors are not completely independent, substantial shifts seem to follow only an introduction of the intervention. Ideally, behaviors should be independent in a multiple baseline design, to prevent the treatment of one behavior causing changes in the alternative behaviors. This can present a dilemma for clinicians who also are interested in furthering the generalization of the treatment effects (see Hartmann and Atkinson, 1973). Moreover, it also is desirable that the order in which each behavior is treated be selected randomly. Finally, the length of baseline and intervention periods should be about the same (see Leitenberg, 1973). To the extent that these conditions are not present, interpretation of intervention effects are unclear.

[2]No distinction is made in this discussion between a multiple baseline and multiple schedule design.

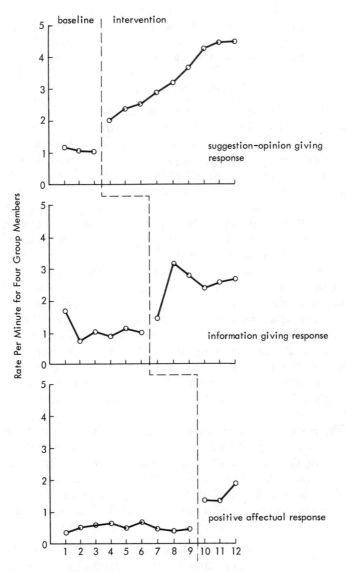

Figure 5.3. Each data point represents one group session. The broken line through the graphs indicates the termination of baseline and the beginning of intervention for each target behavior.

In this example, it appears that increases follow each introduction of treatment (token reinforcement). This alteration adds support to the contention that it is the specific treatment that is producing the change in behavior and not some concurrent extraneous event. The time periods in this example are of equal length, but the categories are not entirely independent.

OTHER TIME SERIES DESIGNS

The therapist is not restricted to the three time series designs thus far discussed. On the basis of evidence accrued in the intervention phase, further intervention in the same way often would seem unprofitable and a new intervention introduced. In a social skills workshop, for example, members appeared unable to express negative feedback to their peers. Following a baseline (A), token reinforcement (B) was used as an intervention. When the data revealed no noticeable shifts, a second intervention—modeling and behavior rehearsal (C)—was introduced. Since a drastic increase in negative feedback followed, a return to baseline (A) was arranged, followed by a return to the modeling and rehearsal condition (C). This ABCAC design, a variation of a reversal design, was dictated by the demands of the situation.

Such trial-and-error variations often are used in clinical practice. Since each variation is planned *a priori,* it is more useful than a simple *post hoc* analysis of the data in explaining intervention effects. However, as the therapist continues to introduce new intervention conditions, he or she increases the probability of finding significant changes purely by chance. The interpretation is further confounded by the fact that the therapist cannot be sure whether the most recent intervention or some combination of interventions is responsible for the shift. Only subsequent replications would answer that question.

Even if the design accounts for major alternative plausible hypotheses, because the sample size is unusually small, these time series designs are limited primarily to drawing inferences about the clients and groups the therapist is treating. Replications across various persons and groups might permit greater generalization of the treatment effects. It is in this way that the clinician can go beyond the collection of data related to the immediate problems and contribute to the growing body of knowledge on the laws governing group and individual phenomena.

CONTROL GROUP[3] STUDIES

Although time series methodology is probably the most practical and useful evaluation model for the practitioner, more traditional control group experiments might occasionally be feasible and/or desired. The principal attraction

[3]To avoid confusion, it should be noted that a control group experiment refers to an investigation in which N subjects are randomly assigned to two or more conditions and then compared. While treatments may be individually administered, the data from each

of control group experiments is their ability to control for many of the alternative hypotheses that may also explain changes in the data (see Campbell & Stanley, 1963). Thus, the practitioner with the necessary resources may wish to conduct this type of experiment to learn more about the relationship between certain phenomena.

In the Group Therapy and Research Project several control group studies have been made. For example, Schinke and Rose (1976) sought to investigate the question, "Is a group assertive training program employing modeling, behavior rehearsal, and contracting procedures more effective than a training group which only discusses assertiveness?" This study had a pre-post design with subjects randomly assigned to either of the training conditions. A behavioral role-play test as well as a variety of self-report measures were used to detect differences between the two conditions. Results indicated that only the role-play test showed the modeling, rehearsal, contracting groups significantly more effective than the discussion control (see p. 200).

This study illustrates many useful features of control group studies on groups as well as some limitations. By randomly assigning subjects to the different conditions, one can assume equivalence of the groups and thus more readily attribute changes at posttesting to intervention rather than to initial group differences. Use of a discussion group allows one to control for such factors as group interaction and expectancy effects as competing explanations of change.

These are just two of many examples of how a control group experiment can provide the therapist with valuable information on treatment effectiveness. Although an extensive discussion of the design and analysis considerations of control group studies is well beyond the scope of this book, many excellent sources fortunately are available (for example, see Campbell and Stanley, 1963; Winer, 1971; and Kerlinger 1973).

Despite its advantages, control group research on group interventions has drawbacks for the therapist desiring to systematically evaluate his or her effectiveness. Probably the most serious limitation is the large number of subjects and resources often necessary to effectively carry out such investigations. For example, even after extensive recruitment Schinke and Rose were able to find only a total of 36 suitable subjects available to complete the training. Once a sufficient number of subjects were found, investment of resources was channeled into such areas as measurement instruments, handouts, and recruitment and training of persons to rate assertiveness role plays. Obviously many practitioners will not have such resources at their disposal, rendering comparable studies unfeasible.

In addition to problems of recruitment and resources, the clinician might

---

condition are usually combined to form a group of scores. In contrast are studies in which a group is the medium of intervention; that is, persons actually meet in groups. This group data can be combined with the data of other groups in the same condition as part of a control group experiment or studied separately as in the time series experiment.

also face obstacles to the random assignment of subjects to different conditions. Ethical considerations and agency policies regarding the withholding of treatment from individuals may force the therapist to abandon the research plan or to use a less controlled method of investigation (see Campbell & Stanley, 1963, and Campbell, 1969, for a discussion of "quasi-experimental" designs and related issues). Obviously this consideration becomes more problematic as the seriousness of the target problem increases.

The clinician wishing to conduct experimental research on groups faces other difficulties unique to control group study. The occurrence of subject attrition, while problematic to all researchers, poses special difficulties for the group therapist. In addition to the loss of subjects from the sample and the change in persons participating in the different conditions, subject attrition also changes the subject composition *within* each group itself. For example, groups of unequal size or differing ratios of males to females may have serious implications for treatment effectiveness. This problem is severely compounded if subject dropout appears not to be random but rather a response to some aspect of the study. Only diligent investigation of the circumstances surrounding subject attrition can answer this question.

A second problem associated with many control group studies on small groups concerns the proper method of analyzing the data. This problem occurs when individuals in each therapy group tend to score more alike after treatment than individuals in other groups *in the same condition.* Essentially, this reduced variability is believed to occur because of the common experience shared by group members. Thus, the more interactive the group treatment, the more likely it is that group members will affect one another's learning. A common result of this dependence is that the usual statistical methods employed lead to conclusions of significant differences more than would be expected by chance (Peckham, Glass, and Hopkins, 1969).

A potential solution to this problem is to use the group itself as the equivalent of a single subject as in the Schinke and Rose study (1976). Unfortunately, while solving the analysis problems, this approach creates its own difficulties through the loss of subjects and information (Peckham and others, 1969).

The aim of this discussion is not to convince practitioners of the futility of control group research on groups, but to point out some of the problems potential researchers should consider. Obviously, there are few simple answers to these and other questions raised by group research; however, awareness of these pitfalls can lead to better, more appropriate research studies as well as to more accurate, albeit cautious, interpretations of results.

In this chapter we have sampled only the potential research designs that were used or considered in the group treatment program. No one design or any one project will answer all research questions satisfactorily. Often it will be necessary to use these and others in combination to begin to develop further the basic technology of behavioral group therapy.

This chapter is only an introduction to the problems of evaluation of the effects of group intervention. More extensive knowledge of various design and analytical methodologies is necessary before the therapist can adequately deal with these and other problems. Many may question the role of practitioners in the research process. Their budget often is limited. Their first responsibility is to provide quality treatment for their clients. Nevertheless, each clinician can contribute to the complex process of testing and retesting the assumptions of the field. Mahoney (1974) succinctly states:

> Our knowledge of effective therapeutic procedures will grow only if we take an active role in its harvest. The age-old dichotomy of "clinician" versus "researcher" should be buried with many other bifurcations which currently polarize our search for knowledge. The most effective therapist is one who is in close touch with the "data" and who sensitively adjusts therapeutic strategies to the ebb and flow of relevant feedback.

In group therapy, research designs usually involve only a part of what is occurring in the group. One design may involve only one or two clients. Another may deal only with one of the many group attributes that are occurring within the group. Differing designs may exist for evaluation of the effectiveness of different treatments. Although limited designs do not answer all questions, clinicians can contribute significantly to knowledge if they deal each time with only one small aspect of treatment in every group they treat. When this is common practice, the accumulation of results from clinicians will produce a highly developed technology and theoretical framework, and clients will be provided highly effective treatment.

As pointed out earlier, collecting data for the purpose of contributing to knowledge is secondary to the purpose of evaluating the effectiveness of the various components of treatment, so that, if necessary, treatment procedures and session formats can be revised. Evaluation is an essential ingredient in the process of treatment planning. It forms the foundation on which plans are developed, criticized, and revised. In the next chapter, we will discuss the other ingredients in planning for intervention.

6 Goal Setting and Treatment Planning

By the end of treatment, George will carry on conversation with his friends while maintaining eye contact with them at least 50 percent of the time.

By the end of the session, the members of the obesity group will be able to demonstrate how to refuse dessert when their friends or family press them to eat it.

By the end of the meeting, each member will have made at least one treatment suggestion to another member of the group, and no one person (including the therapist) will have made more than five.

Once a baseline has been set, it is necessary to determine explicit agreed-upon expectations of what the client or group should achieve at some designated future time. The specifications of desirable changes in frequency, duration, latency, and other patterns of behavior are essential to evaluate whether or not treatment procedures and treatment as a whole has been effective.

GOAL SETTING

By identifying goals, both the client and the group can be active and informed participants in the process of treatment planning. Goal setting is a preliminary step to planning; plans are developed with an eye to the achievement of goals. The examples at the beginning of this chapter represent three of the most important kinds of goals in group therapy. The first goal is an individual treatment goal. The second is a common treatment goal, which several members hold jointly. The third is a group goal, which involves a change in the interactive pattern among the members. Interactive behaviors occur when the behavior of at least one person is contingent in part of the change of behavior of the other. Because of the importance of these three categories to group therapy, we will examine them in more detail.

Individual and Common Treatment Goals

How does one obtain a list of treatment goals from each client? First, the members examine the baseline data of the behaviors they have identified as potentially problematic. Sometimes during the group discussion, members will decide that a given behavior is not at a problematic level and requires no further attention. In other cases, a member will decide that a behavior not previously baselined very well may be problematic and that a baseline is required to determine whether a treatment goal should be set. In most cases, the client will decide that a change in the behavior from the baseline level is desirable; this will be formulated as a treatment goal.

For example, Janet, a 25-year-old administrative assistant in an insurance office, complains that people enter her small office smoking or begin to smoke while there. She is allergic to the smoke, but she is unable to complain. Her sneezes and tears seem to go unnoticed. A baseline self-observation revealed that she said nothing to any one of the 25 smokers who entered her office during the past two weeks. When the group members asked her what she would like to achieve, she responded that she wanted to tell every smoker either to put out the cigarette or pipe or go somewhere else to smoke. The following treatment goal was established: by the end of the treatment, Janet would make the above statement to any smoker who entered her office or anyone who smoked while in her office.

A well-formulated goal describes clearly who is going to change his or her behavior, what behavior is going to be altered, what the conditions are under which that behavior is going to be altered, and the estimated time period required for the change to take place. The goal also contains the criteria by which the client and outside observer could ascertain that the goal was achieved. Thus, the above goal is well formulated. Janet is the subject whose behavior is to be altered; the behavior to be increased is the demand for no smoking in her office; the conditions under which that behavior will occur is when a person enters smoking or when he or she lights up a cigar or cigarette while in her office; the time period is the duration of treatment (in this case, six weeks); and the criteria for success is the number or percentage of desired responses when the above conditions occur (in this case, 100 percent).

Initially in training the members, the therapist provides them with the criteria and examples of good goal formulation. The group members learn these criteria as they assist one other in the formulation of their own treatment goals. As in all other treatment processes, the members are encouraged increasingly to take the leading role in determining each other's goals. It also is important that the person who is to change his or her behavior be the client him- or herself, except in the case where parents are being trained to be managers of their own children's behavior (and even in this case there is an increasing tendency to focus not on changing the children's behavior but on having the parents change their own). In many cases, clients wish to place blame on others for their inadequate baseline level of performance. "If only the spouse, friend, or boss would act differently, everything would be better!" In these cases, the therapist points out that often a change in one's behavior will indeed cause a change in the behavior of others, but there is no guarantee. The behavior that the client has best control over is his or her own.

Often goals are incorrectly stated in terms of the therapist's actions. For example, "the goal of treatment is to provide the client with insight into his or her situational conditions, which are causing the problem." It is the therapist who is providing insight in this example. The action is an intervention rather than a goal. In the behavioral approach, it is essential that goals and methods for achieving them are separated clearly to evaluate the effectiveness of the treatment procedures (Gottman and Leiblum, 1974). Goal achievement provides the criteria against which method effectiveness is evaluated. A goal statement should be examined to determine whether the behavior to be changed is that of the client (or client's child) or that of the therapist. Therapist behaviors are always interventions. Occasionally some client behaviors or group interaction also may serve as an intervention. For example, when the client reinforces him- or herself for desirable performance, self-reinforcement is the intervention. Performance of a certain level of the desired behavior would be the goal. Thus, only careful examination will preclude the error of mistaking a goal for an intervention.

One can make only an estimate of the time period in which the change is to be achieved. In a group discussion, the client estimates a period during which he or she realistically thinks the goal can be achieved. In the author's clinical experience, the time periods set often become the exact limit for many clients in achieving the desirable goal. As noted in the above examples, the length of time stated in the goal varies considerably. Some goals are stated to be achieved by the end of a given session, others in a few weeks, and still others by the end of therapy.

Long-range goals or those of an indefinite length usually must be broken down into intermediate goals. For example, Marge Edwards, a resident of an institution for the past five years and presently in a transition group, has as her treatment goal the completion of two job interviews. She must describe her work experience both in the institution and prior to institutionalization. She also has to explain the reason for being in an institution and why it is no longer necessary. This goal will be attained by the end of group therapy. Such a goal is both too complex and too difficult to attain readily. Therefore, the following intermediate goals were formulated: by the end of the third of six sessions, she will be able to role-play what she will say about her work experience in a simulated interview; by the end of the fourth session, she will have role-played an explanation of why she no longer requires institutional care; by the end of the seventh session, she will have carried out the first interview and reported back to the group about her experience. These goals form a successive progression in difficulty; the achievement of each plays a part in achieving a final goal.

One can criticize the inflexibility of such a goal approach; our concern is that if such a specific achievement level is stated, the client may not go beyond that level even though he or she has the skill to do so. This argument is legitimate, and, in fact, such intransience has been observed in practice. To deal with this, some clinicians are beginning to state goals in terms of a range or set of alternatives rather than as one specific level. For example, a client in a transitional group was one of several members working on social conversation. The goal was that by the end of treatment he would carry on at least one conversation per day with someone other than his roommates. The client worked gradually toward the goal and achieved it near the end of treatment without difficulty. For this reason, it appeared that a much more complex goal could have been achieved. But because of a pattern of meeting minimal expectations, he achieved only the level required of him.

In this case, a goal should have been set that by the end of treatment the client would be carrying out one to five conversations per day, each of 3 to 20 minutes; at least one of these each week would be with a staff person and would be concerned with further planning and preparation for discharge. By setting more difficult alternatives, even if not achieved, the client can work toward the more difficult alternatives after treatment has terminated. Moreover, he or she can achieve success without attaining the more difficult expectations.

In many groups, two or more members may have the same individual treatment goals. An example is the goal of developing refusal responses, shared by all members of an obesity control group. When members hold identical goals, common treatment procedures can be used within the group meeting. Thus, common goals are a convenient but not necessary condition of group therapy. However, common treatment goals pertaining to more than one member are distinctly different from group goals, as demonstrated below.

Group Goals

In group therapy, clients do not work alone. They interact with the therapist and other group members to achieve their individual treatment goals.

Therefore, the therapist and group members must determine not only individual treatment goals but also interactive or group goals. The attainment of these will facilitate the attainment of individual treatment goals. Examples of group goals are the following:

> That all members will participate at least twice in the meeting's group discussion, and that no one member will participate more than 25 percent of the total time.

> That the members by the end of the next session will increase the total number of suggestion/opinion-giving responses by at least 10 percent over their joint baseline.

In both of these goals, the assumption is that increased interaction will facilitate individual treatment. The group allows members to practice those behaviors that they will need later in other social groups. The behaviors are interactive rather than common in that the participation or opinion-giving responses in part depend on the degree to which these categories are performed by others. Moreover, goal achievement involves a shift in the way members are interacting with each other.

It should be noted that all other criteria stated for treatment goals also are necessary in the formulation of group goals. In the first goal stated above, the target of change is the group interaction pattern. It denotes a change in the relative participation of each member. The condition under which it is going to be changed is the group meeting, and the criteria for success is participation at least twice by all members and no more than 25 percent by any one member. The time period for the change to occur is the duration of one meeting. Just as in the case of treatment goals, group goals may be broken down into intermediate group goals, although in the above example that probably would not be necessary.

The major difference between treatment goals and group goals is that in the latter case the target social system is the group, and the behaviors are interactive ones among the members. In a treatment goal, the target social system is the individual client, and the behavior to be changed is his or her individual behavior.

It should be noted also that group goals are usually temporary. Because they are primarily facilitative of treatment goals, the therapist usually is not concerned with maintenance of the group goal beyond the duration of the group. There are some exceptions to this.

On some occasions, group goals may be regarded as group treatment goals. For example, when the group is a complete family, it may have as its goal an increased number of praise responses from each member to every other member. This is an interactive goal, which at the same time is the treatment goal.

In this case, maintenance of the goal level beyond treatment would indeed be important.

One can identify several types of group goals commonly encountered in group therapy.

1) Modification of the frequency of overt manifestation of affect among members.

2) Modification of the affectional pattern (who likes/dislikes whom) within the group.

3) Establishment or modification of the pattern of distribution of work or the performance of group functions.

4) Establishment or modification of the procedures by which groups are governed or controlled.

5) Increasing or decreasing general or specific intragroup activities.

6) Establishment or modification of procedures for planning group activities.

7) Modification of a given group goal or procedure by which a group goal is selected.

8) Carrying out a given project and realization of its outcome.

Once individual and group goals have been formulated, it is possible to develop plans for attaining these goals. In the following section, we will discuss the major principles of treatment planning.

TREATMENT PLANNING

Treatment planning is the process of design and explication of the procedures and conditions of treatment to be used in the attainment of treatment and group goals. The plan often includes the rationale for the use of these procedures, as well as the ways in which the procedures are to be used. The planner draws upon previous research and experience to select procedures and determine appropriate conditions of treatment. He or she constantly evaluates the plan and revises it on the basis of data pertaining to the progress of member and group toward goals.

Planning in advance provides the therapist with an opportunity to prepare adequately for the job he or she is required to perform. The therapist need not know everything about all possible procedures or problems on the day the group begins. If, for example, several persons in the group have a persistent drinking problem in certain situations, and the literature has suggested that covert sensitization and covert reinforcement might be good ways of dealing with the problem, the therapist can review the techniques before using them in the group, and if necessary rehearse their application. He or she can seek assistance from consultants or colleagues who have more experience with the procedure than the therapist does.

In group therapy, one can identify at least two kinds of treatment planning. The first is the treatment plan oriented toward achieving individual treatment goals. The second is the treatment plan necessary to achieve session goals. Let us first examine an example of an individual treatment plan.

> Goal: to increase the amount of time I spend talking to men.
>
> Method: During the group meeting and once afterward with my father, I shall rehearse at least three different conversations with men.
>
> At the end of the day, I will review the amount of time I have spent with men. If I have spent more than 30 minutes, I will allow myself the right to watch the 10 o'clock news. So I not cheat, my roommate has agreed to check me out on who it was I talked to and what it was I said, before I am allowed to watch the news.
>
> If I fail to talk at least 30 minutes, I must rehearse with my roommate at least three more conversations. I cannot watch the news.

This is a treatment plan for one week. It involves the client rehearsing the desired behavior in and out of the group and reinforcing herself if she attains the daily goal. The plan is concerned with such details as avoiding cheating by the client and the consequences for failure. Moreover, it provides the client with a number of ways of achieving the goal. Although the written plan does not contain a rationale for the procedures, the therapist and client probably have discussed it already.

The procedures selected are strongly influenced by what is available in the group context, such as rehearsal and partners to consult. But the above plan has individual components as well, such as self-reinforcement and extra group monitoring by the roommate. It was conceived and developed primarily by the given client. She used her buddy as a consultant and got feedback from the therapist and other group members when she presented it to the group. Of course, since this plan was developed around the fourth week of treatment, the client already had been taught the use of rehearsal and self-reinforcement. The group session plan had included the suggestion that each person rehearse at least one aspect of the behavior he or she wanted to modify. In this way the therapist brought about an integration of individual and session planning and maintained personal input into the individual planning. Ultimately, however, the client will develop a plan for a behavior without consultation or feedback from the group. She will have to look only at the data she collects as the basis for modifying the plan. This level of autonomy does not occur until the final regular session and subsequent follow-up sessions.

As in this case, most clients are asked to put their treatment plans into writing so they can review the plan between sessions. Moreover, the written document provides a final arbiter of what was discussed and agreed upon as the contract. It prevents arbitrary shifting of details of the plan (see Chapter 7 for a more detailed discussion of the use of contracts.)

This does not suggest that shifts cannot occur. If the client, on the basis of conditions encountered during the week, finds that the plan is inadequate, it may be revised with the client's buddy. The client is urged to give the plan an adequate test before making such a shift. Clients who end up every week with several revisions are confronted with this pattern as a problem; often a plan is developed to help them to adhere to any program they develop for continually longer periods of time.

Session Planning

Of equal importance to group members is session planning, in which the therapist draws upon the evelutions from the previous week, the productivity of the members, their satisfaction with the meeting, and the goals that were achieved and not achieved at the last meetings. The therapist then reviews each client's treatment plan to discover what common procedures should be used in the group. On this basis, a session plan is drawn up in the form of a set of session goals, an agenda, and a set of recommended assignments from which clients can choose. Following is an example of the goals and agenda for the third session of a parent training group.

GOALS

By the end of this meeting each member will be able to:
1. state two ways of counting behaviors.
2. describe the events that occur before the behavior he or she is counting.
3. describe the events that occur after the behavior he or she is counting.
4. write a contingency contract for completing home assignments.

AGENDA

I. Review—20 min. What went on last time?
   A. Read goals.
   B. Evaluation and observer data.
   C. Review major concepts from previous session.
   D. Reading review and discussion.
   E. Buddy calls—how did they go?
II. Monitoring. How do I count the behavior now that I have defined it? 15 min.

    A. Handout and examples.

    B. Members develop plans for counting behavior in a case example.

III. Report on behavior-in-a-situation—40 min.

    A. Describe behavior in specific terms

    B. Members read their examples of antecedent and consequent conditions (what happens before and after).

    C. Members develop categories for antecedent and consequent conditions.

    D. Members report on any counts taken during week.

    E. Members develop a plan for counting the behavior each has chosen.

IV. And now, at least, let's make a deal: contingency contracting—30 min.

    A. What? Handout and example.

    B. Verbal contract for home chores.

    C. Write a contingency contract for next week's assignments.

 V. What do I do for next week? Assignments.

    A. Read pages 47–56 in *Parents are Teachers.*

    B. Count (monitor) the behavior you have chosen.

    C. Call buddy, see how his or her monitoring is going.

    D. Carry out the contingencies in your contingency contract.

VI. What I think of this session. Evaluation—5 min.

This plan was developed primarily by the therapist. However, based on the evaluation from the previous week, additional time (Zander, 1974) was allowed for contingency contracting. Before the following session, a planning meeting took place involving the therapist and several members. At this time the members input into the planning began to increase. By the final sessions, the meetings are largely planned with the help of the members.

The question may be raised whether the plan prevents the therapist from dealing with unpredicted situations as they arise in the group. In spite of careful planning, such situations do arise occasionally. When they do, the therapist must consider dealing with them immediately.

For example, in a transitional group in an institution, the original plan was to deal with the problem of finding a place to live when the group members returned for a given meeting in the community. The plan had been devised by several of the members and agreed upon by the rest. That week, however, one of the members found out at the last minute that he was going to have a job interview. He was quite anxious about it. The therapist suggested to the members that they change the agreed-upon agenda and deal with the more pressing problem that Arnold was having. Since job interviewing was something that several of them faced, the agreement came quickly.

In this example, since the initial agreement on the agenda of the meeting was determined by the members, the members had to agree to the shift. If they had not, the original program would be held to and Arnold would have to get his emergency training for job interviewing outside of the group. In either case, it is the responsibility of the therapist to introduce the possibility of altering the program in situations that he or she perceives to have higher priority.

Spontaneity on the part of the therapist is not eliminated. Planning merely protects him or her from having to jump from one major decision to the next throughout the meeting.

It is, of course, impossible to develop a treatment plan without a detailed knowledge of the procedures used to carry out those plans. In the next four chapters, we will discuss the major intervention procedures used in group therapy and the conditions under which they are employed.

7 Reinforcement and Contingency Contracting in Groups

(1)

Stanley: When this guy, this little guy (laughter from others) pushed in front of me, I politely but firmly asked him to go to the end of the line.

Vernon: (with emphasis) Great! You really must have been proud of yourself.

Several others: (nod approval) You should have been. Good for you.

Stanley: I was, I have to admit, but I still couldn't look him in the eye the way we practiced in the group.

Marty: And you still need to work on that, but you've got to admit you've done better than you've ever done before.

Stanley: I think so, too, but I've got a lot to learn still.

(2)

Winnie: I said to myself, I'm not going to feel sorry for myself like I usually do.

Lou: (handing her a token). Winnie, you did a good job.

Winnie: (jokingly) Thanks, I really need that. I'll put it to good use.

Other members: (laughing, all hand her tokens).

(3)

Therapist: It appears that everyone did all the home assignments. As we agreed last week, in that case we would spend the entire meeting role-playing as you requested.

(4)

Annie: (reporting to the group) As I said I would do at the last meeting, I made four phone calls this week, so I earned the new pair of jeans I promised myself.

TYPES OF REINFORCEMENT

In the first example, members are providing Stanley with social reinforcement, or praise and approval, of what he has accomplished during the week. In the second example, Winnie is reinforced not only with social reinforcement but also with tokens for her positive self-references. The tokens may be indicating merely approval or they may mediate the right to attain more concrete reinforcement when a certain number are accrued. In the third example, the therapist provides a reinforcing event for the group because of its completion of the agreed-upon percentage of assignments. This event and its consequence of a group achievement are referred to as a "group contingency." In the fourth example, Annie reports back to the group on the results of her contingency contract in which she awarded herself concrete reinforcement (a desired new pair of jeans) for completion of the contracted frequency (four) of phone calls.

In this chapter, we will see how these and other categories of reinforcement are administered in the group situation and how members are trained in the process of delivering reinforcement to themselves and others. We also will discuss the withholding of reinforcement (extinction) and the type of negative reinforcers that are used in group therapy.

Social Reinforcement

In the first example, only praise, approval, and attention from the group members and the therapist are used to reward Stanley for his achievement. These are commonly referred to as "social reinforcement." Even in this brief example, several principles concerning the delivery of social reinforcement are demonstrated. First, the praise statements were delivered immediately following the report of the accomplishment in loud, clear, unambiguous statements of approval. Second, and especially relevant for group situations, the therapist allowed time for members to indicate their approval. Third, reinforcement occurred even though the achievement was only an approximation of the final goal behavior. At a later date, however, approval would be withheld unless Stanley also looked the person in the eye and spoke in a loud voice.

There also are several potential problems in this example. Since the therapist and group members are reinforcing Stanley's verbal description of what happened and not the behavior itself, they must be careful that they are not reinforcing lying behavior. Members may not be accustomed to praising others. In this case, training in appropriate praise response first would be required to involve members in mutual social reinforcement.

Where praise is excessive and/or indiscriminately given, the effect of the reinforcement is diminished by satiation. In training in reinforcement, appropriate timing also must be considered. Either because of satiation or inexperience with praise and approval, these may not be serving as effective reinforcers. To discover whether this is, indeed, what is happening, the therapist often resorts to a technique called "checking." The checking can lead to a training opportunity as in the following example:

> *Therapist:* I notice that on the evaluations last week, one member noted that I do a lot of praising in the group. I couldn't tell whether he liked it or didn't like it, or whether he found it useful. It would be valuable to me to hear what the rest of you think.
>
> *Tony:* (after some hesitation) Well, you do praise an awful lot, but this is one of the few places I hear something good about myself. I like it. Still, sometimes I get the impression that, since you're the therapist, you're just giving us therapy.
>
> *Therapist:* That's a helpful answer. What do some of the rest of you feel?
>
> *Sherri:* I don't know how to react when you say I did something good. I just get embarrassed. But that's the way I am, I guess.
>
> *Lon:* Is it really natural for you to make all those compliments? I know you're supposed to reinforce us, but do you really mean all the things you say?
>
> *Therapist:* Absolutely. Otherwise what would be the use? (Others nod in agreement; discussion follows in some detail on the criteria for the meaningful use of praise.) This has been a very useful discussion. I think one conclusion can be that I have to be perfectly honest in my praise and that perhaps more of you should begin to praise each other. If anyone has anything he or she feels wasn't covered in the discussion, why don't you add it to the meeting evaluation?

In this example, the therapist evaluates with the group members their perception of the reinforcement process. This type of evaluation should follow any evidence of members' concern about the use of social reinforcement. The therapist used the evaluation to initiate a discussion of greater group involvement in mutual praising, as the absence of mutual reinforcement reduces the effectiveness of the group as a pressure toward change.

In reviewing the data collected on the degree to which members praise or show approval to each other, the therapist may conclude that this is a skill in which they require training. After reviewing the data with the members, he or she will usually develop with them a list of praise and approval statements. If the suggestions are meager, the therapist will use "brainstorming" (see Chapter 10) to increase the list. Members also may assign themselves the task of each discovering at least three praise statements during the week and bringing them in writing to the next meeting.

Once such a list has been developed, a skit or role-play may be used to practice using the praise statements. Eventually, token reinforcement may be delivered everytime someone makes a praise statement. Following each presentation, the group members discuss the immediacy, affect, audibility, and the sincerity of the delivery of the praise statement. The following rating scale often is distributed to the group members to facilitate their participation.

Did the reinforcement immediately follow the target behavior?
    usually _____ rarely

Was the affect with which the reinforcement was delivered appropriate?
    appropriate _____ inappropriate

Did the reinforcement appear to be sincere?
    extremely sincere _____ phony

Could you clearly hear the reinforcement?
    highly audible _____ inaudible

For those groups in which members indicate serious difficulties in praising, the skit is repeated several times until most of the criteria are met. After that a less structured role-play is presented in which only the basic situation is described. During the situation, the reinforcing person must reinforce as often as possible, meeting the criteria to the best of his or her ability. The final step is to give a group assignment to reinforce each other as frequently as is feasible. The therapist may cue the members on when to reinforce, and then gradually fade the cueing. At first the presentations tend to be somewhat stilted, but they soon take on a more natural appearance.

Token Reinforcement

Tokens are often paired with social reinforcement and are administered following each desired behavior. In the following example of a weight loss group, the therapist is attempting to increase the number of new ideas, suggestions, and opinions that the members make. To do this, the therapist awards tokens to each member who presents one of the above verbal behaviors. The tokens serve merely as information or feedback that the desired behavior has been performed.

> *Ruth:* I sure don't know what to do when someone offers me a drink. I usually just hesitate for a moment and then accept, and I know how many calories there are in a beer or scotch. Too many!
>
> *Leader:* Anyone have any ideas? You've been through this before, especially our older members.
>
> *Clarence:* Have you thought about using a card in your purse that reminds you to say no?
>
> *Therapist:* (handing him a token) That's a possibility. What do the rest of you think?
>
> *Roberta:* Well, she might not have her purse with her (receives a token), but it would be better, at least for me, to practice what I would say here in the group in such situations.
>
> *Leader:* (as he hands her another token) That sounds like a great idea. Has anyone done that before?
>
> *Dick, Betty* (nod): Me. Yea, me, too.
>
> *Leader:* Any ideas about what she might say in a practice session?
>
> *Bruce:* How about "Look, a beer is nearly 200 calories, and my calories are up for today."
>
> *Leader:* That makes a lot of sense (hands Bruce a token).

The initial presentation of tokens frequently is greeted by laughter and a slowing down of the interaction on the part of the group members. After a short while, however, little attention is paid to the tokens, except when the therapist forgets to issue one as deserved. It always is surprising how assertive even the most shy clients can be in this situation.

After an initial trial, the token system is evaluated by the members. Most groups enthusiastically endorse it, although occasionally individuals are annoyed by it. Only one group with which the author is familiar decided that it was an undesirable procedure. As a result of the evaluation, members eventually may decide to drop the system, to include backup reinforcers, or to move either from or to the use of group contingencies. Tokens usually are employed only during part of meetings and for a limited number of meetings. They are faded as soon as possible; however, social reinforcement usually is continued. The token system may be reintroduced, however, when the therapist or group members discover a clear verbal deficit, such as problem talk, opinion giving, or feedback. But once the problem is solved, tokens may be eliminated, unless, of course, they are part of a specific research design.

Tokens also have been used by Shoemaker and Paulson (1976) in working with nonassertive mothers who were failing in parent training programs due to their lack of assertiveness in various family situations. A discriminative token system was employed to shape appropriate assertive responses. White poker chips were distributed by the group trainer and group members as immediate positive feedback. Red and blue tokens were given as negative feedback for aggressive and withdrawing responses respectively.

Since a cotrainer recorded all the tokens received and given, patterns of receiving and giving could be discussed (at the fifth and tenth sessions). For example, one mother who never gave negative feedback (red or blue chips) was able to overcome this deficit in the group, and the new behavior ultimately was transferred to the family situation.

Group Contingencies

In most of the previous examples, contingencies have been delivered to individuals. The tokens either have provided feedback or they have mediated concrete reinforcers or reinforcing events. In some groups, however, tokens either are delivered to the group as a whole or to individuals. In either case, they mediate concrete reinforcers or reinforcing events shared by the entire group. These are called group contingencies. Although in adult clinical groups there is little research to indicate whether group contingencies are more powerful than individual contingencies, in children's groups there is considerable evidence that the group contingencies work somewhat more efficiently (see Wodarski and others, 1973, for a review of the literature in this area). It appears from anecdotal evidence in adult groups that group contingencies for ingroup behavior are more effective than individual ones, especially in the middle and later sessions.

The use of group contingencies is never imposed by the therapist. They are presented for discussion either by the therapist or one of the members; before using them, the group must agree that the contingencies are worth trying in terms of what members are aiming to achieve. For example, in one group, every time a member perceived that he was being reinforced by another member, he threw a token into a box in the middle of the table. When the box contained 20 tokens, the members were permitted to talk about off-task subjects. Individual behaviors resulted in individual tokens, which ultimately purchased a desired group event.

Late arrival was a problem in another group, so members agreed that the group break and refreshments would be contingent on all members arriving on time. The plan was later modified to require at least two persons to be late before the privilege of the break was withdrawn. As can be seen here, tokens are not a necessary requisite for the use of group contingencies.

Thus far, we have discussed how individual and group contingencies are administered within the context of the treatment group. Equally important is how they are administered by each client to him- or herself. One vehicle for this is the contingency contract.

CONTINGENCY CONTRACTS

Contingency contracts are written agreements between two or more persons in which consequences following the performance of specified behaviors by one or more of the parties are administered by another party. This procedure has been used especially with individuals and families (see, for example, Stuart, 1971). It also has been suggested as a regular feature of group treatment (see Rose, 1974a, 1974b, 1975).

There are at least five different types of contingency contracts in group treatment. The first is a negotiated contract between a given group member and a significant person in his or her life (usually not a member of the group). For example, in an assertive training group, Mrs. K agreed to reduce the frequency of yelling at her mother-in-law to once a week in exchange for going out to dinner once a week with her husband. The husband monitored the behavior and administered the reward. The group members merely served as consultants to Mrs. K in negotiating the contract with her husband.

The second type is a self-administered reinforcement contract which the member negotiates with one or more other group members to serve merely as monitors that the behavior was appropriately performed. For example, Tom will reward himself with a ticket to the Packers football game if his weight is maintained or lowered for three consecutive weeks. Ron, another member of the group, will weigh Tom and will hold the ticket until the weight is at the agreed-upon level.

The third contract is between two (or more) persons, usually members of the group, who are working on the same or similar behaviors and who control each other's rewards. For example, three men who decided to give up smoking gave each other $100, to be forfeited if there was any evidence of smoking in the next month.

The fourth contract, referred to as a behavioral exchange (Rappaport and Harrell, 1972), involves two or more persons who perform behaviors that the other parties find desirable as reciprocal reinforcement. For example, in a couples' group Mr. M spent more time assisting Mrs. M with household tasks (at least two hours a week) in exchange for Mrs. M spending more time playing bridge with Mr. M and others (at least two hours a week).

A fifth type of contingency contract is between all the group members and the therapist or the agency. The members and the therapist, for example, agree that if all the members give tangible evidence that they have completed 100 percent of their behavioral assignments, the fee for that session will be cut in half. There are many variations of this, such as subgroups contracting with subgroups or individuals contracting with outside organizations. The basic principles, however, are the same.

In all types of contingency contracts, the behaviors to be performed, altered, or omitted are clearly specified and the rewards and the conditions under which they are to be received also are clearly identified. The time period in which the desired behaviors can occur are given in the contract whenever possible. And whenever feasible, the target person provides evidence of his or her completed contract to an external monitor. Ideally, the monitor initially should control the reinforcers for the target person.

In the beginning and middle sessions, contracts are designed in the group meeting. The last 10 to 15 minutes of every meeting are spent developing contingency contracts for the next time period, usually one week. If there is not enough time for everyone to develop a satisfactory contract, the one from the previous week is maintained for another week. To speed up the process, the conditions of the contract related to learning the treatment procedures can be stipulated by the therapist and included as part of the agenda. This is usually a reading and/or observation assignment.

Most items are negotiated with one's buddy or with the therapist in terms of the time available to the client. Group norms, however, tend to pressure members to assume about the same number of items on their contracts. Occasionally, the members will feel that the recommended readings or other assignments are too difficult or too long and will ask for a revised amount. This always is acceptable—the proposals of the therapist are meant as guidelines, not requirements.

Sometimes a longer period of preparation is necessary to develop the contract. A whole meeting may be devoted to preparing unassertive group members to try out one assertive behavior. The contingency contract provides a vehicle for integrating other procedures with reinforcement in developing individual treatment plans for each client. To see how this integration occurs, let us look at the following example.

> I, Martina K, within three weeks agree to ask my employer for a raise. If I succeed in making the request in a clear and self-assured tone of voice, I will purchase the new spring coat I saw at Gimbels. If I do not make the request, I shall forego a new coat until next year. To assure success in my venture, I shall observe in the group other people who will role-play how to ask for raises, and I will rehearse in at least five different situations what I shall say to my employer.

In this example, Martina has included in her plan how she intends to train herself to be comfortable in carrying out the new behavior. She has included modeling and rehearsal (to be discussed in more detail in the following chapter). She also has included what she considers to be a very powerful concrete reward. So that she does not obtain the reward anyway, she has clearly indicated that she will not make the purchase if she does not achieve her goal. Thus, a number of procedures have been integrated into the contract, increasing the probability of success. In many cases, the procedures of training are not included in the contract. They are only inferred. In this case, although modeling and rehearsal were made explicit, procedures such as cueing, shaping, and use of a buddy system also will be used.

One of the more common errors occurs when the client negotiates contracts that are either too difficult or too easy to perform. A too-difficult contract builds in the likelihood of failure. In one that is too easy, no demand is placed on the client beyond his or her present level of functioning. Unfortunately, there are no rules on how to find the happy medium. It is helpful, however, to ask the clients, and eventually encourage them to discuss with each other, whether the contract is realistic in terms of the level of difficulty.

The process of negotiation is crucial to the success of the contract as an intervention procedure. Yet members are often deficient in this extremely complicated skill. As a result, the therapist unwittingly may impose the conditions of the contract on them. One way to avoid this problem is to provide models on how to negotiate and to create opportunities for members to reject suggestions by the therapist. Occasionally, a therapist may perceive this rejection as resistance when, in fact, it is an indication of improvement in assertiveness and even in negotiation skills. This does not imply that the therapist should abdicate responsibility to propose conditions of the contract. Rather the members should be encouraged to weigh the recommendations, to substitute alternate conditions that they perceive to be more relevant than those suggested by the therapist, and to seek advice from other group members. In this way, the members are being trained toward the goal of independent functioning and the contracts gradually moved from something created largely by the therapist to a plan designed completely by the given member.

Eventually, however, the entire contract is eliminated. As the individual members meet with success in their short-term, highly specific contracts, the time periods for which they contract are extended, and the conditions of the contract become more general. In the final phase, written conditions are replaced by verbal agreements. At the same time the schedule of reinforcement (see the following section) is thinned, and eventually reinforcement is eliminated, although many clients have indicated that they continue to reinforce themselves when faced with undesirable tasks. Thinning usually occurs item by item in the contract rather than with the contract as a whole. In this process of gradually eliminating specific conditions of the contract, backsliding may occur. At any time that behaviors fail to occur in desirable frequencies, or maladaptive ones begin to increase to earlier levels, the contract should be renegotiated, as in the following example.

Mrs. P was a member of a weight loss group that met weekly for six weeks. Because monitoring her caloric intake was now a matter of regular habit at the end of every meal, she no longer stated this item in the contract, although she did tell group members of her intention to continue monitoring.

After the success of this first fade-out, the members suggested that she no longer monitor her exercising, but that she make a commitment to the group to continue her half-hour of daily exercise. Finally, Mrs. P eliminated the written contracted prohibition against eating high caloric snacks and desserts, although she resolved to continue avoiding those foods. She soon noticed a tendency to renege on her verbal agreement about snacks, however, if no written contract and contingencies were set up. So the following week she once again included the elimination of snacks into the written contract. Success in this endeavor would earn her points to buy a new book that she had wanted for a long time.

Self-Reinforcement

As contingency contracts are faded, the client increasingly gains skill in self-reinforcement. Ultimately the client must learn to gain a great deal of the deserved approval from him- or herself rather than from others. The contingency contract is a means of organizing oneself, and the people about one, to receive reinforcement. Eventually, the client becomes the major source of that reinforcement, and ultimately, the major type of reinforcement he or she uses is self-approval. The concept of self-esteem (see Rimm and Masters, 1974, p. 426) is closely related to the ability of an individual to appraise his or her actions and attitudes favorably. In training clients in self-reinforcement, the therapist increases the frequency with which clients praise themselves and their actions, and in so doing increases the self-esteem of the clients.

Inititally, clients tend to depreciate their behavior and attitudes. Often there are good reasons for this low valuation, but in many cases the problem is one of inaccurate self-appraisal. In learning new, more useful skills and attitudes, the clients in the first category can reinforce themselves more easily. By hearing group praise of their actual accomplishments, often those in the second category also find a basis for more frequent self-praise and higher self-valuation.

Most clients learn how to praise themselves in the process of using contingency contracts and in observing the praise of members and therapists among each other. However, some clients require a special training in self-reinforcement. In the group, praising of oneself aloud for real achievement may be carried out in role-play demonstrations and rehearsals, and contracts will be negotiated in which the individual agrees to practice the self-reinforcement so many times a day. Some clients can reinforce themselves overtly but in such a way as to make themselves disagreeable to others. This often is discovered by the other group members in the group exercises. To correct this behavior, the given client is provided feedback from the others on the quality of self-praise, in addition to the role-play training already mentioned.

BUILDING A REINFORCEMENT REPERTOIRE

One of the major problems in contingency contracting with adults is finding effective reinforcers. Obviously, in almost all cases there are many available that the individual has not been able to identify. To facilitate this identification, the following questionnaire is distributed at about the third session. The members usually are asked to fill it in at home as one of the behavioral assignments. It should be discussed at the meeting, however, in case there are any questions. The therapist also can provide a completed example similar to the following form.

Name _____   Date _____

SURVEY OF REINFORCERS

Record all items according to preferences, beginning with the most preferred items.

A. People

    List below the 2 people with whom you spend the most or a lot of your time each week. In making the list, consider children and friends (exclude job-related people).

1._____ 2._____

    There may be other people (acquaintances, coworkers) with whom you would like to spend more time each week but don't get a chance to. List below 2 people with whom you feel you would like to spend more time than you presently do.

1._____ 2._____

B. Places

    List below the 2 places where you spend the most or a lot of your time each week. In making the list consider such places as the bedroom, family room, kitchen, out-of-doors, garden (exclude your job/office).

1._____ 2._____

    There may be other places where you would like to spend more time, but don't get a chance to. List 2 such places below.

1._____ 2._____

C.   Things

List below the 2 things with which you spend the most or a lot of your time each week. In making the list, consider such things as specific books, sewing, musical instruments, stereo, bicycle, and so on.

1._____   2._____

List below the things you do not own that you would most like to have and can afford (book, album, new shoes, and such).

1._____   2._____

List below your 4 best-liked foods and drinks. Include candy, desserts, and so on. Include items you may not have very often.

1._____   2._____

3._____   4._____

D.   Activities

List below 2 activities on which you spend the most or a lot of your time—such things as housework, working crossword puzzles, reading, going to the movies, playing cards, watching T.V., walking, riding a bike, taking a bath, talking to other people, going shopping, being alone.

1._____   2._____

List below 2 activities you would like to engage in more frequently than you do now.

1._____   2._____

You have listed numerous people, places, things, and activities that you value. Of all of these, select 2 or 3 that are the most powerful and that you are able to offer as reinforcers to yourself.

1._____

2._____

3._____

At the following meeting the various categories are discussed and members are encouraged to modify their answers in any way after hearing the answers of others. The group quickly establishes the norm that everyone is to have reinforcers and certain events appear to be shared generally as reinforcers. From this list members are asked to select events that they or someone else in their environment can control steadily until the time that they perform the contracted behavior.

The following week each member contracts for a relatively high probability behavior (one that he or she can perform readily), for which he or she receives either a self-administered, friend, family member, or buddy administered reinforcer. At the next meeting the problems in contracting, administering, or withholding of reinforcement are discussed. The effectiveness of the reinforcers also are discussed, and often it is necessary to use more powerful contingencies than the client orginally selected. If the client sees that other group members are successful in controlling their own behaviors with contingencies, he or she is more likely to risk more of his or her material goods or recreational activities on behalf of behavioral change.

In a few cases individuals are still unable to find adequate reinforcers. Either the ones they have selected in the questionnaire are too general, unavailable (for example, flying lessons when they have very little money), or they would not withold them because they claim that the given reinforcers are vital to their absolute minimal life satisfaction. Or they may have a limited number of reinforcing events in their repertoire. In this case, reinforcement sampling (Allyon and Azrin, 1968, p. 91) often is used. This is a procedure in which the client is confronted with an event or material stimulus prior to its being used as a reinforcer. For example, the group members in the obesity group ate a low calorie meal together at the second meeting. Generally, in spite of some initial anxiety, this turned out to be an enjoyable experience for all. As a result, the therapist could use a second dinner as a group contingency. Similarly in a mental hospital group, the therapist took the members shopping and to a film in a nearby town. They also went to a restaurant and a laundromat. At a later date, all of these events were used as individual reinforcers for the completion of behavioral assignments in the group.

The purpose of reinforcement sampling is to provide the clients with initial experience with a given event. Following an initial sampling of an event, clients usually claim that they find it more satisfying. Events used as reinforcers often are those that the therapist is aiming to increase anyway. The mere act of using an activity as a reinforcer seems to make that activity more attractive. For example, the members of the obesity group learned that low calorie meals can be enjoyable.

Reinforcement procedures primarily are used to increase behaviors in which the client is deficient. Now we will discuss procedures used to decrease behaviors that the client has in excess (surplus behaviors).

Procedures for Decreasing Behavior

Some verbal behaviors in the group need to be decreased in frequency. For example, a certain amount of complaining by the client is appropriate, but a high frequency of such behavior attended to by the other members both reinforces the behavior and increases the other members' dissatisfaction with the group. Similarly, continued responses of blaming others for one's situation and nonspecific aggressive statements fall into this category.

Within the group, a number of procedures such as extinction, negative feedback, and response cost can be used to reduce the frequency of such behaviors. Extinction, the withholding of positive reinforcement, commonly is used in group treatment to deal with those undesirable behaviors that tend to disrupt the group. However, the therapist alone cannot use extinction without involving the entire group. For example, although the therapist conscientiously ignored the complaining behavior of one of the clients, the other members consoled the client and attended to the behavior in a number of other ways. As a result, complaining failed to be eliminated and, in fact, increased in frequency. In the following example, the therapist first attempts to teach the members how to apply extinction procedures to behaviors that they find annoying in the group.

> *Therapist:* Let's review the kind of statements we discussed last week as being annoying or not helpful to the group.
>
> *Charles:* Criticism without giving evidence!
>
> *Ed:* What about complaining without adding on a plan to change one's own life?
>
> *Frank:* Down-in-the-dumps talk. All that does is get the rest of us down.
>
> *Therapist:* These are good comments. How should the rest of us respond to such statements?
>
> *Charles:* I don't know. Maybe that just gives people the attention they're looking for. I think it would be better if we either ignored them or just went on to the next person. That's what you seem to do, Leo (therapist).
>
> *Therapist:* Do the rest of you agree? (Further discussion.) Well, we seemed to have bought a rule. We can try it out for a while and see how it works. And we can always change it if it doesn't serve our purposes.

Where tokens are used, occasionally response cost (the withdrawal of reinforcers or tokens) is administered. In this case, the clients are fined a certain number of tokens for the performance of previously agreed upon, undesirable group behaviors. For example, in a transitional group several members consistently failed to bring their assignments sheets. Tokens are acquired for a number of reasons in the group and could be used to purchase refreshments in the canteen. Reinforcement for bringing the sheets did not seem to work. When the therapist discussed this with the group, the members proposed that those failing to bring such sheets be fined five tokens for each failure. When implemented, the number of assignment sheets returned each meeting was 100 percent.

In working toward their own individual treatment goals, clients occasionally elect to use self-administered response cost. They will incorporate a system of fines into their plan, often to be managed by others in the event that they do not comply with their own demands.

For example, in a self-control group one member stated that positive reinforcement simply was not helping him to lose weight. He gave every member in the group a predated check for five dollars. Each week that he did not lose at least one pound, the member holding the check for that week was to send it to the charity of his or her choice (see Ferster, Numberger, and Levitt, 1962).

The important principle is that *the client* initiate and organize the procedures for the administering of his or her response cost. In this way some of the undesirable side effects of such a punishment procedure can be avoided.

Another means of limiting undesirable behavior in groups using tokens was demonstrated by Shoemaker and Paulsen (1976). By providing the members with one color tokens for negative feedback and another color for positive feedback, members received a mild form of punishment for undesirable behaviors. Because the positive feedback was high in proportion to the negative feedback, it avoided the pitfalls of some of the following procedure.

Another form of negative feedback is confrontation. Usually this is a description of what the client is doing and how the other members appear to be responding to it. This is used primarily to give clients information on which to base an accurate assessment of their presenting problems. Although for some clients such confrontation by group members serves as a positive reinforcer, for many it is a highly punishing experience. As such, the clients may become quite anxious and on occasion may fail to return for subsequent meetings. Still others find the bearer of such unfavorable tidings aversive as well, and the relationship to the group becomes unproductive. To protect the client from these side effects, they are discussed with the members usually prior to the use of confrontative procedures. Those who do not want such feedback are not required to receive it. Others while receiving it may ask at any time to discontinue confrontative comments directed at them. Although these protective devices rarely are called upon, the clients find these rules reassuring.

Schedules of Reinforcement

The schedule with which reinforcement is delivered in a learning situation has important implications for both the speed of learning and the degree to which a response is maintained once reinforcement has been discontinued. Since a full account of the research and implications of the many variations are quite elaborate (see Ferster and Skinner, 1957), only the implication of schedules for group therapy will be discussed here. Following are a few examples of schedules that have occurred in groups.

In an early session when problem talk is highly desirable to determine the focus of treatment, every time any member talks about a problem he or she is having with others he or she is praised or given a token—continuous reinforcement.

Every 30 suggestions, group members make to each other results in their having a dinner out together—fixed ratio schedule.

The timer is set for successive periods of five minutes each. Every time it goes off, if one or more members has praised other members, the group receives one token—fixed interval schedule.

Occasionally, when a member makes a good suggestion to another member, the therapist points this out to the group. The therapist tries to praise them at least every three to six occasions—variable ratio schedule.

The timer is set between 1 and 10 minutes. Every time it goes off, if any member has demonstrated one leadership behavior, the therapist increases the break time by one minute—variable interval schedule. There is a great deal of praise in the group by the therapist and members, but no noticeable pattern can be discerned—a mixed schedule.

Because continuous reinforcement is the quickest way to increase the frequency of a behavior (see Ferster and Skinner 1957), in the beginning of treatment a client should receive reinforcement as often as possible. But continuous reinforcement (the reinforcement of every behavioral event) can be only approximated in the group situation. The client may find it difficult to reinforce him- or herself or have others reinforce him or her at every opportunity. In the group, members may assist the therapist by participating in the mutual reinforcement of each other. This increases the number of people watching for desirable behavior as well as those actually doing the reinforcing. In the extragroup environment, such sources usually are not available. The same difficulty prevents the exact use of fixed interval or fixed ratio schedules. For these reasons, only approximations of either the continuous or fixed schedules are used. Because of the approximate nature of the use of schedules, only the broadest principles can be considered.

First, continuous schedules, very brief intervals, or very small ratios are used initially in building a behavior into the repertoire of the group members. Once a behavior has been demonstrated clearly by the given members, a gradual increase in the ratio and/or interval occurs. A gradual increase in the irregularity or variability of the schedule is increased as a means of maintaining the behavior or making it resistant to extinction (see Staats and Staats, 1963, pp. 61–68). Perhaps as we gain more experience in the administering of reinforcement in groups and in the monitoring process, we eventually will be able to utilize the finer principles involved in the application of the various schedules of reinforcement that have been explicated by Ferster and Skinner (1957) based on their research in highly controlled environments.

CONCLUSION

It should be evident that reinforcement is a key intervention in the behavioral approach. Not only does the therapist reinforce, he or she teaches the members to reinforce each other and individuals in their everyday world. Even more importantly, the therapist teaches the clients to reinforce themselves. The person who is able to praise him- or herself readily should have more self-respect than the individual who is quick to condemn him- or herself and others. (Of course, a person must develop the skills that earn his or her own praise.) Thus, reinforcement is both a tool and a behavior to be learned. But in spite of its importance, it is not the only intervention procedure used in this approach. In subsequent chapters, we will discuss other procedures commonly used to attain both individual and group goals. Even these, however, widely incorporate the principles of reinforcement.

8 Modeling and Behavior Rehearsal in Groups

Therapist: Virginia and Bob, who were in the group last fall, now will demonstrate to the group how they settle arguments. Although they are role-playing, the following incident has happened to them quite often.

Virginia: You were late for dinner again, and you didn't call. You know how I worry. Besides, dinner's cold.

Bob: Well, you'll just have to learn not to worry. I'm only an hour late, and if I were to call I'd have been an extra 10 minutes late. You make me feel like an infant, reporting in every 10 minutes.

Virginia: Well, I don't think that's very considerate.

Bob: Well, let's get out the old paper and pencil, before we get into a shooting match.

(Both get out paper, begin to write.)

Virginia: Okay. I've written all I want is that if you're going to be more than 10 minutes late, I would like a phone call.

Bob: All I want is that I have a little leeway so that if I get into a traffic jam, I don't have to panic that you are worrying.

Virginia: Would 20 minutes be reasonable?

Bob: Half an hour.

Virginia: Agreed. Thirty minutes and I get a phone call, but don't expect dinner on the table when you get home.

Bob: Fair enough.

Therapist: Perhaps we can discuss what Virginia and Bob did to work on their argument and see if there is any behavior each couple here can duplicate in their own discussions.

Learning through observation of models is one of the most powerful tools at the disposal of the group therapist (see Goldstein and others, 1973). In every group, not only does the therapist provide him- or herself as a model, but members provide models for each other. Moreover, other models, real or symbolic or covert, can be introduced readily into group sessions to maximize the opportunities for observational learning.

The therapist in the previous example invited two former members of the group to demonstrate to the multicouples group one way of dealing with arguments. By means of this demonstration, supplemented by discussion, practice by the group members, and reinforcement, some of the couples will learn this or a similar pattern of interaction. This process, by which persons acquire behavioral patterns of others primarily through observation, is called modeling. What they learn is referred to as observational learning or imitation.

MODELING TECHNIQUES

In group therapy, modeling is an important tool in the treatment process. The group lends itself to the procedure. Models who possess desired characteristics and who have desired skills can be brought into the group as in the previous example. Tapes of models can be shown to the group. The therapist can model certain behaviors for the group. The members can model behaviors in which they excel for the other members. Although the literature is replete with empirical evidence for modeling (see, for example, Bandura, 1971; and Flanders, 1968, for a review), only a few studies are available that use modeling in group therapeutic situations (Whalen, 1969; Schwartz and Hawkins, 1965; Truax and Wargo, 1969; Goldstein and others, 1966; Truax and others, 1966; Fiske and others, 1970). However, each of these has demonstrated the efficacy, of modeling procedures in the group context in comparison with other approaches.

As Bandura (1971) pointed out, research has demonstrated that modeling has produced three distinguishable types of effects in subjects, each having therapeutic equivalent. First, the observers may acquire new patterns of behavior. Second, modeling may serve to strengthen or weaken inhibitions of responses that already exist in the observer's repertoire. Third, modeling may facilitate responses already in the repertoire of the observer but which are not inhibited for any reason. In clinical practice it may not always be possible without laboratory controls to determine to which class a given behavior may belong.

It is clear that modeling can be used to produce a wide variety of effects. In most groups in the Group Therapy and Research Project, the modeling has been used as one of the procedures to train members in social skills in which they are deficient, such as how to reinforce their children, how to refuse an unreasonable request, how to carry on a conversation with someone in authority, and how to carry out a job interview.

To make maximum use of modeling, the therapist can manipulate a number of attributes of the modeling situation; the clarity of the modeling cues, the characteristics of the model, the reinforcement of the model, the variety of models, the frequency of modeling, and the reproduction of the modeling event by the members concerned with the behavior. To insure attention to the modeling cues, the therapist must be certain that they are distinct, audible, and interestingly presented. The therapist should select a modeling procedure in which he or she can control these characteristics of the model's presentation. These procedures are discussed in the following section.

The model characteristics most commonly associated with effective outcome are similarity in such variables as age, sex, general appearance, race, and socioeconomic class. If the client is too different from the model in many of these areas, the client often perceives that the attributes he or she lacks are those needed to imitate the model. As one unskilled, black male put it, "My white, female group therapist can make it all seem so easy, but she should try to say those things at my house with my friends and my family." Where such differences exist, the therapist must seek people other than him- or herself for models. There also is evidence to suggest that within a reasonable range of similarity in the above areas, clients are more likely to imitate high power than low power models. The use of guests similar to but more powerful than the clients may serve as better models than the group members themselves, who tend to be low power in their own communities.

Dependency on the model by the clients also has been shown to increase the probability of imitation (Bandura, 1969, p. 137). Other relational factors, such as the perceived warmth and attractiveness of the model, increase the likelihood of imitation. For this reason, therapists tend to increase dependency on themselves through advice-giving, giving of physical assistance, and large amounts of positive reinforcement in the early phases of treatment. Of course, as treatment progresses clients must be trained in more independent behaviors.

Far more powerful than any of the above characteristics, however, is the incentive control of observing behaviors (Bandura, 1969, p. 137). For this reason, wherever possible the model is reinforced in the presence of the client. In the initial example, Virginia and Bob were reinforced for their behavior by arriving at a mutually satisfying solution. Moreover, following the successful imitation of the model either in rehearsal or real life, the client is also reinforced, as the members do with Evie in the following examples.

Although modeling has the potential of occurring in every interpersonal situation, what the participants learn in most instances is largely left to chance. For this reason, therapists have utilized a number of controlled procedures as a means of increasing the probability that specified observational learning takes place. These procedures include role-played demonstrations of adaptive behavior and the use of in vivo models in prescribed ways, films, tapes, or other symbolic models, covert modeling, verbal instructions as to behaviors that should be learned, and negative modeling. Since the operations involved in each are somewhat different, we will discuss each one separately.

Role-Played Modeling

There are many advantages to role-played modeling. It is a procedure that is relatively easy to incorporate into the ongoing program. It is an attractive treatment procedure. Clients repeatedly claim that they particularly enjoy meetings in which role-playing occurs. It is a flexible procedure in that following a role-play modeled demonstration, the members can discuss the situation in terms of its usefulness to them. On this basis it can be adjusted and replayed. Because of the discussion, the members are more sensitive to the cues they should be attending to. Thus, in spite of the lack of spontaneity and the sometimes inappropriate tones of voice, role-playing is by far the most common form of modeling used in group treatment.

The role-players in the modeling session may be the therapists, guests, as in the previous examples, or, more frequently, group members who already have skills in the behavioral area being demonstrated. There is an advantage to using either former or present clients who have demonstrated competence in the problem area. By virtue of their similarity to the clients who are experiencing problems, they may serve as more effective models. However, if the therapist serves as a model, he or she has more control over the situation.

Once the therapist decides who will be the role-players, he or she must decide how the technique is to be applied. In most cases modeling is not used as an isolated technique. It often is preceded by a discussion of the problem, followed by a role-played demonstration by a person dealing with the problem situation.

The modeling presentation usually is followed by a discussion with feedback to the role-players. They usually will repeat this sequence several times, either demonstrating alternative or improved responses to the situation. Occasionally, the models will be replaced by those who have made alternative suggestions. The modeling demonstration ultimately is followed by a behavioral rehearsal or set of rehearsals by those members having a problem in the given situation.

Let us look at some of these steps in an example similar to those commonly found in therapy groups. Evie has described a situation in which Augustus, a fellow employee and a married man, has called her late at night on several occasions and asked her to have a drink with him. To prepare the role-play, she coached another member in the behaviors that Augustus had manifested. When it was Evie's turn to present her problem, the other members were given the assignment to take notes on what she did well and on what she might have done differently. A part of the initial role-play is presented below.

Evie: Oh, it's you, Augustus.

Aug.: Say, I'm here at Harry's Bar and there's a great little band. Real country music! Can you hear it? Why don't you come on down?

Evie: It *is* nice music, but it's late. I don't think I should.

Aug.: C'mon, honey. You'll have a great time. Don't be a stick-in-the-mud.

Evie: I have to work tomorrow, Augustus. I'd better not.

Aug.: Well, I'll call you on the weekend sometime. But you sure are missing a good time tonight.

Evie: Well (hesitating), yes, I suppose I am. Goodnight.

In the group discussion that followed, it was pointed out by the other members that Evie did refuse—and that was to her credit—but that she was far too tentative in her refusal. In fact, she appeared to encourage Augustus to call her on the weekend. The therapist asks the group members for suggestions as to how she might refuse him with more definity. Evie was interviewed by the others to find out what she would like to say, and once it was determined what words she might use, two members agreed to demonstrate to Evie how to do it.

Mary (in the role of Evie): Is that you, Augustus?

Paul (as Augustus): Yes, say why don't you come down to the bar? There's a great party going on. Can you hear it?

Mary: Yes, I can hear it - and, *no,* I won't come.

Paul: Well, maybe next time?

Mary: Listen, Augustus, I'm glad you asked about next time. I know that you mean well. But there won't be a next time. I don't want any more calls at any time. You're a married man, and even if you weren't married, you're not my type.

Paul: I'll call again. Maybe you'll change your mind.

Mary: Not on your life, and if you continue to call I'm going to have to take serious steps. But I imagine I've made myself extremely clear . . . and I'm not going to get any calls anymore under any circumstances.

Following the demonstration, Evie was encouraged to rehearse the situation. Since she was successful in simulating the initial model presentation, a situation was repeated in which more pressure was put on Evie.

Evie: Oh, not you again, Augustus! (onlookers laugh, indicate approval)

Paul (as Augustus): I won't take no for an answer. Come on down right now. Wow, what a party going on here! Can't you hear it?

Evie: Yes, I can hear it.

Paul: How can you resist it?

Evie: (breaks the role play and talks to the group) What do I say now?

The members suggested that she start over, and when Augustus says, "Can you hear it?" that she not answer the question at all but deal with his position of not taking no for an answer. Evie tried again.

Evie: You're going to have to take no for an answer. I find this phone call an imposition, and if you don't stop calling I'm going to take legal steps if necessary. (Group applauds)

Aug.: When the gang at work hears what a killjoy you are, your name will be mud.

Evie: (prompted by Mary) And when the gang at work hears you've been arrested for disturbing the peace, and your wife hears you've been pestering a single woman, your name won't look so good either.

Therapist: (interrupting) That's great! What do the rest of you think?

After several such rehearsals, the therapist asked whether Evie thought she could handle the call the next time it came. Evie indicated that she could and would take it as a condition of her next contract to handle it in one of the ways it had been role-played, and then report back to the group in detail.

For purposes of illustration, this process has been kept much briefer than usual. However, the role-play should not be too much longer in the first trials to avoid practicing mistakes. If there are too many behaviors that need to be dealt with, it is better to repeat the enactment several times in several different ways or during several periods, each of which is interrupted by discussion. This allows an opportunity for feedback, reinforcement, and revision.

The entire sequence need not be performed always. In cases where the client feels sufficiently competent to rehearse only with simple instructions, no modeling is required. And even when the entire sequence is performed, it is not necessary, as in the above example, to carry out all steps at any one meeting. In fact, there is a high likelihood that if an entire meeting is devoted primarily to one person, the attraction of the group for the others would be decreased.

In Vivo Modeling

On occasion, models are presented who do not role-play the desired behavior. Rather they are allowed to interact with only minor limitations with the clients under prescribed conditions, with the expectation that imitation will follow. The control in these procedures is in the selection of the models and instructions to the observers. These procedures are referred to here as in vivo modeling to distinguish them from covert, symbolic, and role-played modeling. A modification of an *in vivo* procedure developed by Kelly (1955) involves the selection by each client in the group of an individual each admires to serve as model. This is usually someone with whom the client comes in regular contact in everyday life. Following observation of the models, the clients, usually in pairs, and the therapist develop role sketches that contain descriptions of the behaviors, attitudes, and values the client admires. If the client is unable to describe the model in sufficiently specific terms and if the model is still available, the client is instructed to observe the model for several days to develop a more thorough sketch. The sketch goes beyond an overt behavioral description insofar as it also includes feeling, attitudes, and points of view. Even if the client is unable in the first instance to modify the covert phenomena, if he or she is able to learn to manifest the overt behavior, there is evidence that this will result in changes in attitudes and other cognitive activities (Festinger, 1964).

Following role-play, the client for whom the sketch has been developed will rehearse it. The client is then instructed to adopt the role—both behaviors and attitudes—to the best of his or her ability for an extended period. The client is told to act *as if* he or she *were* the model rather than *to be* the model. The assumption is that this instruction will reduce the threat involved in presenting characteristics of a different person. This approach differs from the usual modeling-rehearse sequence described previously insofar as a more complex set of attributes are modeled and rehearsed. Should it be effective, the results would be more dramatic than training situation by situation, in sets of simple operations.

Because of the encompassing nature of fixed-role therapy, many therapists prefer a similar but more limited procedure suggested by Kelly, called "exaggerated role training." In this procedure clients are instructed to adopt prescribed roles limited to cope with highly specific behavioral problems. For example, a group therapist instructed one of her clients complaining of social anxiety to view all members of his club as if he had been the club's president. The client reported that his anxiety disappeared during the meeting that he played this role. To prepare him for the role, the other members of his therapy group discussed the attitude and behaviors that a president might assume. In the same assertive training group, other members decided on the assumption of similar roles in various situations in which they participated. However, most met with limited success and returned to the briefer, step-by-step approach described earlier.

Another type of *in vivo* modeling has been referred to as participant modeling (Rimm and Maloney, 1969; Rimm and Medeiros, 1970). In this form, the therapist or other model physically guides the behavior of the client. In an assertive training group, all the members accompanied one member, who was afraid to go to places with a large number of people, to a film that they knew would be attended sparsely. One of the members took the arm of his anxious colleague as the group escorted him to his first film in many years.

In all treatment groups, *in vivo* models are plentiful. However, in those groups in which problems are similar, the behaviors that need to be demonstrated may not be in the repertoire of any of the members. Although the therapist may model the desired behavior, the dissimilarity between the therapist and the members may mitigate against efficient learning. As Mowrer (1966) has pointed out, clinicians characteristically present themselves as models for a narrow range of social behavior within the therapy setting. What they do demonstrate usually has limited applications for their clients. The therapist may supplement his or her own modeling with guests, usually former clients of similar groups as in the initial example. Also in parent training groups, it is common procedure to invite former members to early meetings to discuss the problems they dealt with, the procedures they used, and the results they obtained. The guests are invited back from time to time to demonstrate, occasionally with their own child, new procedures. It is imperative in the use of models to rehearse their presentation prior to their talk to the group. On one occasion the "outstanding" mother of a previous group told the new mothers that she had learned to reinforce and to use time out, but all that was really important was to punish consistently (a message her therapist claimed he had never taught).

A variation of this procedure was used by Mash, Lazere, Terdal, and Garner (1970) in their group program for parents. A mother who had completed a course of instruction interacted for 15 to 20 minutes with her own child. During this, she was observed by the other group members, who sat behind a one-way mirror. As the demonstration progressed, the group leaders pointed out the various effective and ineffective techniques used in the demonstration. Following the modeling session, the demonstration mother joined the group to discuss the tactics she employed.

Symbolic Models

Another set of procedures used to delimit the behaviors to be imitated involves the use of symbolic models. These include audio and videotaped models as well as films of models. Even cartoons have been used. Extensive research has demonstrated the efficacy of symbolic modeling over control groups (Eisler and others, 1973) in training psychiatric patients in assertive behavior and symbolic modeling, and symbolic modeling plus instruction, over instruction alone and two control groups (Eisler and others, 1973). In each of these analog studies, the model subjects were trained by presenting them with video tape models of appropriate responses to a number of interpersonal interactions requiring assertiveness.

A symbolic model approach provides the therapist with efficient control of the model, because the model's behavior can be reviewed repeatedly before presenting it to the clients. This also allows the therapist to plan easily how he or she can use the material. Furthermore, the results of several studies reveal no differences between live or symbolic models.

At present in the group therapy project, several video tapes have been prepared to demonstrate parenting skills and appropriate assertiveness in a number of situations. In all these tapes, the demonstrations are brief and followed by the identification of the desired behaviors in a group discussion. Selected excerpts from the film by Mager (1972) called *Who Did What to Whom* have been used to model specific reinforcement procedures to parents and to provide examples of how reinforcement could work against the parent if not used appropriately.

Truax and Carkhuff (1967) have used symbolic modeling in the form of a 30-minute audio tape to train clients in groups in good patient therapy behavior. The tape shows how clients explore themselves and their feelings. Truax and Wargo (1969) show reliable differences between five therapy groups of outpatients who were exposed to the taped models and five groups who were not. In behavior therapy groups, therapists could provide a tape of behavior appropriate to that situation, such as being problem-focused and behaviorally specific to reduce the time spent in getting oriented. The modeling would probably increase in effectiveness if the taped models were reinforced for their activities (see Bandura, 1969).

Covert Modeling

Cautela (1971) has recommended another means of modeling in which the clients imagine the model engaged in various activities. Not only is there evidence that such covert modeling does alter behavior, but that the laws that govern the process of alteration of behavior are the same as for overt or symbolic modeling (see Cautela and others, 1974; Kazdin, 1973, 1974a, b). One advantage of covert modeling is that the therapist can control the external stimuli quite readily. Another advantage is that it is relatively easy to administer and can be carried out readily with groups of people or in pairs at a large savings in time. The major disadvantages are that the modeling stimuli presented by the therapist may not be the same or even similar to those ultimately used by the client, and there is no external check on what the client is imagining.

Nevertheless, because of its utility, covert modeling should not be overlooked. One therapist used the procedures in the following way. All the members in the group wrote down the description of an individual whom they admired and respected. They then described how that chosen individual would handle a situation involving a refusal. As a group they were then instructed to imagine the model refusing in each of the situations they had listed. They were further instructed to note the model's facial expression, tone of voice, the speed with which he or she responded, eye contact, and posture. Although no data was collected on the procedure, the members claimed that they found the experience a valuable one.

Instructions and Modeling

One of the major problems of using modeling in group treatment is the amount of time each sequence requires. Although in groups of persons with similar problems there is considerable savings in time, modeling of the way each person would handle the specific situation often is unique to that person, and each may need a unique training experience. For this reason, modeling often is replaced by detailed instruction on how to deal with each client's problem situation. These may be developed with the client and his or her buddy, and presented to the group for additional suggestions.

There is some evidence that symbolic models alone and instructions alone, although each contributing to behavioral change, may not be sufficient to produce it. Whalen (1969) studied the interaction of 128 students in leaderless groups of four students each under four different experiment conditions. One set of groups was exposed to a film model of interpersonal openness, a second to detailed exhortative and descriptive instructions, a third to both detailed instructions followed by the film, and a fourth to neither instructions nor film. The 12-minute film portrayed four students talking at a highly personal level "describing their anxieties and feeding back their impressions, whether positive or negative or neutral, to the other group members." The film group was highly similar in appearance, age, sex, and dress to the experimental subjects. In the instructions the subjects were told how to be open and honest with each other. The data indicated that exposure to both instructions and symbolic model was the only condition effective in producing the expression of interpersonal openness and in inhibiting inpersonal discussion. In fact, there were virtually no differences between the control groups and the groups receiving only film or only instructions.

Bean (1971), on the other hand, discovered in a similar experiment that modeling was significantly superior to instructions in eliciting self-disclosure. In contrast with Whalen, Bean used a live model, and his instructions were far less persuasive than Whalen's. This may indicate that for some populations, at least, live models may be more powerful elicitors of behavior than symbolic ones.

The implication of these studies for the group therapist is that some form of instruction to the clients could accompany the modeling process. The addition of rehearsal procedures might enhance further the effectiveness of the modeling procedures. It is clear from the literature that no one procedure alone is effective ubiquitously in producing complex behavioral change.

Negative Modeling

Thus far, we have discussed only the presentation of models whose behavior is expected to be imitated. Occasionally, modeling procedures are used in which the model's behavior is to be avoided or reduced in frequency. Such a presentation, usually role-played or presented on videotape, is used in the same way as the assessment role-play. It is a stimulus to discussion and a means of differentiating adaptive from maladaptive behaviors.

In a parent training group, the therapist played the role of a parent who had no training in behavior modification. Prior to the demonstration, the parents were instructed to take notes on what they would do differently. Following is an excerpt from that role-play.

> *Parent* (as played by therapist): Johnny, if you don't pick up all your toys, I'm going to put you in your room for the rest of the day.
>
> *Johnny* (as played by a member): Nyaa, Nyaa (dances around mother). I don't care, I don't care!
>
> *Parent:* (disgustedly) Oh, do what you want!
>
> *Therapist* (as himself): Well, what did I do as a parent that could have been improved upon?
>
> *Mrs. M:* You certainly should keep from making idle threats. Either follow through or don't threaten.
>
> *Therapist:* Good!
>
> *Mr. K:* And putting a child in a room for the rest of the day doesn't make sense, in any case. Shouldn't time out be 30 seconds or less? (Other parents nod agreement.)
>
> *Mrs. T:* And telling a child to do what he wants after you've told him what to do is like telling him you can't do the job.

Following the completion of this discussion, the therapist incorporated their suggestions into a positive role-played demonstration by one of the other mothers. Note that therapist in his role as parent was punished by the child with noncomformity for both making an idle threat and not carrying through on it. Although the research is not clear on this principle (see Bandura, 1969), it would appear that punishment of the model in the presence of the observer should serve to reduce the likelihood of imitation. Whenever negative modeling takes place, it should be followed by a discussion of what is wrong and what the alternatives could be. In addition, a positive modeling demonstration would put into action the alternatives thus developed.

BEHAVIOR REHEARSAL

An essential step in the modeling process as a means of insuring retention of the modeled behavior is motoric reproduction of the behavior (Bandura, 1971) or behavior rehearsal. As in the earlier example of Evie, an overt rehearsal follows the modeling demonstration and, in most cases, a group discussion of the demonstration. Overt behavioral rehearsal involves an enactment by the target client of the desired behaviors in a simulated situation. The goal is to prepare the client to perform the desired behavior in its real world context in the absence of modeling cues. In rehearsal the client can try out not only the appropriate words and affect but also the accompanying motor activity. Since the rehearsal represents a simulation of the real world, it is possible to protect the client from aversive consequences while he or she is learning and to include positive reinforcing consequences, which should increase the probability of his or her trying out the behavior in the real world.

In addition, rehearsal permits the therapist to train the clients through successively more difficult trials to master a complex behavioral pattern. For example, in learning job interview behavior, the members of a transitional group in an institution first had to rehearse asking the secretary for an appointment. When this was mastered, they rehearsed social greeting responses. This was followed by learning to describe one's experiences. After this the members rehearsed how to answer questions about their commitment and their present ability to function in the job. Finally, they rehearsed the entire sequence.

Another particular advantage of rehearsal in groups is that each rehearsal serves as a model for the other members. Thus, every member is able to obtain a multiple modeling situation from which to select the most suitable cues for his or her own performance.

For many of the above reasons, some authors (Underwood and Schultz, 1960; Goldstein and others, 1966; Bandura, 1971) strongly recommend that desired responses be practiced repeatedly during therapy sessions. Moreover, even though it is usually difficult to investigate an isolated technique systematically and empirically, there are a number of experiments in which the efficacy of behavioral rehearsal with adults has been examined systematically. Because of the centrality of this procedure, we will review briefly several of these projects.

Lazarus (1966), comparing behavioral rehearsal to nondirective therapy and advice-giving treatment, found that behavioral rehearsal was by far the most effective method of resolving specific social and interpersonal problems. He assigned 75 outpatients to three treatment conditions: behavioral rehearsal, reflection-interpretation, and direct advice. One problem only was treated in each of the three conditions in four weekly sessions of 30 minutes. If there was no evidence of change or learning within the month, the treatment was regarded as a failure. The criterion of change was objective evidence that the

patient was performing adaptively in the area which had previously constituted a problem. The results showed that 32 percent and 44 percent of the
patients, respectively, benefited from behavioral rehearsal. Of the 31 patients
who did not benefit from reflection-interpretation and advice, 27 were later
treated with behavioral rehearsal, 22 successfully.

Wagner (1968) found that reinforcement of role-played expressions of anger
resulted in an increase in the expression of anger among mildly inhibited
hospitalized patients. In this study, he divided 29 patients into three treatment
groups, which were equated on the basis of scores on an anger-expression test.
In the experimental group, subjects were encouraged to express anger in
role-played situations. All expressions of anger in the role-play were reinforced
in the sense that the "other" submitted to their anger, and, if appropriate,
apologized for giving cause for anger. In a contrast group, the "other" retali-
ated with greater anger than the subject had expressed. In a control group,
expression of anger was neither encouraged nor reinforced nor punished. The
results showed significantly greater expression of anger for the experimental
group, with no significant change in the control or contrast group.

In a study by McFall and Marston (1970), two behavioral rehearsal treatment conditions were compared to a placebo and a control group. One of the
experimental conditions involved a feedback procedure to the subject; the
second did not. All subjects had requested help in becoming more assertive in
their social relationships. Tested on four different instruments, the experimental conditions resulted in significantly greater assertiveness than either the
placebo or control condition. There was no significant difference between the
two experimental conditions, although the behavior rehearsal with feedback
showed a somewhat stronger effect.

Continuing in the same line of research, McFall and Lillisand (1971) trained
nonassertive students in refusing unreasonable requests by means of behavior
rehearsal therapy. This approach consisted of overt *or* covert response practice
and symbolic verbal modeling *and* therapist coaching. The behavior rehearsal
therapy was compared to an assessment-only control. After two sessions, the
behavioral rehearsal S's improved dramatically in their assertive refusal behavior on self-report and behavioral laboratory measures in comparison to the
control group. Covert rehearsal tended to be somewhat more effective than
overt rehearsal. In a third study consisting of four separate experiments,
McFall and Twentyman (1973) evaluated the additive effects of behavioral
rehearsal coaching and modeling on self-report and various behavioral measures of assertiveness. As in the previous study, they found behavioral rehearsal and coaching each were effective but more so in combination.
However, in contrast to the work of Hersen and others, (1973), they found that
the addition of modeling yielded no increment in assertiveness. (This inconsis-
tency may be due to the difference in population.)

Building on the above studies, Goldsmith and McFall (1975) compared an interpersonal skill training group of psychiatric inpatients to pseudotherapy, and an assessment-only control group. The interpersonal skill training involved the patients in modeling, rehearsal, coaching, recorded response playback, and corrective feedback. It covered such interpersonal tasks as initiating and terminating conversations, dealing with rejection, and being more assertive and self-disclosing. After only three hourly sessions, skill training was found to be superior to the other two conditions on a number of behavioral and self-report measures, both in the training context and in a more real life context.

In the research by McFall and his associates (see above), the efficacy of coaching, prompting, and feedback as an adjunct to rehearsal has been established convincingly. As a result these elements are used increasingly in the clinical setting. All of the McFall clients were trained individually. In the Group Research and Therapy Project, DeLange (1977) used similar procedures but added group feedback, which according to the clients enhanced the value of the experience.

Coaching seems to work best when the coach sits behind the individual rehearsing. When the client is at a loss for words, the coach, a fellow group member, whispers suggestions. Occasionally, the coach may model an entire sequence before returning to this role. Before a client is prepared to perform the role in the real world, the coaching must be faded. Not all role-players need coaching, and if the client prefers or feels comfortable enough, he or she should play his or her role without them.

Another variation is the use of cue cards with written messages on them. These have advantages over the personal coach insofar as the client can use the cue card, if sufficiently unobtrusive, during the everyday situations. An example of the use of the cue card was by a client who, when she went shopping, carried a card in her purse that read "Look the clerk in the eye."

Occasionally, behavioral problems such as lack of eye contact or speaking inaudibly detracts from the effectiveness of the role-player. Although the usual modeling/rehearsal sequence may be adequate to train an individual in the correct words, prompting may not be sufficient to increase eye contact or audibility to the degree that the individual would be effective in the real situation. To deal with this, Brockway and others (1972) developed a procedure called the "paired reinforcement-rehearsal system (PRR)," which aims at increasing the frequency of such microbehaviors. In the PRR, two therapists or the therapist and a member are used. One therapist role-plays the protagonist role and the client plays his or her own role. The second therapist (or a member) sits next to the therapist and prompts the client and then reinforces the desired behavior. For example, finger to eye was a cue for more eye contact for the client; finger to mouth was a cue for speaking louder. When the client was giving appropriate eye contact or speaking sufficiently loudly, the trainer verbally reinforced or used tokens to reinforce the individual. This approach has two advantages. It makes it possible to provide the actor with immediate feedback and reinforcement for small units of desired behavior and, within the context of a role-play, to shape more complex behaviors.

Since this is a highly structured procedure, the trainer-reinforcer prompter must be faded at the first opportunity. Once the client consistently demonstrates the desired behavior in a nonprompted role play, the rehearsals are eliminated for the given behavior entirely.

One of the problems of role-played rehearsal in a group is that only a few people are rehearsing at any one time. If the situation does not have direct relevance for the others, they sometimes become bored, impatient, and occasionally (in the case of older adolescents) disruptive. To prevent this, an operating principle has been established. Whenever role-played rehearsal (or assessment or modeling) takes place, the nonperforming members are given an observational task. In the project's most recent assertiveness groups, the members are required to rate the rehearsing member on a scale of 1 to 10 on the crucial variable, such as assertiveness, audibility, appropriate facial expression, and/or eye contact. Following the role-play, these ratings are discussed. Once an observer announces a rating, he or she must give evidence for it. "Your strong voice sounded very convincing; that's why I gave you an eight on assertiveness." In addition, he or she may jot down sentences that could be used as alternatives to those used by the rehearsing member. Or the observer may jot down other responses of the protagonists that also might occur in the interaction. Both the alternate responses are then given to the role-player, who may choose to repeat the role-play or, if he or she is satisfied to assume a home assignment to carry out the role in the real world at the first opportunity. This procedure has increased the vigor as well as the quality of the discussion that follows the role-play.

Thus far we have assumed that all members are willing to participate in a simulated situation. Occasionally, however, this is not the case. To get some clients involved in behavior rehearsal, it is sometimes necessary to model the process for them. Experienced group members or two staff members may demonstrate a rehearsal of a situation relevant to them. The therapist may then use short "warm-ups" where the members each in turn will rehearse one sentence to the other members. This also may occur in pairs. Gradually, the length of the role-play is extended.

Occasionally, even after warm-ups and demonstrations by others, members still may be too uncomfortable to role-play. Under these conditions, they should be encouraged to describe prior to acting what they would do. Jeanne has just described a situation in which the fellow next to her in class had talked to her. She would like to practice what to say to him, but she has indicated that she doesn't think she is ready to role-play.

T: That's not necessary, but why don't you tell us what you would like to say, Jeanne?

J: I would like to say that I thought that the course was a bummer, too.

T: And then if he should say that he found it difficult to take notes, what might you say?

J: I suppose I could say that I could lend him my notes since I didn't have any difficulty?

T: That's good. Now what if he should say he accepted them.

J: Gee, (hesitates) I don't know.

T: Can anyone help Jeanne, any suggestions?

F: Try this. My notes are hard to read. Why don't we go over them at the Union after class?''

J: I'd like to say that, but I don't know if I could.

T: Why don't you just repeat what Frank said? Once you've said the words, it might be easier to role-play them later.

J: (hesitatingly) Frank said that I should say (pause) that my notes are hard to read (long pause) and maybe we could go over them after class (pause) at the Union.

T: That's a good start. Would you feel comfortable about doing it again?

This system allows a high frequency of reinforcement without interrupting the ongoing process as one would have to do in a regular role-play. At the same time it provides the client with adequate protection from too much pressure. If Jeanne refuses to try it again, the therapist will go on to someone else at this point and come back to Jeanne when she claims she is ready.

Covert Rehearsal

In a large group it is often difficult for each client to participate in sufficient rehearsal trials so that he or she feels comfortable in trying out the behavior in his extratherapy world. To facilitate multiple trials, a procedure developed by McFall and Lillesand (1971)—called covert rehearsal—often has been used to supplement and on occasion to replace overt rehearsal procedures. As pointed out earlier, they demonstrated that covert rehearsal was somewhat more effective (although not significantly) than overt rehearsal. In group therapy, the procedure consists of the therapist presenting a general situation that would be stressful for most of the members in the group. One example from an assertive training group was the following:

You are walking down the street and you see someone whom you know and would like to know better, but you can't remember his/her name. You are not sure whether he/she has seen you.

Following the presentation, the members are asked to respond covertly, that is to think and imagine exactly what they would do. Often they are instructed to write down their responses. Afterward the leader and the members may suggest several alternatives to each other. Then the situation is repeated, and the members covertly rehearse their new responses, incorporating those ideas that best meet their personal style. The procedure is repeated several times with each situation. The members for whom the problem is still difficult or uncomfortable will practice the covert procedure with their buddies or friends at home. Some of these situations have been put on audio tapes with several variations of each situation. The client can practice with the tape at home until he or she feels comfortable with all the variations.

Modeling, Rehearsal, Coaching, Corrective Feedback

Both in the use of modeling and rehearsal in most of the successful experiments reported in this chapter, the procedures were combined with some form of coaching, prompting, or instruction (these words are used interchangeably) as a means of insuring adequate performance. In addition, in many cases following a rehearsal the client was provided with corrective feedback, such as suggestions for improving performance. In some cases, the feedback has been combined with audio or video playback of what the person actually did. In our clinical model, many of these features have been combined with the purpose of obtaining an additional effect of each of these procedures separately.

Thus, the members will observe models, usually multiple ones. They will discuss what they have found useful in the model's behavior. They will coach one another on how each should rehearse the given situation. Each will then rehearse a situation relevant to his or her problem. Members will provide each client with corrective feedback. The rehearsal will be repeated interspersed with corrective feedback until mastery is achieved. Where video or audio facilities are available, some therapists will provide the given role-player with a playback to both check and enhance the corrective feedback.

Interspersed with each performance by the group members is ample reinforcement for successful approximations of the desired behavior. And, finally, in most groups each member will contract to perform some component of the desired behavior before the next session. This is a summary of the entire treatment process when the major problem is an overt skill deficit. In the following chapters, we will discuss some alternative methods used primarily in the treatment of anxiety-related or other covert problems.

9 Anxiety Management in Groups

Okay, let's divide into pairs as we did last week. Those who were the coaches last session are now the trainees. Trainees should be sitting in the chairs as comfortable as possible. Coaches, stand to one side. That's right. Coaches will be watching to see that the trainees are following instructions, and the second time around you'll be instructing. Let's begin. Coaches make sure belts and ties are loosened. Now trainees extend your right arm, a little more. Good! That's it. Now clench your fists. Harder. Feel the tension in your arm, shoulder, and fingers. Check them out, coaches. Now hold it a few seconds longer. As I count to 10, gradually relax the arm, the hand, and the fingers (pause). At one point your arm will fall to your lap. Let it collapse completely. (Count slowly to 10.) Okay, coaches, pick up the arm at the elbow just an inch; That's it; now let it fall. Is it a dead weight? Okay, good, now this time the coaches while working on the left arm will go through the same procedures with the trainees. If you have any questions, I'll be walking among the pairs.

The group members in this example are learning and teaching relaxation procedures. In this chapter we will discuss relaxation and other procedures commonly used in the treatment of problems related to excessive anxiety and other covert problems. In addition to relaxation, these procedures include systematic desensitization and cognitive restructuring. Although many group therapists have used these as the primary intervention procedure in their approach (see, for example, Lazarus, 1971), these anxiety management procedures in the Group Therapy and Research Project generally have served as a

120

supplement to the procedures of modeling, rehearsal, coaching, reinforcement, and group intervention.

RELAXATION TRAINING

The most commonly used anxiety management procedure is relaxation training. Although an integral part of systematic desensitization, muscle relaxation is an important procedure in its own right. It has been used to treat such problems as insomnia, headaches, back pain, menstrual cramps, mild forms of depression, and generalized anxiety (Rimm and Masters, 1974, p. 46). For this reason in heterogeneous groups, it is taught as a common skill, which most clients find profitable to learn.

Muscle relaxation usually is experienced when muscles throughout the body are loose and flaccid. Although few people are able to bring on this state naturally, most can be taught readily to do so. One procedure involves training in the alternation of tension of the muscles in each large muscle group, with the release of that tension as in the example that opened this chapter. As one muscle group is tensed and eased, the trainer moves to other muscle groups until the entire body is relaxed. This may occur in one or several sessions. Multiple trials are necessary before an individual can bring on complete relaxation at self-command, which is the ultimate goal of the training. Once this is achieved, relaxation becomes a tool for dealing with a large variety of stress situations, or it can be incorporated into systematic desensitization.

Relaxation training in groups can occur in several ways. The therapist can go through the procedures with all the members at the same time. However, it is difficult to observe carefully more than two or three at a time. Members may practice inappropriate actions without any feedback. To insure closer supervision, the group is divided into pairs. One person in each group is the relaxer and the second is the coach. The coach is instructed what to look for each step of the way. As in the opening example, once the therapist has modeled a set of instructions for one part of the body, the coach will then give the same instruction for a parallel part of the body. Thus, the therapist and coach alternate giving the instructions. After the one subgroup has completed the procedure successfully, the roles are reversed. The use of pairs puts each client in the role of teacher as well as client. This appears to facilitate his or her conceptualization and concern for small details, as well as the quality of the teacher's relaxation.

If the coach is not certain of the appropriate correction, he or she calls over the therapist, who usually rotates among the various pairs as he or she goes through the relaxation instructions. There are many types of instructions, but most are similar (for details see Wolpe, 1973; Rimm and Masters, 1974; or Rose, 1972). The procedures most commonly used by the author involve successive tension and relaxation of feet, calves, knees, thighs, hips, trunk, small of the back, stomach, chest, hands, forearms, biceps, shoulders, neck, mouth, tongue, eyes, and forehead. After several groups are alternatively tensed and relaxed, the therapist quickly goes over all of them with the relaxation instruction only. After the entire body is relaxed, the therapist relaxes all the muscle groups without the tension instruction. Tension is best achieved through clenching or extending the given muscle group. However, before having clients tense for the first time, the therapist must check to see whether a certain area is given to knotting or whether breaks or other injuries have occurred in the area. In these cases, the client is advised to ignore the tension part of the instruction to the given muscle group.

To estimate the degree to which clients are relaxed, the coach asks them to indicate the degree of anxiety (SUDs) on a scale of 0 to 100 before and after the relaxation exercise. For those who have indicated no change, the method may have to be revised.

Once the members achieve relaxation, they must be instructed to come out of it slowly—first by wiggling the toes, then the fingers, increasing gradually the rate of breathing, moving the arms and legs a little, then the head, increasing the motion, then stretching. In the event that certain areas are more difficult than others to relax, special attention must be given to these. Often by breaking down these areas into even smaller units (see Jacobsen, 1938, for the most detailed analysis of muscle groups), relaxation can be achieved. If not, additional practice may suffice. The coach plays a major role in detecting these problems, although each member is encouraged to report them as well.

Except in groups where desensitization is the major treatment procedure, training in relaxation occurs only during the first or last 15 minutes of a given group meeting. As a result, only a few muscle groups are taught each session. Thus, several sessions are required before the entire procedure is learned. A common error caused by the limitation of time is to rush too quickly through the process. A full 10 seconds of tension followed by at least 15 seconds of relaxation is required for each muscle group (compare with Rimm and Masters, 1974, p. 51) to maximize learning. Otherwise members may never quite achieve a reasonably relaxed state.

Learning to relax is largely a function of practice. The more frequent practice sessions a member can be encouraged to put in, the more rapidly and effectively the skill is learned. For this reason, members are encouraged to agree to daily practice sessions of 5 to 10 minutes in their contracts. In many groups, this encouragement has not been sufficient to obtain such practice without the stimulus of other people. The discipline required to practice alone is often more than many clients are able to muster regardless of their level of motivation. To deal with this, special relaxation practice sessions between regular meetings may be made available to clients. Where buddies live in close proximity, they are encouraged to get together for practice sessions. Members also may be provided with tapes of the relaxation instruction to be used at home. Where there are persistent difficulties, group aides or former members may be enlisted to assist the clients immediately before or after the regular sessions. All of these should be viewed as temporary "crutches" to be faded as soon as an individual learns to practice on his or her own.

Cautela (1966) points out that the level of anxiety in pervasively anxious clients is increased readily by any threatening situation. There is a tendency for the anxiety to generalize to all other phenomena present at the time of the increase in anxiety. To break this cycle, Cautela (p. 102) teaches his clients the following adaptation of the relaxation procedure. When the client is completely relaxed in the presence of the therapist, he or she is instructed to say to him or herself, "I am calm and relaxed." Each time that the client says this and has a compatible feeling of calmness, he or she is instructed to raise a finger. This procedure is repeated 10 times at the first session and assigned as homework every day for a week. After three weeks and approximately 300 trials of associating the words "I am calm and relaxed" with the inner feeling of calm and relaxation, the client usually is able to bring on the inner state by voicing the words that represent it. Following Cautela's recommendation, therapists in this project also have taught members to pair the thought of relaxation with the behavior. Many clients have reported that this procedure does, indeed, ultimately facilitate the elimination of the alternation of tension and relaxation in obtaining a relaxed state.

As all other procedures, relaxation training is evaluated regularly. The self-reported SUDs level, the evaluative responses on the session evaluation form, the reported number of extragroup sessions, the observed skill in achieving and teaching relaxation provide extensive data on which to base a judgement of the effectiveness of the training program. Once relaxation has been learned effectively, it can be used as a treatment procedure in its own right, or it may be used as a part of systematic desensitization for clients with clearly identified phobias.

SYSTEMATIC DESENSITIZATION

As it is most commonly employed, systematic desensitization is a technique that pairs imagined scenes of anxiety-provoking situations with deep muscle relaxation. These scenes are usually presented by a therapist to the client, who is in a relaxed state from the least anxiety-producing to the most anxiety-producing event. Each scene usually is presented several times. If during these presentations there is no unusual amount of anxiety elicited, the therapist goes on to the next item in the hierarchy. There appears to be a correlation, although not perfect, between successfully imagining a scene with a low degree of anxiety and successfully encountering that scene in real life with a low degree of anxiety. For a detailed account of procedures commonly used in systematic desensitization, see Wolpe (1973). For a critical review of research findings, see Paul (1969).

The scenes are developed by the client in consultation with the therapist and ranked by the client in order of the anxiety they elicit. If possible, each client attributes a given level of anxiety (SUDS) from 0 to 100 to each scene.

Although primarily used in the treatment of phobias, systematic desensitization also has been used successfully with sexual disorders, speech problems, somatic complaints, emotional aberrations, and many other disorders. However, there appear to be several prerequisites for successful completion of treatment (Rimm and Masters, 1974, p. 55). First, the client should suffer from only a few phobias. The client should be able to achieve a state of deep muscle relaxation. Finally, the client should be able to imagine the anxiety-producing scenes mentioned above with the appropriate emotion. In the first few sessions, the client's ability to meet these conditions is readily determined. Since most clients meet these requisites, it usually is possible to employ this procedure in groups.

Systematic desensitization in groups was first described by Lazarus (1961). In this procedure, several individuals while relaxed are presented with a hierarchy at the same time. Either the hierarchy is standardized or it is developed in group discussion with the clients. Usually the therapist takes an upward step in the hierarchy only when all patients successfully have experienced the previous step. As a result, the procedure is slower (average, 20.4 sessions) than individual treatment, but in the long run it is a savings in therapist time. However, from the point of view of building in stability of the change, overlearning through extra trials and observation may have added usefulness. One problem is that occasionally the pace of one client is so at variance with the pace of others that he or she cannot remain in the group, but this is equally true of most other therapies. Another problem is that hierarchies often are idiosyncratic. Even so, this does not seem to influence the outcome of such practices as noted in the studies below.

On the basis of findings from an experiment in which group systematic desensitization is compared with individual systematic desensitization but without a control group, Ihli and Garlington (1969) report that desensitization in groups is as effective as desensitization with individuals in the treatment of test anxiety. The implication of this equality in outcome is that the group is more efficient in terms of the costs of professional time.

A number of other authors using desensitization procedures with groups of clients noted that the group interaction seemed to facilitate the reduction of anxiety. Katahn and others (1966) indicate that their clients (in this case, students) invariably reported that being able to talk to other students in the treatment context, being aware that others had similar problems, and learning better study habits were the crucial factors in the reduction of anxiety. Since

Katahn combined desensitization and group discussion, it was not possible to ascertain which variable was the more significant. Lazarus (1961) noted, as a result of his experience with desensitization in group situations, that desensitization is facilitated by talking to persons with similar problems in a relatively nonthreatening situation.

Paul and Shannon (1966) developed a hierarchy list for social evaluative anxiety by group discussion. The hierarchy thus contained elements from all the members of the group. At the beginning of each session, they also provided the group with an opportunity to discuss some of the situations that provoked anxiety and to alter the hierarchies somewhat. Although the method proved significantly better than either insight therapy or a placebo, as in the above studies, the combination of discussion and group desensitization confound the interpretation of the results. To deal with this problem, Cohen (1969) compared the effects of group interaction, desensitization, noninteraction desensitization, and no treatment. His instructions to the subjects in the group interaction condition were as follows (p. 17). Subjects in this group were encouraged to discuss particular problems and alternative means of handling them. The discussion was directed toward issues of test anxiety, and the experimenter structured discussion so that the members of the group interacted with each other. The interaction took place during the nondesensitization periods and included discussion of intraexperimental situations (for example, process of relaxation as well as extraexperimental experiences, performing during the actual test). He discovered that although both desensitization procedures were more effective than no treatment, group interaction plus desensitization was more effective than desensitization alone in reducing test anxiety. Although only with limited data, the above mentioned authors provide some evidence to conclude that the combination of behavior modification procedures (in this case, systematic desensitization) and group discussion of problems within a group context is an effective procedure for reducing anxiety.

In a study by Kondas (1967), 23 sixth to eighth grade children and 13 college students were desensitized in groups to reduce "stage fright" and examination anxiety. The combination of imagination and relaxation brought about significant changes not achieved by simple imagination or relaxation alone. Moreover, the results were still stable five months after the end of treatment.

In summary, it appears that group systematic desensitization is at least as effective as individual desensitization in the treatment of several types of phobias, including interpersonal ones, and is more effective than either insight therapy or no treatment or placebo conditions. Furthermore, relaxation and hierarchy presentation both appear to be necessary in this kind of treatment. Another condition in groups that seems to contribute to a positive outcome is discussion among the clients of the types of situations that seem to bother them and the different ways each has of dealing with them.

In Heterogeneous Groups

Most agencies do not have a large number of persons with the same phobias who request treatment at the same time. If there are sufficient phobias to organize a group, they acknowledge a wide variety of anxiety-producing events. For this reason, the author has produced a set of procedures that permits the development of hierarchies tailored to the specific phobias of each member, but that nevertheless employs the group structure and group discussion as additional means of treatment.

The first method makes use, once again, of the buddy system. Following a demonstration by the therapist, each member, using his or her buddy as a consultant, develops his or her own hierarchy. The therapist checks out the hierarchies and makes suggestions where necessary. Where pairs or triads of members have similar phobias, they will be encouraged to develop common hierarchies.

Once the hierarchies have been developed, each item is placed on a separate card. Each card is numbered in order of difficulty. After relaxing all the members, the therapist gives them the following instructions.

> Clear your mind. Now I want each of you to imagine the content on card one. Okay, imagine each detail. If you can clearly imagine card one, indicate this by raising your left index finger. How much anxiety do each of you feel?
>
> Okay, once again. Clear your mind, relax (then repeats once or twice more before going on to item two on the hierarchy).

The members must be completely familiar with their cards, although they may look at them, if necessary, during the instructions. It is usually a good idea to have them memorize the situations on each card between sessions.

Another approach is to have each partner desensitize his or her buddy. When the first of the pair is finished, the second runs through the hierarchy with the first. Before this is possible, the therapist must train the members in the procedure, usually by demonstrating on several clients how the procedure works. A practice period ensues in which each person goes through one item in the hierarchy for another member in the presence of the rest of the group. Suggestions are made as to how he or she can improve the procedure, and the member repeats the practice until he or she has developed a reasonable style.

A third approach is to use professional therapists or group aides to desensitize subgroups with similar problems. In a group of 5 to 8 members, there are probably no more than three subgroups of problems that would require three therapists or aides for that part of the meeting. In this approach, each subgroup is treated as if it were a homogeneously composed group.

The entire group or a subgroup also may be used to accompany a given client when he or she tries out the imagined scene in real life. Rimm and

Masters (1974, p. 146) refer to this procedure as "contact desensitization." In children's groups, evidence has shown this to be a powerful procedure in reducing fear of snakes (Ritter, 1968). Not only does contact desensitization in groups make use of a modeling effect, but it provides both group pressure as well as reinforcement for successful completion of the approach response.

Although relaxation, systematic, or contact desensitization are major procedures used in groups to deal directly with problems of anxiety, a set of cognitive procedures is being used increasingly as an auxiliary or major method of dealing with these problems. These cognitive procedures also may serve to change a person's perception of him- or herself and other cognitive targets and to modify his or her overt behavior.

COGNITIVE RESTRUCTURING

It is becoming more and more evident that what persons say to themselves, their thoughts, their beliefs, and their information impinge upon their behavior and their levels of anxiety. These internal statements are referred to as "cognitions." They serve as both discriminative, as well as reinforcing, stimuli to both overt and covert phenomena. Moreover, cognitions appear to be controlled by the same laws that govern overt behavior. As we can observe in relaxation and systematic desensitization, both procedures are in part governed by cognitive imagery and subvocal self-instructions. In recent years, a number of behaviorally oriented authors have attempted to expand behavioral approaches to include cognitive targets of change as well as cognitive change procedures. Some of these targets and accompanying change procedures are reviewed in this section. For a more complete discussion, the reader is referred to Bandura (1969, Chapter 9; 1971) and Wilkins (1971).

Some cognitive phenomena often are associated with high anxiety, and as such commonly have been selected as targets of change in group and individual therapy. Some clients possess inadequate or incorrect information that directly may cause them to be anxious. Had they possessed the correct information, they would have realized that their fears were unjustified. Some clients have persistent or obsessive thoughts, often accompanied by anxiety, over which they feel they have little control. Other clients hold to self-defeating, irrational beliefs, such as the assumption that one must be loved or approved of by everyone. Failure to achieve this impossible standard results, then, in high levels of anxiety. Still other clients inappropriately label their own behavior or that of others, which also causes them unnecessary discomfort. Fortunately, a number of procedures have been developed to deal with these problems, although because they are covert they do not level themselves readily to systematic research. They are primarily supported by anecdotal evidence. The simplest procedure among these is corrective information.

CORRECTIVE INFORMATION

Some clients have anxiety or act the way they do simply because of a lack of correct information or an excess of misinformation. Part of group treatment is the discovery of beliefs based on inadequate facts and the correction of this informational problem. Parents believed that excessive thumbsucking would cause intellectual impairment in their five-year-old; a couple refrained from sexual relations because of inadequate knowledge about birth control; a member of an assertive training group was convinced that the recently discovered lump in her breast meant certain death, and thus refused to go to the doctor. These are a few of the many examples where corrective information has sufficed to decrease anxiety and increase appropriate behavior.

In the group, it is possible to deal with general topics such as sex, birth control, diet hazards, health, and child development without forcing individual members to admit their ignorance. For this reason, guest expert speakers often are called in to deal with topics about which members suggest they know little. Where individual clients have specific informational needs that they are willing to talk about in the group, members often are able to supply it or to find outside sources to provide it.

THOUGHT STOPPING

When a client has difficulty in controlling thoughts, and these persistent thoughts result in a high level of anxiety, often many of the procedures discussed in earlier chapters may result in better control. When this is not the case, a procedure called "thought stopping" may be called for (see Wolpe, 1973). In this technique the client is instructed to concentrate on the given persistent thoughts. After several seconds, the therapist suddenly yells, "Stop!" After several repetitions, the client is told to stop his or her own thoughts in the same way. And, finally, the client thinks "stop" subvocally in response to the persistent thoughts. The client is informed that he or she may have to repeat the procedure several times to maintain control. To check what the client is thinking, it may be advisable to have him or her vocalize his or her thoughts the first few trials.

Since most anxious clients claim to have some difficulty controlling their thoughts, thought stopping often is taught as a self-control procedure to all group members. As in teaching most other skills, the rationale is explained, the procedure is demonstrated, the members try out the procedure with each other in pairs or triads. They discuss any problems that may have occurred in the subgroups when the group gets back together. For those members for whom obsessive thoughts is a chronic problem, a behavioral assignment will be given to use the procedure between sessions.

Rimm and Masters (1974, p. 434) also recommend that the clients be taught an alternative adaptive or assertive thought to be used in place of or in response to the obsessive thought. For example, in response to the persistent thought,

"I'm going crazy," a client was trained to say "Screw it, I'm perfectly normal" (see Rimm and Masters, 1974, p. 434). Other types of internal sentences also may be taught either in conjunction with thought stopping or as independent covert behaviors. These internal sentences may be self-reinforcing statements (Boy, did I do a good job in controlling those thoughts!) or self-cueing statements (Look out, here it comes, now handle it right!).

In the group, members are asked to describe how they talk to themselves. The members give suggestions to each other about what other sentences they might use to reinforce or cue themselves more effectively. The rest of the training to learn covert sentences is the same as in learning thought stopping. First, the sentence is vocalized to the group. If the client feels that it serves his or her purpose, he or she practices it (often with a buddy) subvocally under role-played or rehearsal conditions. And, ultimately, the client tries it out whenever the situation calls for it.

Dispelling Irrational Beliefs

Ellis (1962) describes a number of irrational beliefs often held by clients in this culture, which are usually self-defeating. These include beliefs that one should be loved and approved of by everyone; that one should be perfectly competent, adequate, talented in all respects; that one should blame oneself and others for mistakes and wrongdoings; that it is catastrophic when things are not the way one likes them to be; and, finally, that emotion is uncontrollable. To deal with these in the group, members are asked to check which of the assumptions seem to guide their view of the world and then to give evidence to support their position. All the members then pick two people in the group who know them best, and they do the same thing. Finally, a client may give the same list to people who know him or her outside of the group. The results are discussed in the group. There is a danger of imposing the therapist's or even group members' perceptions on the client. To avoid this, in the absence of agreement among the members, it may be better not to pursue the therapist's or a single member's isolated hypothesis as to what assumption governs a given client's behavior. However, when there is agreement among several members and where each can point to specific behavioral evidence to substantiate that opinion, it may be valuable to go further with the client.

The next steps would then involve the client in a discussion with the other members of the rational or irrational basis of his or her beliefs. The members point out the ultimate and eventual consequences of maintaining the given belief. They even may give the client the role-play assignment of acting *as if* he or she did not have the belief. Once the client accepts the invalidity of the belief, he or she is given the assignment of handling situations as they occur outside of the group *as if* he or she no longer had this belief.

Although there is only limited evidence as to the effectiveness or ineffectiveness of this approach, group members have evaluated it as extremely useful in the several groups in which it has been incorporated into the Group Therapy and Research Program.

This method is drawn from Rational Emotive Therapy (RET) by Ellis (1962, 1971). The behavioral approach differs from that used by Ellis in that the former stresses role-playing while the latter stresses confrontation.

Relabeling

Another cognitive procedure that appears to be effective in influencing perception of behavior is relabeling, which involves the replacement of inappropriate maladaptive labels with appropriate adaptive ones attributed to one's own behavior or characteristics or that of others with whom one interacts. For example, in a parent's group, Mrs. L called her child, Petey, age 3, "hyperactive," because he ran around the house and yelled a lot. On learning that most of the three-year-olds belonging to the group members exhibited the same behavior (and that one member whose child was more subdued was equally worried), she now labeled Petey as "healthy active." No further modification was necessary. In assertive training, one member labeled himself as "crazy" because he was isolated and didn't go out much. When he indicated that he did enjoy reading and playing chess with a neighbor, cooking, and listening to classical music, members told him that he wasn't "crazy," just "different," a title he accepted readily. Because the members are similar to each other, the group is a much greater force than a therapist in helping an individual member to accept a new label. But even the group is not always successful. In these cases, behavioral change through self-control procedures may be required before the client is convinced that his or her self-depreciating label is inappropriate. In most groups, the therapist helps members to examine labels they attribute to themselves and others. They are required to justify these labels to the other group members, who are quick to point out the inadequacy of the evidence.

SYSTEMATIC PROBLEM SOLVING

All of the above methods require that a client be able to deal with a problem rationally and systematically, that is, that he or she have problem-solving skills. Often, however, this is not the case. Clients must be taught a systematic problem-solving paradigm. This covert framework gives the client a structure for dealing with inevitable problems that arise long after treatment has ended. (Since this is an important step in maintenance of changes, it is discussed in detail in Chapter XI.) One type that requires such a problem-solving paradigm for solution is group problems. To deal with group problems, group goals must be formulated.

According to D'Zurilla and Goldfried (1971) there is a remarkable degree of agreement among investigators and theorists about the operational stages involved in effective problem solving. These stages include (1) a general orientation, (2) problem definition and orientation, (3) generation of alternatives, (4) decision making, and (5) verification. As a person solves a problem, he or she may go back and forth among these phases until they reach the final phase. The paradigm merely suggests a model for organizing therapeutic procedures; it does not establish how problems are solved.

General orientation refers to the way in which the therapists orients the client to his or her problem. First, the therapist helps the client to view the existence of problems, which usually can be dealt with, as a normal way of life. Second, the clients are oriented towards identifying problems as they occur, and third, they are encouraged to limit their impulse to deal with problems as they occur. The group members are taught this orientation through case examples, through the analysis of ongoing problems they themselves are experiencing, and through group discussion. The specific topic, problem solving skills, is an agenda item in several meetings.

In order to define the problem and formulate it appropriately care is taken to identify in observable terms all the elements of the problem. This is necessary since it has been observed that often individuals with a given problem do not respond to the relevant cues, which prevents them from resolving it.

In the generation of alternatives, a procedure called "brainstorming" is often utilized. In this procedure the members attempt to develop a large number of solutions to the problem. In order to generate creative solutions, all criticism is ruled out and wild ideas are encouraged. Once the ideas are on the table the members then suggest how they might be combined or revised in such a way as to make better ideas. In decision making the given client is helped to evaluate each of the final sets of tactics and general strategies proposed in the previous phases in terms of their likely consequences and their general usefulness.

Finally, the client must do something about the problem. In the verification phase, he or she commits him-or-herself to the trying out the general strategy and specific tactics developed in the group, and to report back to the group the results of this trial. On the basis of this experience the plan may be revised in which case the client tries out the revised strategy until a successful outcome is obtained.

After all members have successfully negotiated at least one problem by means of the problem solving process, the steps are reviewed in the group, and the members are encouraged to go through the process on their own. By the end of therapy members are expected to be able to articulate and use all steps in the problem solving paradigm. (See Goldfried and D'Zurilla, 1971, for greater detail.)

In the last three chapters, we have discussed the major means of achieving individual treatment goals within the context of the small therapy group. In the next chapter we will discuss how these same procedures, as well as additional group techniques, can be used to facilitate the attainment of group goals, and thus to resolve group problems.

10 Modifying Group Interaction

Therapist: As you see on the chart, three of us seem to talk more than 75 percent of the time, and the remaining five talk about 25 percent of the time. It seems to me that those not talking aren't getting their share out of the group. And those doing all the talking may be preventing those who aren't as assertive from getting their share. What do the rest of you think? (Discussion follows in which general agreement occurs.)

Therapist: Since we all seem to agree that this is a problem, I wonder if we can't use some of the procedures you've been using to work on your own behavior to help each other to increase or decrease his share of the participation?

Edgar: Well, we could give tokens as feedback to the quieter ones among us. Since I'm the yapper, you'll have to give me tokens to shut up. (Members laugh but also give nods of agreement.)

Vince: How about red chips for the noisy three and white ones for the quiet five? The idea would be to see whether the average number of whites will equal the reds (nods of agreement from others).

Dean: Everyone seems to agree, but I don't always know what to say, and I'll bet that's true for others, too.

Guy: Perhaps before the meeting the buddies can coach each other or even role-play what to say or how to limit what one says.

Tom: What about one meeting devoted to demonstration and practice of talking in groups? Some of those exercises we used two weeks ago might be helpful. (Discussion continues until an agreed-upon plan is achieved.)

Throughout this book we have stressed the relevance of the group not only in the context of treatment, but also as a set of means by which treatment goals are achieved. An earlier chapter demonstrated how the patterns of interaction in the group can both hinder and facilitate the attainment of individual treatment goals. Thus, procedures for altering patterns of group interaction are necessary skills for the group therapist. We will now see how the treatment procedures discussed in the previous chapter can be used to modify patterns of group interaction.

One of the major characteristics of group treatment is that the therapist must use the behavior and perceptions of each of the group members to influence the behavior of each of the other group members. The therapist cannot apply a treatment procedure within the group without cooperation. For example, if the therapist ignores the highly critical statements of one of the members, but the other clients respond to them, the effect of the therapist's extinction behavior is virtually eliminated. He or she must enlist the cooperation of the other members to control the target behavior effectively. For the same reason, each member must become involved with the treatment plans of each of the other members, must aid in their development, and must assist in carrying out these plans.

The concept of interaction is central to a behavioral perspective of the group. All action in the group is in a sense interaction, since it is in part stimulated by previous actions of others and is a reinforcement of the previous actions of others. Thus, each given behavior is both a consequence and a stimulus to a response. Since the group therapist is aiming at modifying responses of the members, he or she cannot isolate individuals in the group. The therapist must identify and deal with the pattern of interactions in order to predict and control the behavior of group members. A molecular analysis in which each action and interaction is analyzed, although academically of interest, would be far too cumbersome to prove useful. It is necessary to hypothesize the actions that are relevant and amenable for analysis and to evaluate and deal with them. It is the purpose of this chapter to identify those patterns, content, and correlates of interaction that have been demonstrated to be both relevant and amenable to analysis and treatment.

PATTERNS OF INTERACTION

The most apparent question the therapist must ask is the degree to which each member overtly participates in the group interaction. If a member fails to participate, his or her problems cannot be assessed, treatment plans cannot be developed, and homework assignments cannot be designed or monitored. Thus, it is important that the group develop a distribution of interaction in which each person initiates sufficient interaction that his or her problems are dealt with adequately. Yet, just as in the introductory example, in many groups there are sizable disparities among members in the amount of interaction initiated. Some disparity is due to certain members having fewer problems or being more efficient in presenting their problems than others. But more often disparities are a result of differences in the skill of talking in social situations and in degrees of anxiety in the face of social stimuli. Another interrelated cause of a discrepancy may be verbose and assertive members, who allow little time for less assertive members to participate. Whether a person is prevented by his or her own behavioral pattern or the behavior of others, gross disparities signal a group problem that must be introduced by the group therapist and dealt with by the group.

There is considerable evidence to show that combined behavioral methods are effective in increasing social interaction among both normal and psychotic small group populations. In at least one study with psychotics, the researchers also demonstrated both a transfer and a maintenance effect (Bennett and Maley, 1973). Because of the importance of manipulating the interaction in therapy groups, a brief review of the literature that deals with this problem is presented here.

In a study by Bennett and Maley (1973), four chronic mental patients, selected because of persistent patterns of withdrawal from social interaction, were residents of a token economy treatment unit and were assigned to an experimental or control-simulated group therapy condition of ten 30-minute treatment sessions. For the two experimental subjects, reinforcement was contingent for four distinct types of interactive behavior: talking to another person, attending and talking to another person, asking and answering questions in a dyad, and working cooperatively in the dyad to solve problems. The two control subjects had instructions to perform the same behaviors but received no reinforcement for their performance. Not only was the contingent reinforcement effective in increasing the interaction significantly over that of the control group, but in a follow-up study there was evidence of maintenance of the change and transfer of the change to other situations. Since chronic mental patients are notoriously poor interactors (Maley, 1974), these results were all the more significant.

The patients in the study were residents on a token economy ward prior to and concurrent with group treatment; therefore, one must ask what the small group effect of contingency plus instruction might have been to increase their interaction. One can postulate a powerful modeling effect in the small group. The dyad forced patients to observe others who were being reinforced for appropriate behaviors. The patient could escape this pressure on the ward. Moreover, it appeared that considerably more verbal reinforcement could be used in the dyad than on the ward, which also may have contributed to the increased interaction.

In simulated or real group therapy situations, a number of other projects have used reinforcement to increase other classes of interaction. Williams and Blanton (1968) showed that patients in psychotherapy would increase the expression of statements with discriminable feeling content if such statements were reinforced. The effect of the group, although not explicitly stated, was that insofar as each person could be a model for other persons in the group, reinforcement of the model in the presence of the subject should increase the probability of imitation (Bandura, 1969). Dinoff and his associates (1960) were able to increase the number of personal group references with verbal elicitation and reinforcement techniques. Heckel, Wiggins, and Salzberg (1962) increased interaction in a therapy group by eliminating silences through the surreptitious introduction of noxious noise every time the group became silent. The elimination of noise served as a negative reinforcement for speaking or breaking the silence.

Bavelas and others (1965), in a series of experiments, demonstrated the efficacy of differential reinforcement of group members in modifying the distribution of interaction in the group and in changing the sociometric structure. More specifically, in a laboratory study they observed without intervening the interaction of four men in a group. Following a brief interaction period, the men were ranked in terms of their interaction, and one of the two least active persons was selected by the experimenters as the target person (TP). The members also ranked each other in terms of four sociometric questions. During the experimental period, the discussion continued with the members expecting to receive green lights to indicate a positive contribution and red lights if the contribution interfered with the task. In fact, in most instances only the target person received green lights for his contributions. The other participants received green lights only when supporting the statements of the TP. After 20 minutes, the members reranked fellow members along the sociometric dimensions, and a third session was run without lights.

The results showed that the interactional frequency of the TP increased significantly over that of the control subjects and that his sociometric status rose equally. In subsequent studies where only positive reinforcement of the TP or punishment (negative feedback) of the control subjects were used, the results were in the same direction but not nearly as strong. The implication is that if one wishes to modify the sociometric status of the group, the therapist must respond not only to the target person but to the contributions of the others as well.

Lights as reinforcers have been used effectively by other experimenters (for example, Oakes, Droge, and August, 1961; Aiken, 1965; Oakes, 1962) to modify a number of categories of interaction in the group. Oakes, Droge, and August modified the total output of interaction by means of the lights. Using

12 categories of responses (Bales, 1968), Oakes discovered that only one of the categories—"giving opinion, evaluation, analysis; expresses feeling, wish"— was significantly altered. However, this category accounted for 50 percent of the contributions of the group members. Moreover, the number of responses in the other categories may have been too small to obtain significant differences.

In summary, researchers in laboratories and group therapeutic situations repeatedly have demonstrated that contingent reinforcement can be used by the leader in the form of approval, praise, nods, lights, positive feedback, showing of interest, or removal of noxious noise to modify the sequence and/or the content of interaction. They have modified such diverse categories of verbal behavior as the statement of feelings, personal and group references, expressing opinion, leadership behaviors, silences, and so on. Although reinforcement procedures are the common denominator in all of these projects, they also have been used in combination with other explicit procedures, such as verbal elicitation, prompting, and instructions. And it is quite likely that a powerful modeling effect also was operating in most of the groups in which members observed the model, who was another group member, being reinforced. Many of the treatment plans for modification of group attributes described in this book are based on the findings from these experiments.

When an undesirable distribution exists, the following steps usually are taken. As in the initial example, the data are first presented to the members, who discuss whether or not they perceive the unequal participation as a problem. Often, the presentation and ensuing discussion is sufficient to increase the participation of the members.

How does the practitioner determine the distribution of interaction? An inexpensive procedure is to have observers record the number of statements by each participant in the group. Although counters for each person can be used, the observers usually have a segmented circle in which each segment represents a group member or therapist. They record each unit of participation by placing a tally mark in the appropriate segment, as in Figure 10.1. A unit of participation is any statement, regardless of length, that has at least an understood or expressed subject and verb and that is directed to most of the members. Although the number of seconds spoken can be recorded, this is highly correlated with number of units and far more costly. To avoid observer fatigue, time samples of 10 minutes are taken, with a five-minute rest between each sample.

Where it has been determined that an uneven distribution of participation exists among members, and a chart showing member participation scores is not sufficient to alter the pattern, the following steps can be taken. A decision is made as to which participants must attempt to increase their participation, which should attempt to decrease theirs, and which should attempt to maintain their present levels. Once each person has a goal, a 15-minute period is designated as a practice time. The discussion continues with the added instruc-

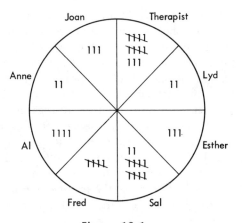

Figure 10.1.

tion that whenever a low participant speaks, he or she is reinforced by the person to his or her right; whenever a high participant speaks, he or she is given negative feedback, usually by the person on his or her right—for example, by putting a hand on the shoulder of the target person.

At the end of the 15-minute time sample, the distribution again is recorded and discussed by members of the group. Usually a second time sample is applied using the same plan. In cases where the high participants completely stop talking, the average is calculated and every person has as his or her goal approximating the average. The right-hand partner may reinforce until one reaches the average and may provide negative feedback after the average has been reached.

In using this procedure, it is helpful to evaluate subjectively the usefulness of the content of interaction during the training periods. If the content does not appear to be task-related or otherwise relevant, the program should be modified to include reinforcement only for task-related topics. In subsequent meetings, procedures are applied during continually shorter time samples until the members voice confidence that they can maintain a desired distribution without the assistance of the procedure.

In some cases where the problem is clearly anxiety or lack of skill of isolated members, individual training programs are developed for those clients within the group. Such programs usually involve modeling and rehearsal of successive approximations of the individual interacting in stressful group situations, and on occasion group desensitization of covert thoughts of these approximations may be employed.

Not all interactive problems need to be resolved by the therapist. Often the group members will deal with their own problems, as can be seen in the following examples.

A weight loss group consisted of nine women and one man, who was the husband of one of the members. At first, whenever he spoke, people would listen to him. But after a short period there were clear signs of disinterest, as indicated by the women talking to one another, or looking off into the distance, or shuffling their chairs every time he spoke. The reason for this, the therapist hypothesized, was that the male client was prone to give advice in a pedantic and fatherly tone, which annoyed the other members. However, after the fourth or fifth time that he gave advice, it was disregarded. No further change apparently was necessary, because the absence of response from the other group members seemed to extinguish the behavior. As a result, the man gave less advice and talked at a much lower frequency than in the original meeting.

Had the male client's behavior continued, it would have been necessary for the therapist to intercede. Otherwise the membership might have dwindled because of the aversive interaction. Where a group problem exists, action is required, but it is preferable to wait, at least briefly, for the group to mobilize its own resources for dealing with its own problems, as shown in the above example. A therapist-perceived problem may not be viewed in the same way by the clients, as we see in the following example.

> In an anxiety management group, participation was unevenly distributed after three sessions (i.e., some people spoke often, while others rarely spoke at all). The therapists were concerned that this might be annoying to the members, even though no evidence appeared on the weekly evaluation. As a result, at the fourth meeting they showed the data to the group and asked if the members felt that a problem existed. The relatively inactive members claimed that they would talk more only if they had more to say, and that they appreciated the activity of the more active members. Since the members were, in fact, being more assertive outside the group and fulfilling the conditions of their weekly contracts, the matter was appropriately dropped by the therapists and the members.

SEQUENCE OF INTERACTION

Members may be prevented from participating in the interaction because of the prevalence of the leaders' activity. To obtain what is assumed to be vital information for assessment or to help members formulate problems more behaviorally, therapists may interview each member one at a time. This is an especially common problem with therapists whose previous experiences have been solely in one-to-one therapeutic situations. One of the side effects of this approach is that the observing participants tend to lose interest. In group meetings where the therapist-member interaction is high in proportion to member-member interaction, the members have evaluated the meeting as unproductive on the session evaluations and have indicated their discontent in other ways as well.

To determine whether such a problem exists, the sequence of interaction is recorded by an observer (or one of the members). The therapist's activity is designated by an L (for leader) and the members by an M. Usually no distinction is made among members or between therapists (if two are present). However, in some cases such distinctions may be desirable. Three or four 10-minute time samples per hour seem sufficient to get a meaningful sample of the interaction without overloading the observer.

Thus, a two-minute time sample might look as follows: L M M M L M L M M M L L. By analyzing each letter and determining what the letter is that precedes it, each pair can be classified as LM (ML), MM, or LL. No distinction is made between LM or ML. In this example, the following pairs are obtained: ML, MM, MM, LM, ML, LM, MM, MM, LL, or 6 LMs (MLs), 4 MMs and 1 LL. The minute rate would be obtained for a two-minute sample by dividing by 2. Thus, the ML rate per minute was 3, the MM rate was 2, and the LL rate was O.5. A high level of LL would indicate that the leaders are talking too much to one another, a problem discussed in more detail in the section on leadership.

In the initial phases of treatment, one would expect a high level of leader-member interaction in proportion to member-member interaction. As Bales (1968) has demonstrated in problem-solving groups, the first treatment phase is concerned with orientation. The members ask questions to which the leaders respond, and vice versa. The leaders check to see whether the members understand certain concepts, and the members respond. However, if there is not a gradual reduction of leader-member and a concomitant increase in member-member interaction, it is clear that members are being prevented from assisting one another and from adequately trying out their newly acquired knowledge. The following illustration (Figure 10.2) indicates a group problem during the baseline period. After dealing with the problem, a reversal of rates was obtained.

After the third meeting, the therapist reviewed the data with the members. When several indicated that they thought the therapist, indeed, was talking too much, he asked them what they might do to restrain him or to increase their own help in giving behavior to each other. The members expressed the opinion that they ought to be reinforcing more, giving more suggestions to each other from their own experiences, and raising more questions. These were acts that the therapist alone was performing. One member suggested that the therapist pause before making any comments so that the members have at least the opportunity to enter the discussion. A system of prompts was suggested in which the person next to the therapist would show him a cue card that read "pause." In rejecting this, the members decided to observe whether or not a change would occur merely because they were aware of the problem. At the following meeting, no significant change occurred, and the group agreed to prompting the therapist and for the therapist to indicate his approval of their

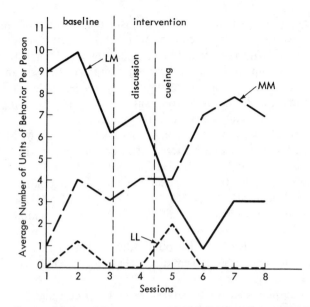

Figure 10.2.   Minute rate of LM (ML), MM, and LL sequence.

participation nonverbally. As a result, there was a radical decrease in therapist-member interaction, although member-member interaction remained the same. The program was dropped after the eighth meeting because the ratio had begun to stabilize, and the members felt that the program had achieved its purpose.

TASK ORIENTATION

Even when appropriately sequenced or distributed, interaction may not be particularly pertinent to the group task. Relevancy is determined by the relationship of the content of the interaction to session, treatment, and group goals. Interaction related to these goals may be considered on-task; all other off-task. Obviously, not all interaction need be on-task. Some discussion of subjects that are not related to formal goals may enhance the attractiveness of the group for its members and also may lead to assessment of problems not originally considered within the more formal goal-related discussions. An occasional joke may lighten an overserious mood. However, the ratio of on-task to off-task behavior in a goal-oriented therapy group should be extremely high to achieve even the minimal task requirements at any one meeting of monitoring the contracts of the previous session and developing new ones for the next session. When goals are not achieved and a particular member's achievements not reviewed at a given meeting, there is dissatisfaction with the group. And since most behavioral groups are time limited, it is important to limit off-task behavior, which can prevent the group from accomplishing very much. One need not use an iron fist to keep persons to the task.

Simple praise or, in most cases, the statement of session goals and an agenda of items related to those goals usually are sufficient to keep the group on-task. Because some off-task discussion is important to the members, a certain amount of time is allotted for such talk either during an extended break or following the meeting over a beer or cup of coffee. During the formal session, however, deviation from the session goals are pointed out by the therapist, who first attempts to relate it to the topic at hand. If it appears in any way relevant, in spite of being off-task, the therapist will make a note to include an item in the agenda in which the subject can be discussed at a subsequent session.

On some occasions a more elaborate group treatment plan is called for, as in the following example concerning a group of mothers. The trainer noted that there was considerable group discussion of the children's recent escapades, but agenda items were rarely if ever completed in the early meetings of the group. The trainer paid little attention to this off-task behavior at first because she wished to maintain the cohesiveness of the group, but as meetings continued little progress was being made toward attaining the group goal.

To deal with the problem, the trainer showed a video tape of a segment of the previous week's meeting. She pointed out how the off-task discussion prevented the members from achieving the agreed-upon goals. However, she noted that social contact with each other was an important part of coming to the group. She wondered how the members could meet both aims—the achievement of the task goals and the satisfaction of informal discussion. One member suggested that they plan to stay a few minutes longer after the formal session to discuss their children. The trainer agreed to increase the break between the first and second hours to 15 minutes. The group members then tried to define task-oriented discussion. They decided that it referred to any verbal contribution that related to the agenda item being handled at any given point in time. If it was not related, it was off-task. One member agreed to review the tapes with the trainer to monitor the off-task behavior. They then decided that each person would remind her buddy if she were off-task. The trainer suggested that if the agenda items were finished early, the meeting could be ended early, which would give them more time for socializing. In this way, they gradually designed a plan acceptable to all.

REINFORCING AND COERCIVE INTERACTION

There is a high degree of mutually reinforcing interaction in some groups, that is, sequence of events in which the behavior of one person is reinforcing for the behavior of another person, whose behavior in turn is reinforcing for the behavior of the first. For example, one person gives a suggestion for modifying one facet of a treatment plan; the second points out that the first has a lot of good ideas; the first in turn indicates appreciation for getting that kind of feedback. In other groups, mutually punishing or coercive interactive sequences seem to prevail, that is, a sequence in which two or more persons present aversive stimuli to each other to control the behavior of the other (Patterson and Cobb, 1971). The pattern is maintained by ending the aversive stimulation following its presentation by the other person in the sequence. For example, one member of the group criticizes another for unfeeling responses to others; the first member begins to yell at the second, who in turn shouts, "You see what I mean?"

In most cases, members present initial patterns of interpersonal responses already in their repertoire. If these are coercive, the interchanges may prevail after the initial introductory phase of treatment. Groups characterized by such interchanges usually are highly aversive and tend to dissolve quickly or at least to be limited in effectiveness. For this reason, such interchanges within the group must be dealt with at once.

To monitor the problem, it is easier to count the number of reinforcing and punishing statements than to analyze specific sequences. It also is more effective to involve the members in determining what is reinforcing and what is aversive to each of them than to utilize an outside observer. It is done in this way: Each person records all statements which he or she experiences as reinforcing or punishing. At the end of the first hour of the meeting, the minute rates are calculated, and if the ratio of rates is high for coercive, overreinforcing statements, a treatment plan is developed.

In the following example, the monitoring process alone modified the ratio of mutal reinforcement to mutual coercive statements.

The therapist for a group of highly confrontative patients, all of whom had previous experience in encounter groups and group psychotherapy, asked the members to record the number of statements they regarded as "put downs," insults, or in any other way aversive. The results were startling. Not only did the members experience a high number of "put downs" from each other, but each perceived the therapist as primarily a punishing person. The group developed a plan. When a person experienced a "put down," he or she would toss a white poker chip into a large can in the middle of the room. In that way each person knew when another felt punished. If a member felt complimented, praised, or otherwise reinforced, a red chip would go into another can. The mutual reinforcement increased, and mutal aversive exchanges decreased, almost immediately. The program was maintained for part of several meetings. To ascertain whether or not the behavior was maintained, an observation in the group was made four weeks after the exchange program had been terminated. Although the mutual reinforcement decreased somewhat, it never returned to the baseline levels.

AFFECTIVE STATEMENTS

Many clients have problems in verbalizing affective statements that describe how they feel about themselves, others, or situations they encounter. These problems may be characterized by a deficit, surplus, or inadequate discrimination as to the persons, time, and place such statement can be expressed most appropriately. The group provides a unique laboratory for learning appropriate, interpersonally expressed, affective statements. Some of these statements may overlap with the expression of praise or of criticism of others as described above. However, the broader category of positive and negative affective statements may be more relevant for clients in this area. Brockway and others (1972) find that these categories can be observed with a high degree of reliability.

The categories may be observed as a part of a role-play situation, simulating situations that clients typically encounter, such as being imposed upon by one's child or being complimented by a friend. They also may be observed in the ongoing interaction in the group by the observers. However, negative affective statements rarely tend to be observed in behavioral groups under these conditions. Groups using more confrontative methods, however, do evoke both positive and negative affective statements in large numbers, and such procedures may be called for where there is a deficit or inadequate discrimination in the use of these categories of behavior.

In addition to the use of confrontative cognitive methods described in the previous chapter, all of the other techniques to increase interactive categories commonly have been used.

A number of other interactive categories (p. 50) have been observed in treatment groups, depending on what the therapist hypothesized as a group problem. For example, in some groups there was a deficit of opinions and suggestions to other members of the group. In one group, questioning for any purpose was rarely practiced and hence became a target of change (Linsk and others, 1975).

LEADERSHIP

Many categories of interactive behavior are concerned with the facilitation of group and individual treatment goals and the maintenance or morale of the group. These goal-facilitating and group-maintaining activities are referred to as "leadership functions or behaviors." Examples of leadership behaviors are making suggestions on how to deal with a problem, encouraging members, giving positive reinforcement for task completion, limiting off-task behavior, limiting disruptive behavior, and even arranging the seats so that everyone can see everyone else. The specific characteristics of leadership behaviors vary as to the goals of the group and the theories of the therapists and members as to what behaviors are necessary to maintain the group. But it is possible in each group to decide what leadership behaviors might be for that group.

Leadership behaviors can be performed primarily by one person in the group or they can be distributed among several or even all of the members. In the beginning of therapy, most of the leadership behaviors are performed by the therapist. Clearly, in the discussion on the sequence of interaction, this is not always a satisfactory arrangement. It is necessary for members to learn the leadership behaviors and to share in their performance, not only to increase their satisfaction with the group but also to facilitate their learning skills to administer their own treatment when the group therapy has terminated. For these reasons, one of the principles of behavioral treatment is a training in, and gradual delegation of, leadership behaviors to members of the group.

To carry out this principle, the relevant leadership behaviors are performed by the therapist in the initial sessions. Later in treatment, these behaviors are identified in group discussion, at which time the therapist encourages members to perform those behaviors. He or she also may provide the members with examples of what they can do or may provide them with exercises in leadership. The chairperson's role may be distributed among members in order to train and evaluate their skills as leaders (a detailed description of this procedure follows later in this chapter).

As the behaviors are performed by members, they are reinforced with praise or simple feedback. At the end of the first meeting in which delegation of leadership functions takes place, the therapist evaluates the degree to which leadership behaviors have been performed by members of the group. Plans are made to increase the distribution of leadership behaviors. If particular behaviors are difficult to perform, more formal behavioral treatment programs may be established to train the members in these.

Several group problems that require special attention may be noted in the evaluation. First is the problem of one or two persons dominating the leadership behaviors to the exclusion of others. If this is the case, a program similar to the ones used to increase the distribution of participation can increase the distribution of leadership behavior (see p. 136). Another problem commonly occurs when cotherapists follow each other excessively in the performance of leadership behaviors. They are constantly amplifying each other to the exclusion of the group members and often to their discontent. Such a problem can be detected most readily if the sequence of interaction is counted, as was discussed earlier. A minute rate of leader-leader interaction of higher than one is usually an indication of such a group problem. Working on it provides the therapists with the opportunity to model a relevant program that modifies their behavior as well as the behavior of the members.

Several programs have been used, each developed with the group members. The most common procedure is to instruct therapists to write down anything they wish to say following the statement of the cotherapist. They usually discover that either members of the group say what they have written or that, as the discussion progresses, their statement was not as important as they thought it was. A very effective—but somewhat aversive—procedure is to have one of the members press a buzzer every time one therapist follows the other.

As the reader may have noted, the major difference between the experimental literature on groups and the treatment plans suggested by the author for clinical practice has been the clients' involvement in clinical groups in the evolution and carrying out of the treatment plans and the use of as many procedures as possible to attain the desired group change. One procedure for increasing involvement is rotation of the position of discussion leader (or chairperson) among the members. In many groups the discussion leader for the meeting is not necessarily the therapist. It may be one or two members who have demonstrated special competence or, more frequently, it may be all members, who are rotated into the role of discussion leader. The discussion leader, when a member, also may assist the therapist in the establishment of session goals and the drawing up of the agenda. The leader usually leads the discussion for all or part of the meeting. The length of time is determined on the basis of previously demonstrated leadership. His or her skill as a leader is evaluated by the therapist and members. The focus is primarily on what he or she has done well, although suggestions indicate what behaviors might be increased. Where necessary to obtain sufficient information or to practice newly learned skills, a discussion leader may be kept on longer than his or her official turn.

The advantage of using members as discussion leaders is that it provides them with an opportunity to learn and practice leadership skills in a highly supervised situation. Each member receives feedback on his or her leadership but with protection by both rules and the therapist from more confrontation than he or she can handle.

The disadvantage, of course, is that unless members already possess some skills in discussion leading, the meetings usually (but *not* always) are less efficient and sometimes less attractive than when a professional leads the group. To deal with this problem, in some groups only short periods of time are allotted to leadership for members. As the members themselves decide, the periods are extended until the entire meeting and all meetings are led by members. As in all procedures, the crucial variables are whether the productivity of the group remains high.

Little has been done with this procedure except in children and adolescent groups where the experience has been evaluated positively and the added cost in terms of outcome has been insignificant. In the several adult groups in which the procedure has been applied, all were assertive training groups, and the leadership behaviors were important for the members to attain. For this reason, further experimentation with its use is recommended.

Buddy System

Another promising procedure that allows every member to perform leadership behaviors is the buddy system, which we have mentioned throughout this book. In this procedure, each client is assigned or chooses another as a monitor and coach in the treatment process. A triad system also may be used, but it tends to reduce the intimacy of the situation and to give opportunity for temporary withdrawal from interaction by one of the members. Dyads, however, are used most commonly.

To select buddies, clients are first told the purpose of the procedure, and, if the buddy system is used in the first few meetings, buddies are randomly assigned or assigned in terms of proximity. In later sessions, clients may be asked to indicate two persons with whom they would like to work as a buddy. (This also provides sociometric data, which can be used to observe who have the weakest interpersonal relationships in the group.) Some therapists ask the clients to rate each member on a scale of one to five as to the degree to which they would be able to work with that individual. Brinkman and others (1973) used these scales to determine partners on the basis of the least possible average discrepancy between the two. They began pairing those people who appeared to be the least attractive. The person who assigns the partners is given the rough data without the names of the patients, to prevent him or her from using private criteria or perceptions as the basis of pairing.

The assignments given to buddies to work on together are quite varied and are used in all phases of treatment. In assessment, the pairs are asked to define together the behaviors that concern each the most. Each one evaluates the other's formulation in terms of the criteria of relevance, specificity, and observability.

Buddies may serve as extragroup monitors to each other, or they merely may remind each other between meetings to keep up their self-monitoring. In either case, they provide each other with reinforcement for carrying out monitoring assignments.

Buddies may help each other to develop treatment plans during, as well as between, group sessions. They provide between-meeting support for carrying out those plans. Buddies develop role-plays, carry out contact desensitization, or go to a new organization together. They often plan and help carry out transfer of change and behavioral maintenance programs, not only while the group is ongoing but sometimes long after it has terminated.

To evaluate whether the buddy system is being effectvely used, the partners are asked to record the amount of time spent together between meetings and the degree, on a 10-point scale, to which their meeting goals were reached. In that way the therapists get a weekly overview of the difficulties and progress occurring in the use of the subgroups.

Although the buddy system is an excellent device for most clients, it seems to be unacceptable to those who have well-developed social skills and a history of satisfying social experiences. Such people feel that the procedure is an intrusion in their lives and not necessary for treatment. Most clients, however, do not have such social skills, and they seem eager for social contact. For them, the buddy system is a prescribed—hence safe—social interactive situation. The behavior of each party is stated in advance and required. This tends to overcome any anxiety that they may have about participating in the system. The therapist, however, can use the buddy system to increase social skill practice by reducing gradually the prescriptions for interactive behavior.

Not all professionals agree with this author's enthusiasm and wide usage of the buddy system. Lawrence and Sundel (1972), for example, develop a rule in their behavioral groups that members do not contact each other outside of the group. However, they work with extremely heterogeneous groups and may find that the absence of commonality precludes the effective use of extragroup contacts. They also may be concerned with the unstructured and unmonitored nature of the contact, which can be protected by adequate preparation. On the other hand, the buddy system was a major procedure in a job finding group program developed by Azrin, Flores, and Kaplan (1975). They also stressed mutual assistance in job seeking, family support, and sharing of job leads. When compared to randomly selected control within two months, 90 percent of the group-trained job seekers and 55 percent of the control group had obtained employment. Moreover, the average salary of the group-trained job seekers was about one-third higher than the control group.

In summary, the buddy system represents an extension of the group into the community, during and sometimes following group treatment. It can be a source of mutual support as well as mutual planning and monitoring. But the client is not tied to a given buddy or to the system. As with all other procedures, contined use always is evaluated in terms of goal effectiveness. Often buddies are rotated, and occasionally the buddy system is dropped. As clients develop extragroup relations, buddies dissolve of their own accord. But as they enter their new relationships, the clients take with them the skills they learned with their partners in therapy.

DEVIANCY, GROUP PRESSURE, AND GROUP NORMS

One common behavioral problem in groups is nonconformity to the rules or therapeutic expectations of the group. Members may attend irregularly or come late. They may fail to prepare for meetings. They may be sloppy in carrying out weekly assignments. Where the majority of members adhere to these expectations, it is possible to use the group to bring about conformity. For many of the participants, treating their deviant behavior in groups has direct implication for their behavior in the everyday world, where they are punished for deviancy from the norms of the social groups to which they belong.

This does not imply that deviancy in itself always is either maladaptive or nonfunctional. But in those situations in which deviancy from norms defeats the individual's expressed personal goals, the group provides the client with the opportunity to learn alternative ways of examining and dealing with the world about him or her. Deviancy that facilitates the attainment of personal or social goals may be useful in triggering a re-evaluation of the immediate group structure or the larger social structure to which the client belongs.

Where the majority or even the large majority of group members deviate from therapist expectations, the expectations may be considered either poorly communicated or meaningless to the participants, and they must be evaluated with the entire group to determine whether these expectations are reasonable and functional in the attainment of treatment goals. It is primarily when only one or two members deviate from given expectations that the use of group pressures is appropriate.

Before discussing the procedures to bring about conformity to therapeutic expectations, we will examine some of the more recent literature on experimental attempts to analyze and deal with the problem of nonconformity and its resolution in small groups. There is a vast amount of conformity and deviance literature; therefore, this discussion is restricted to those few articles written within a behavioral framework.

For example, Endler (1965) attempted to influence subjects by having them answer questions after each had heard the opinions of three confederates of the experimenter. In one condition the experimenter reinforced the subject whenever the subject's answer conformed to the answer of the three confederates. In another condition the experimenter reinforced the subject only when the answer deviated from the replies of the three confederates. Thus, under one condition the experimenter joined the subject, and in the other condition he joined the confederates. The results of the experiment showed that his reinforcement (approval) was the critical factor in increasing the number of times that the subject conformed to the confederate. When conformity was reinforced, it increased. When deviance was reinforced, it increased. The author also discovered that simple facts and perceptual items were more resistant to the experimenter's influence than statements of attitudes.

In a replication study by Tolman and Barnsley (1966), the fact that identical results were obtained despite the variations in details of procedures strengthens Endler's main findings. In both sets of studies, the effects of group pressure and leader reinforcement were confounded. In a subsequent study, Endler and Hoy (1967) attempted to separate out these two variables. The authors found that social pressure per se was sufficient to produce conforming behavior. However, reinforcement by the leader had an additional effect on conformity. The greater the degree of reinforcement (100 percent versus 50 percent versus 0 percent) for agreeing with others, the less frequent the conforming behavior. In reviewing this and previous studies (Endler, 1965; Endler and Hoy, 1967), the author concluded that differences in a conformity as a function of types of stimuli represent an unstable phenomena.

Hollander, Julian, and Haaland (1965) developed a somewhat different experimental paradigm to measure the conformity process. The subject was asked to report which of three lights came on first. In the first part of the experiment, the subject reported his observations prior to those of three confederates of the experimenter; in the second part, after those of the three confederates. By manipulating the number of times the confederates agreed or disagreed with those observations of the subject in the first part, the experimenter controlled the degree to which the subject was at variance with the majority. During the second part of the experiment (20 trials) when the confederates consistently disagreed with the subject's judgment, the subject made independent judgments only if in the first part of the study, their choices conflicted with those of the group.

It appears that if subjects are reinforced for deviance from group norms, they will continue to deviate; if they are reinforced for conformity, they usually will continue to conform. Of course, the stimulus conditions in each of these studies is relatively simple. In therapy groups, the stimuli are often quite complex. One can realistically question whether the experimental findings are transferable to the clinical setting. Although only anecdotal evidence is available, the observations of clinicians seem to support the conclusions derived from experimental data. Until such time as experimental data on complex stimulus situations or research in clinical settings suggest the opposite, the clinican should use the agreement of the majority and the reinforcement of the leader as strong change procedures in the group treatment process. The following sections contain examples of how group pressure is stimulated to bring about individual conformity to group expectancies.

One patient in a transitional group, whose members were preparing to leave a mental institution, was opposed to going on furlough. He had many reasons, and nothing the staff said to him seemed to encourage him to spend a few days outside of the institution. The group members, however, had decided that since theirs was a transitional group, furlough participation was essential. To operationalize this decision, the group established a rule that to remain a member, an individual must spend at least one day every two weeks outside of the institution. Discussion in the group surrounded the topic of furlough preparation, problems on furlough, and accounts of what one achieved on furlough. Because the group was valued by the deviant member, he submitted to going on highly structured off-grounds visits for the minimally required time. Before he made that decision, however, members had discussed with him in and out of the group how much they hoped that he would stay in the group. They offered to escort him, if necessary, if he would go on furlough, an idea he readily accepted.

A number of principles are operating in this example. First, for group pressure to work, the group must be highly attractive for the individual. Otherwise, under pressure—an aversive stimulus—a member simply would leave the group. Second, pressure is a relatively complex operation. It consists of a majority decision to carry out a given activity, an operational rule, a set of clear procedures by which the given activity can be carried out, and usually some system of positive reinforcement for compliance, as well as something punishing for noncompliance. Third, the principle of small steps can be used to gain compliance to therapeutic expectations. In this example, the members facilitated the target person's achievement by accompanying him on furlough. Later he would have to go alone.

Following is an example of deviancy that was not only reinforced but in which the deviant from group norms was protected from group pressure.

One member of a social skills workshop disliked the location of the meeting at the clinic. His complaints fell, at first, on deaf ears. Later the members began to tease him about it. Nevertheless, he persisted. The therapist suggested that he find an alternative, and if the group agreed it would be acceptable to use the new location. He found a lounge in a nearby church, and when he presented his idea, the members would scarcely let him speak. The therapist praised his resourcefulness and insisted that the patient at least be allowed to describe his idea. The plan was well though out and included ideas about availability of bus transportation. The other members were impressed with his proposal and ultimately accepted his idea.

PRODUCTS OF GROUP INTERACTION

There are several important and measurable products of interaction in a treatment group. First is behavioral change in the direction desired by the patient. Second is the number of behavioral assignments or components of behavioral assignments generated at a given meeting. A third is the number of assignments actually completed between each meeting. Behavioral change is the ultimate objective of behavior therapy and as such is the best criteria for evaluating whether a group has been effective or not. However, it is difficult to observe whether a given meeting is productive because actual change of target behaviors often does not begin until late in therapy. To evaluate the productivity of meetings, the number of assignments generated seemed to give a better picture. Unfortunately, assignments may not be equivalent. For example, how many pages of reading is equivalent to a daily one hour self-observation and recording assignment? A second problem is that often people will generate assignments that they do not complete. For this reason, most therapists use the number of assignments and the percentage completed prior to the subsequent meeting as an indication of the productivity of the individual and the average for the group as an indication of the productivity of the group. In spite of the problem of relative nonequivalence of assignments, the number and percentage of completed assignments gives at least a rough indication of what the group seems to be achieving and provides an empirical indicator of whether the procedures should be altered. If productivity is high, the fact that the interaction pattern in the group is not evenly distributed does not warrant intervention. When productivity is low, the therapist together with the group must consider what can be done to increase it.

For example, in a social anxiety group, which the members evaluated each week very highly, the average percentage of assignments was less than 70 percent and the two lowest people in the group were completing at a rate of less than 40 percent of the assignments for which they contracted. This was a signal for the therapist to examine all other sources of data. He discovered in interviewing the members that the assignments were too difficult, and that for the most part they took on the assignments to please him. The members decided to alter the problem in two ways. First, all assignments would be checked out with a buddy to ascertain whether they were both achievable and understandable. Second, contingencies were attached to the completion as well as the noncompletion of assignments. As a result, the productivity of the group increased to 85 percent at the next meeting and 100 percent at a subsequent meeting.

Another outcome of group interaction is whether or not clients return to group meetings and how much of each meeting they attend. Obviously, if members do not attend meetings, the discussions can be of little value to them, and if they arrive late, part of the content of the meeting may be lost to them. Moreover, such problems have implication for the other group members. If part of the group comes late, it often results in the other members coming late at subsequent meetings. If several members attend irregularly, this may result in a similar pattern by the remaining members and a general devaluation of the group by all the members. Moreover, the program that is often planned sequentially is difficult to administer if all members are in different phases of treatment.

From the point of view of those who come late or who attend irregularly, the group probably is relatively unattractive or has a lower priority than other activities in which they may be participating. The group also may not be serving what clients perceive to be their purposes. Thus, these data also provide important clues as to group cohesiveness.

Where the problem is isolated to one or two persons, the annoyance of others may be allowed to operate. Where it is a general pattern, an evaluation by the group is called for. Occasionally, technical problems such as medical appointments or previous commitments may be the trouble. In most cases where the problem is more endemic, the entire program may need to be overhauled.

Fortunately, in most groups attendance is regular, promptness is the norm, and productivity per meeting is high. In these cases, the therapist usually is less concerned with minor aberrations in group interaction. However, he or she always is concerned with preventing problems by keeping the program attractive and increasing involvement of the members in their own treatment and in the management of the group, and ultimately in preparation of clients for leaving the group. In the final chapter of part 1, we will discuss this and other principles involved in terminating group treatment, and beyond.

11 As the Group Ends, and Beyond

Ron: A situation occurred today that really would have thrown me a month ago. The parking lot attendant started yelling at me because I parked the car in the wrong place and didn't leave my keys. I just told him that if he wanted me to listen to him, he'd have to cool it, and he did!

Therapist: You seem to have mastered your assertiveness. What's happening to the rest of you, now that we're approaching the end of the group?

Steve: I'm working hard on self-reinforcement. That's one thing I can take with me when the group breaks up. And, at least for me, it's really helping.

Stan: Well, I finally joined the A.A. The group helped me to find some other ways to get along without drinking. But if I'm going to keep it up, I'm going to need whatever help I can get hold of.

Janice: And I joined the Y. I've met some neat people already in my karate class. And it's one class I'm not afraid to walk home from.

Joanne: I haven't joined yet, but I did go with Janice to the Y to look around while she was in her karate class. I think I might join the art class. That's a little more my speed.

Therapist: It sounds to me like you all have something going for you when we call it quits in a couple of weeks. I suspect those surprise role-play situations I promised you for this week will be a kind of graduation exercise. They're tough ones; let's see how you do.

In this group, the members have been preparing for termination. Some are joining new groups. Others are practicing skills they need to maintain the behaviors they have learned in the group. The therapist is about to train them by means of role-plays for unpredictable types of stress situations they might encounter once the group is over. Actually, preparation for termination, the transfer of change from treatment to extratreatment situation, and the maintenance of gains obtained in the group began early in the sessions through the use of role-playing simulated situations, assignments to practice group learning in the real world, and group discussion of the general principles involved in learning. But as the group approaches termination, the entire meeting becomes increasingly concerned with these areas. Transfer of change usually refers to the performances in extragroup situations of behaviors learned and exhibited in the group. It also refers to the generalization of these behaviors to similar behaviors not originally worked on in the treatment setting. Maintenance of behavior refers primarily to the continuance of behavioral levels achieved in the treatment setting long after treatment has terminated.

Where transfer effects have been evaluated systematically (Kazdin, 1974; Hersen, Eisler, and Miller, 1974; McFall and Marston, 1970) in assertive training, the results were extremely weak. Although this may have been due to the problems in the measures and to the analog and brief treatments the subjects received, it is clear that the therapist cannot leave generalization to chance.

Transfer of learning from the therapy setting to performance in the face of the feared situation was studied by Agras (1967) with five severe agoraphobic (having a fear of open spaces) patients. Although transfer did occur in four of the five patients, there was a lag between performance in the treatment situation and in the external criterion situation. The authors concluded that transfer does present more of a problem to the therapist than previously had been considered and that part of treatment must attend to the problem of transfer if it is to be attained.

Where operant problems of children have been treated, there was evidence that unless fading procedures (O'Leary, Becker, Evans, and Saudargas, 1969) were used or efforts were made to reprogram the environment (Walker, Mattson, and Buckley, 1969), behavior would not be maintained automatically. In conclusion, both transfer and maintenance may be possible provided only that these programs are established to achieve those ends.

PRINCIPLES FOR TRANSFER AND MAINTENANCE

Through the years several writers have become concerned with the problem of achieving transfer and maintenance (for example, Goldstein, Heller, and

Sechrest, 1966; Gottman and Leiblum, 1974). They have explicated a number of principles that can be used by practitioners as guidelines for their work with individual clients or in groups. Most of these principles have been extrapolated from research on cognitive learning of simple concepts. Although in most cases there seems only anecdotal evidence for their application to complex motoric sets of behavior commonly the target of behavioral therapeutic endeavors, these principles are still the best available guidelines to the practitioner. In this chapter, we will discuss the principles that seem to have major implications for achieving transfer or maintenance of learning gained in treatment groups. Among these are varying the conditions of treatment, simulating as nearly as possible the context of the real world, increasing extragroup incentives, preparing for possible setbacks, preparing for an unsympathetic environment, learning the general principle, and learning the skills to function independently. Although there is some obvious overlapping in these principles, each is sufficiently distinct to warrant separate discussion.

Varying Conditions of Treatment

Before a behavior can be transferred from group to extragroup performance, it must be learned adequately. That is, there must be more trials and more situations than are minimally required to produce initial behavior changes (Goldstein and others, 1966, p. 219). For this reason, it is necessary to provide multiple opportunities for practice in a variety of treatment conditions.

Behaviors learned under a limited set of environmental cues often can be emitted only or primarily under those cues. Therefore, it is desirable that a given target behavior be practiced repeatedly under many different environmental cues. The therapist can create a large number of simulated conditions through manipulation of instructions to the role-players in the behavioral rehearsals that the group members are to perform.

For example, assertive training groups often have as many as 18 rehearsals of different situations requiring refusal responses at a given meeting. Thus, a subject will participate in three rehearsals directly and in 15 more vicariously. Similarly, in a transition group, the members practiced job interviewing in 12 different situations over two meetings before they indicated that they were sufficiently comfortable to try out the behaviors in the real world.

Similarly, the conditions of the group also may be manipulated. In later meetings, the therapist may introduce new group operating procedures that require members to become more businesslike in their meetings. He or she may increase or decrease therapist demand and therapist activity. Each of these changes would require performance of the newly learned behaviors under slightly different group climate.

More radically, the therapist may replace him- or herself with a new therapist. Several authors (for example, Rimm and Master, 1974; Goldstein and others, 1966) recommend the use of multiple leaders as a means of encouraging transfer of change. Since the therapist represents one set of cues associated with behavioral change, it would appear that a number of therapists would result in change being associated with many types of people. Moreover, undesirable behaviors often are inhibited only in the presence of the therapist. Multiple therapists would expand the number of persons associated with the inhibition of this behavior.

According to Bandura (1971), the use of multiple models should promote the transfer of treatment effects. If only an individual model is presented, the client may assume that the individual has special characteristics that account for his or her ideal behavior. With multiple models, such reasoning is difficult to retain. Not only do group members present such models for each other, but the therapist also can introduce multiple symbolic models on tapes or films to provide variable sources of ideas for each client.

Simulating the Real World

The ideal way of varying the treatment situation is to change it to approximate more nearly the real-life situations of the clients. Boocock (1967, p. 142), in a review of educational research on the effect of simulation games, noted that simulated methods were superior to traditional teaching approaches in terms of attitude change retention and transfer of learning to novel situations. For these reasons, extensive use is made of simulation methods such as role-playing.

Some therapists have even changed the treatment meeting from the more usual office or meeting room to situations under which problems occur. For example, weight loss groups have met at a member's house for a potluck dinner for one meeting and at a restaurant for another. Members of an alcoholics group have met in a bar. Schaefer, Sobell, and Mills (1971) have introduced a portable bar into a therapy room to simulate real world conditions for alcoholics. A dating group met in a dance hall one week and a singles bar the next. A job seeking group met occasionally in the lounge of employment agencies.

Simulating the real world involves fading those unusual or extreme treatment procedures not commonly found there. For example, if token reinforcement is used, it is faded early in treatment. However, it may be replaced by self-reinforcement, which can be used long after treatment has ended. Even the activity of a therapist must be faded, as discussed under training for leadership behavior. All of treatment is faded gradually by having continually shorter meetings and by spacing them at consistently greater intervals. One way of simulating the real world is to begin to shift reinforcement from the group to the extragroup environment, as Goldstein and others (1966), recommend.

Increasing Extragroup Incentives

If possible, one should look for the natural reinforcers in the environment to maintain the newly learned behaviors. In fact, if there is little or no reinforcement, it is unlikely that the new behavior will be maintained at all. For this reason, the therapist helps the group members to identify the natural reinforcers in their environment and the behaviors they need to obtain them. Moreover, if a behavior is unlikely to result in such natural reinforcement, it is usually a poor target.

One way of shifting reinforcement to the environment is to help clients with previously unreinforcing social situations to find new social interactive conditions that might be reinforcing. In many cases, social recreational groups give such reinforcement, provided that the client displays minimal social skills required to participate in such groups. Assertive training group clients may turn to dancing clubs or intellectual discussion groups. Weight loss group members often join weight watchers organizations. In the final meetings of most groups, clients are encouraged to explore several such groups and ultimately to try out at least one to see if it provides what they are looking for. To develop a resource book for each other, the members of one group divided up the city's social recreational organizations and investigated what each had to offer.

Membership in these alternative groups usually is encouraged prior to termination of the treatment group. This is an opportunity, at least for the socially less facile clients, to have a well-prepared entry into the new groups. They can be helped to deal with unexpected or new problems that such membership may cause. Thus, one of the major sets of assignments as the group approaches termination is to explore such memberships, to select one group for a visit, and to join one group. For many, seeking reinforcement in groups to which they already belong may be the preferred strategy. Where possible, shifting treatment focus to the family might provide training in reinforcement for the entire family unit. In some cases, as with transitional patients in institutions, parent or relative groups may be established to assure a sympathetic and reinforcing environment for the returning person. Others may be taught directly how to deal with their environment. Positive reinforcement usually does not continue unabated for the rest of the client's life. Often he or she is confronted with unusual stress in many forms, which the client does not know how to deal with. This may result in setbacks by which the client may be overwhelmed if he or she is not prepared to expect and deal with them.

Preparing for Possible Setbacks

Therapist: Tim, you were in a group like this last year. I wonder if you could tell the members what happened after you left the group.

Tim: Well, for a while I really felt on top of things. I used a lot of the ideas I learned in the group, like relaxation and thought stopping, and my eye contact in conversations was devastating (laughter from group). I even called my buddy from time to time to see how he was doing and tell him how I was conquering the world.

Therapist: You say, "for a while." You mean the program failed you?

Tim: No, but I had some trouble at work I hadn't expected, one of my children was sick at the same time, and the doctor bills were more than we could handle. So for a short while I was really down. I had the feeling that therapy had been a waste of time and that nothing could help a guy like me.

Therapist: How did you get out of it?

Tim: I remember someone in the group saying that there might be times like this and that you had to be prepared for them. As somebody also in the group had suggested, I made a list of all the things I could do about it and all the things I had no control over, like little Peter's illness. Then I used thought stopping for self-blaming thoughts and used self-praise everytime I had an idea about what I could do. I called my buddy and told him what I had done, and he had some other ideas, too. By the end of the day I felt like I had the situation pretty well under control. Action really destroys depression.

This therapist has begun to prepare the members for a possible setback after the group has terminated. By introducing a former client who has struggled with a problem and resolved it, the therapist provided a model of what could be done should a setback occur for them. It also provides a basis for discussing the probability of such setbacks and a wide variety of techniques that could be used to deal with them. Also, an important part of the process is the clear statement that therapy does not promise perfection, but that in spite of temporary failures due to problems either under or not under the client's control, something can be done about it.

The usual techniques employed under these conditions are a systematic analysis, often in writing, of what a person can control and what is out of his or her control. If the client cannot do it alone, he or she is encouraged to try it with someone else. After this, the client lists procedures for controlling his or her own behavior and takes on the assignment of picking out one area where he or she might initiate action. For those problems over which there is little or no control, the client must decide what attitude would be most effective in achieving his or her purpose. Members often will use a buddy for this discussion, but ideally the client will act as manager of his or her own new program. The client also is provided with a list of other resources that may be appropriate to the given problem, including an agency emergency service number. This list also may contain the number of the local A.A., financial support agency, family services, a local community center, day care center, job employment agencies, and so forth. Where such agencies are, indeed, relevant to members of the group, each of these services are discussed in a meeting prior to the members' departure. The therapist goes over each agency, its purposes, goals (if any), and types of help given. In some cases, agency staff are invited to the meeting to provide this information and to handle any questions the members might have. The guest establishes a familiar liaison between the client and the agency should it ever be needed.

One dramatic form of preparing clients for setbacks and unusual stress has been to role-play situations in the last few meetings for which the clients are totally unprepared, as in the first example in this chapter. The therapist, drawing on experiences from previous groups, introduces a vignette describing a number of circumstances such as job loss or serious illness in the family. The members in subgroups are asked to develop role-play situations, filling in the details as nearly as possible from their own situation. These are then given to members of the other subgroups to role-play without preparation in front of the entire group. Since role-playing is time-consuming, only a few such situations can be enacted at any one meeting. To supplement these, an extensive list of similar vignettes may be presented to the clients. As a home assignment, they are asked to read them and to indicate how they respond to each of them. At a subsequent meeting, their solutions are evaluated and compared. The disadvantage of this procedure in comparison to the role-play is that there is less actual motoric participation in the process. Moreover, the procedure is less impressive. On the other hand, many more different types of situations can be handled in this way in a short time. Of course, both procedures may be used if time is available. In maintenance groups this certainly would be recommended.

To develop the vignettes, former clients at a follow-up interview are asked to describe any setbacks or unusual stress situations that may have occurred. This list is edited for duplication and presented to the clients. As such lists are refined and criteria for evaluation developed, they might serve as the basis for measuring the ability of clients to deal with unusual stress or setbacks.

Preparing for an Unsympathetic Environment

Spouse of client: I don't know what's got into you lately. You act strangely. I just don't seem to know you any more.

Client: What don't you like? I'm certainly not as anxious as I was. I don't complain as much, and my complaining used to bug you.

Spouse: I know! I know! I just don't know what it is. Sometimes I wish you'd never gone to that therapy group, even if it did help you.

This spouse had urged the client to go to treatment for months. When at last the client had completed a term of therapy with reasonable success, the spouse was annoyed by the change in the client, even if it was for the better. Previously, the situation had been predictable, and now the spouse no longer knows what to expect. Where the spouse once could be nurturant or righteously indignant, now neither response is justified. This change in a spouse, a close friend, a parent, a roommate, a child inevitably affects the predictability of the relationship and the behavior of the significant other.

Ideally, it would be best to treat all interacting parties in the same situation as does, indeed, occur in couples groups and family treatment. But in many cases this is not possible for financial, time, or other practical reasons. Therefore, therapy is not complete until the client is helped to deal with the reactions of the significant persons in his or her environment. They often lack understanding and even are unsympathetic and, in some instances, hostile. However, sometimes overacceptance and too much praise are equally difficult to deal with. As a way of dealing with these extreme reactions that pressure the client to return to his old patterns of behavior, clients are requested to describe to the group such reactions following their occurrence at home or at work. Each time a reaction is described, the members discuss it and the client is given a plan for dealing with it the next time it happens. If necessary, alternative approaches may be modeled for the client, who may rehearse them as with any other behavior. In this way the members observe a large number of unsympathetic responses and learn various strategies for dealing with them. The learning process is facilitated further by discussing the reasons that the others respond as they do. It is important to the relationship that the client *not* perceive the significant other as vindictive or vicious because of unaccepting responses. Out of this discussion, general principles often are learned to deal with a wide variety of unsympathetic environments. This is not the only area in which the learning of principles furthers the transfer of learning, as we will see in the following example.

Learning the General Principle

Therapist: Don has learned to deal with situations calling for refusal when he is imposed upon. Henry has learned to participate in the many meetings he must attend to do his job. Nancy can let her boss know when he is imposing on her without feeling that the world will collapse. Loretta has been successful in expressing how she feels about situations to her husband to both their satisfaction. And I seem to have done a good job in asking people their names when I've forgotten them without getting too embarrassed. What general principle does all this learning imply for you?

Loretta: That it's possible to assert one's self without being aggressive.

Henry: It's clear to me that when a person is assertive, as we've seen in all these examples, that people respect you more rather than less, as I had originally thought.

Nancy: And it seems that most of us are far less anxious as a result. I know I am.

In this discussion the therapist has reviewed the accomplishments of the members of the group. She has tried through group discussion to use this opportunity to clarify the general principles involved in their learning the one behavior for which they came to the group. It is often the recognition or statement of these general principles that furthers performance of the target behavior in new situations long after the group has terminated.

In this example, the therapist has identified a number of assertive behaviors. She will help the members in subsequent assignments to develop more general treatment targets—assertiveness—and will encourage them to learn to treat the general category of assertive behaviors. For example, the therapist listed all the behaviors that all the persons had learned. Each member was then given the responsibility to note his or her participation in any of those behaviors and to apply the contingencies previously associated with the one specific behavior to any of the behaviors that fell into the general category. In this way the client not only learns one specific behavior but also the general category. The order of this learning sequence is important. There has been little success in trying to teach the general category before clients have had a successful experience with a specific behavior. Learning the general category does not imply that the specificity is ignored. It merely means that the general category is spelled out in terms of a large number of specific behaviors. As in this example, the members not only expanded their learning to recognize many different behaviors under the category of assertiveness, but they also identified some general principles associated with assertiveness as a means of learning. These were the principles elucidated by the members of the group.

One of the general principles that clients must learn is to discriminate among those situations calling for the desired pattern of behavior and those in which it is not desirable. A client may learn to state his or her annoyance when people make unfair or imposing demands. However, he or she also must learn to withhold such responses from an uncompromising and authoritarian employer if the client wishes to hold his or her job. (He or she also may decide that the job isn't worth it!) In addition, the client must learn to find commonalities among situations in order to make diverse situations similar. By labeling these situations as similar, the client more readily can transfer behaviors learned under one set to another. This labeling is referred to as "mediated generalization" (Goldstein, Heller, and Sechrest, 1966. p. 217).

For example, if people learn to express their feelings when they recognize that they have warm positive thoughts toward someone in the group and if they identify these feelings with significant others outside of the group, they will be able to express the feelings to those others as well. For this reason, whenever a client learns a new behavior in the group, the members spend some time discussing appropriate conditions outside of the group for the performance and nonperformance of that behavior. Although the boundaries are not always clear, the discussion tends to facilitate the client in making his or her decision as to the conditions under which the given behavior should be performed.

Another category that clients can learn profitably is how to solve problems in general. They have learned in each case to solve several highly specific problems. They now must learn general paradigm of learning to deal with whatever else may arise after treatment has ended. To teach a problem-solving paradigm, the therapist draws upon the client's concrete experience. He or she points out the steps taken in each case for all members of the group. In the group, the members discuss the following general categories for problem-solving: assessing the problem, spelling it out specifically, monitoring it, developing plans for dealing with it, selecting one plan and trying it out, evaluating the data, revising the plan or selecting another, or, if necessary, continuing with the original plan, and, finally, when a resolution is reached, discontinuing the plan. (See, also, pp. 130–131)

Training in Leadership and Independence

In the final analysis, the client's ability to solve new problems as they arise becomes the essential skill that he or she must learn. Throughout this book, we have seen how responsibility for each step of treatment gradually is delegated to the group as a whole and ultimately to the individual client. This is equally true of assessment, monitoring, treatment planning, and especially in the planning for termination. The more practice the therapist can give in self-planning, the greater the likelihood that the client will be able to develop his or her own treatment plans as the inevitable new problem arises.

The client is placed in leadership positions. He or she works with a buddy whom the client coaches, advises, and monitors, and also receives such actions. In some groups the client may serve as discussion leader for select parts of the program. He or she also may serve as discussion leader of a subgroup during the group meeting.

Leadership skills are discussed, explicated, and the members participation in them is reinforced and otherwise encouraged. (Chapter 10 explained a variety of procedures for increasing the distribution of leadership of these functions.)

When a client is finished with the group, he or she may not have to be regarded by all who confront him or her as a leader. But the client will have had extensive leadership training, and if this training is used only to structure his or her own situation, the program will have been successful.

PREPARING FOR TERMINATION

In preparing the client to function independently, the therapist is preparing him or her for termination, which inevitably comes too soon in the time-limited groups. There are always loose ends that the members and the therapist would like to have cleaned up before the clients departed for the corners of the city. As pointed out earlier, the therapist will describe alternative resources, new groups if necessary, and how the therapist may be used if the occasion calls for it. The therapist also will discuss the difficulties of terminating such an intensive relationship, not only for them but for him or her. However, the therapist also reviews the evidence that they can do it alone.

In some groups, selected members may have not achieved major treatment goals. They will be referred to maintenance or continuing groups or individual therapy. They even may be helped to find alternative approaches to the behavioral one. This referral often is handled in the group because members may be aware of resources not known even to the therapist.

In those groups without a fixed number of sessions—continuous groups—preparation for termination reoccurs for all other members as an old member departs. Usually at the final meeting for the departing member, the group reviews the member's accomplishments, what he or she still needs to work on, and how to work on it. Often members are invited back for a meeting in the future to report on how they are doing and how they have dealt with the inevitable new problems.

THE FOLLOW-UP INTERVIEWS

As a matter of course, some therapists, including the author, employ what Gottman and Leiblum (1974, p. 157) recommend—a follow-up interview either 3, 6, or 12 months following termination as a means of assessing whether changes were maintained or whether new problems have arisen. These serve the additional purpose of a "booster shot" for maintaining the behaviors. Because the client is aware that he or she is returning to see the therapist, and in many cases former group members, there is an added pressure to keep up the discipline that was learned in the group. To incorporate this group pressure, group follow-up interviews are recommended. However, it often is difficult to bring back even the majority of any treatment group for interviews a year or more following treatment. For the long range follow-up, either individual interviews or phone calls may have to serve the above purposes. Some group therapists have used buddies, former members, or group aides to facilitate follow-up interviews.

In preparation for the follow-up interviews or group meetings, an assignment usually is given at the final meeting for the client to work on an entirely new behavior of his or her own choosing, using as many of the procedures as he or she can for dealing with it. The client is encouraged to use his or her buddy or other nontherapeutic resources for the program. Because of the importance of the follow-up, some therapists do not refund a deposit until after the series of follow-up interviews or meetings.

In Part I of this book, we described in detail all the phases of a therapy group from its conception to the follow-up interview of its members. Part II will show how the principles can be applied to a number of specific types of groups: parent training, assertive training, institutional groups, self-control groups, couples communication workshops, and even in such nontherapy groups as group supervision. Each chapter will describe the methods peculiar to that population, the problems encountered, how they were dealt with, and the results of some of the major programs.

Part Two
APPLICATIONS AND RESULTS

12 Parent Training in Groups

WITH continual shortages of trained personnel, the use of parents as a source of change agents for their own children promises to be a valuable means of meeting more of the therapeutic needs of the community. Parents are likely to be the first to encounter and to deal with the problematic behaviors; therefore, those who are trained can begin change actions quickly and continue them as long as necessary. Moreover, because the behavior usually is being dealt with at home, there is no problem of transferring changes that were achieved in the agency or clinic.

Training parents as effective behavior modifiers has been demonstrated by a number of writers. A wide range of behavioral changes, such as decreasing tantrums, self-destructive behaviors, verbal aggression, excessive crying, thumb sucking, soiling, increasing self-help skills, verbal behavior, social approach responses, and play with other children, have been attained successfully by parents trained as behavior therapists of their own children. Although other authors have reported successful experiences in the group training of parents as behavior modifiers (see Cone and Sloop, 1974, for an excellent review of these studies), none of them describes how the group can be used to facilitate treatment.

The group as both context and means of treatment can be utilized to facilitate parents' exposure to a wide range of behaviors beyond those exhibited by their own children. According to the findings of small group research, the group, when highly attractive to its members, puts considerable pressure on parents to conform to therapeutic demands and group norms (Cartwright and Zander, 1968). Group properties such as cohesiveness, norms, interaction, and pressures can be manipulated to increase participation and to facilitate parental acquisition of necessary skills (Cartwright and Zander, 1968). In addition, the group is a source of extensive ideas for reinforcement and other treatment plans. Multiple membership allows for many different types of coactors in role-playing, behavior rehearsal, and modeling, all important training procedures in a broad spectrum behavior approach. Finally, parents in groups maintain each other's high level of enthusiasm for the program. They provide an abundance of social reinforcement for each other's achievements.

In spite of this and other research, there are many as yet unanswered questions related to parent training in groups. One is whether the achievements of individual therapy can be duplicated in the small group. Another concerns the social class of parents who can use group training most effectively. Most published reports detail the achievements of middle class parents. Another question involves characteristics of the children. Can parents of retarded children be trained to modify successfully their children's behavior?

To answer these questions a series of projects has been designed involving more than 50 groups of parents over a four-year period. This chapter will discuss the two projects first completed. One project deals with a comparison of middle class and welfare parents under two types of group composition (Rose, 1974a). The other involves an evaluation of training of natural and foster parents as behavior modifiers of their retarded children (Rose, 1974b). First we will discuss briefly the methods of training parents and leaders, which were similar in both projects.

METHODS OF TRAINING PARENTS

Training consisted of two parts—the group meetings and the homework assignments. At the first meeting the parents contracted to attend all (7 to 10) of the hour-and-a-half parent training sessions and to complete all home assignments that they negotiated with their respective leaders. Home assignments included the following: 1) reading behavioral literature and completing exercises on behavioral assessments; 2) weekly monitoring (counting) of behaviors; 3) application of change procedures and development of maintenance and/or transfer plans; and 4) autonomous development of treatment plans. These assignments tended to overlap. Parents were encouraged to negotiate only those home assignments that they felt could be completed readily in the course of the week. Although suggestions were given, parents made their own decisions as to the content of the assignment. Once a decision was reached, however, each recorded his or her agreement in writing. The parent kept one copy and gave the other to the therapist. Although no specific contingencies were attached to the agreement, it functioned as an unambiguous set of mutually agreed-upon expectations for the week. Still later, more complex change procedures were assigned along with development of treatment planning by parents without assistance from the group.

Parents read a programmed textbook that outlined social learning theory and, in later groups, Becker (1971) and several supplementary publications pertaining to child management. Group members were tested periodically on the content of these materials throughout the training program. In spite of the staff's initial hesitancy to test adults, the parents claimed to benefit from the feedback they received about what they had learned. They indicated that the test served as a necessary pressure to read.

The meetings were highly organized. Every meeting had a set of goals and an agenda for meeting those goals, which were distributed to the members. (See pp. 83–84 for an example of a goal/agenda statement in a parent training group.) Every group developed from a set of standard goals and agendas an individually tailored set for each group prior to each session.

The agenda of the first sessions primarily concerned assessment and monitoring. A pretreatment checklist facilitated problem definition. In this way, the children's problem behaviors were identified by the parents in brief but behaviorally specific terms before monitoring and treatment began. Conditions that controlled these behaviors were examined during the initial group meetings. To increase the probability of initial success, parents were encouraged to select as initial targets only those behaviors that were identified readily, were relatively simple to count, and lent themselves to simple reinforcement and/or "time out" procedures. It had been observed that early success increases the motivation of the parents to treat more complicated behaviors later on.

To facilitate correct problem formulation, each parent presented an initial description of his or her problem to the group for discussion. This not only resulted in a sharper definition, it provided the parents with practice in dealing with a wide range of different formulations. When many of the parents in a given group had difficulty in the initial session in discovering problems suitable for behavioral treatment, parents from previous groups were brought in to discuss the types of problems they had dealt with. Case studies also were used as models, which the group members read as home assignments and discussed in the meetings.

While the parents were learning to formulate behavior problems correctly and to select an initial behavior problem, they were presented with monitoring procedures. The members performed standard exercises in monitoring in the groups. In more recent projects, group members counted behavior of leaders and/or each other using tallies, counters, and stopwatches. (These data were used later to provide a baseline for problems in interaction.) It appears that the more experience parents obtain in the group, the fewer errors are made in monitoring their own children. Graphing exercises were used in many of the groups very early in treatment. The parents took great pride in showing their graphs to each other.

As soon as parents demonstrated that they were able to count, they were assigned to do a baseline measurement on their children. This measurement broke down if the parents either had not adequately defined the problem or the conditions under which the problem was to be observed. Failure often was due to small engineering problems such as the location of the counter or paper and pencil. Incidental problems often arose such as illness or vacations. Parents were encouraged to report the problems to the leaders by telephone as soon as they occurred, in order to develop alternate plans. All these aspects of monitoring were discussed in the group. (At present we have begun to require premonitoring for a week or even just two days to iron out the kinks in the monitoring plan. In this way failure to achieve accurate counts on the first trial does not become aversive because it is allowed for in the plan.)

While the baseline data were being collected, parents were trained in various treatment procedures such as reinforcement, time out from reinforcement, extinction, prompting, modeling, and behavior rehearsal. Along with brief lectures and discussion of reading materials, role-playing, modeling, and behavioral rehearsal also were used to prepare parents for the ensuing week's assignments. Group leaders and, at times, the parents themselves served as role-playing models to demonstrate various management techniques. Behavior rehearsal involved the parents in practicing these techniques on each other before using them at home. Modeling and behavior rehearsal were particularly useful in training parents in the expression of appropriate affect in the application of reinforcement and time out; some parents tended to praise with too little enthusiasm or to apply time out with too much affect for these procedures to be maximally effective. Leaders also made frequent use of praise to reinforce members for active participation, for being task-oriented, for reinforcing another parent, and for completion of assigned tasks during the previous week. Following is an example of how behavior rehearsal was integrated into the training program with group discussion.

For two weeks Ms. N had monitored the trash-emptying behavior of her 13-year-old foster son, Joe. He was supposed to empty six wastepaper baskets each day between 3:30 and 4 P.M. Baseline data indicated that Joe had not emptied any baskets on one day and on the remaining days had emptied four or less baskets. Since the possibility of the behavior occurred so regularly, Ms. N decided to reinforce Joe only when he emptied all six wastepaper baskets, but she was not sure how to carry it off. A rehearsal was then organized.

One of the coleaders of the group played Joe, and Ms. N played herself. She began by saying, "Joe, you know it's one of your duties to empty the wastepaper baskets after you come home from school. I know that sometimes you forget, and I have to spend a lot of time nagging you about doing this chore. I have an idea of a way to get you to remember to empty the waste baskets." Ms. N then told Joe that they would keep a chart posted on the refrigerator. Each day Joe would get a check if he emptied all six waste baskets. After getting so many checks, he would be able to go to the store to buy something he liked.

Ms. N was praised by the members for her explanation of the treatment and for presenting treatment in a positive way. However, she was unable to answer Joe's questions about how many checks he needed and what he could buy. Group members suggested to Ms. N that she decide ahead of time how many checks were needed for the backup reinforcer and what the backup reinforcer could be. It also was suggested that she have some examples of reinforcers ready in case Joe couldn't think of any.

As in this example, each parent developed a treatment plan to deal with his or her child's problem behavior. Before such a plan can be put into practice, the member usually must demonstrate either by a verbal description or in a behavior demonstration exactly what he or she will be doing and the affect to be used. As many details of the plan as necessary must be included to make it vivid for the other group members.

Once the plans were approved by the group and put into practice, the weekly meetings were used primarily to evaluate results with the members and to recommend changes if necessary.

Most plans consist of concrete reinforcement paired with enthusiastic praise; often simple shaping or, on occasion, backward chaining are used. However, others combine the reinforcement with time out or extinction of the undesirable components, modeling, rehearsals, cueing, and any other procedure that might seem efficacious and could be delineated clearly. The following treatment plan with an eight-year-old mongoloid child who did not chew food utilizes primary reinforcement with praise, modeling, cueing, reinforcement of the model, and shaping.

In the presence of the child, the parents and the siblings took turns producing audible "crunches" on the edge of a graham cracker. After each member crunched the cracker, he was immediately rewarded with the target child's favorite food (cottage cheese baby food). At the end of each round, the target child also was offered the graham cracker to crunch. If he failed to do so, another round was begun. Each training session consisted of five rounds. At the fourth session the target child began to crunch and was reinforced with cottage cheese baby food and family exuberance. (See Butterfield and Parson, 1973, for more detail of this example.) The family soon thereafter shaped normal chewing behavior in a wide range of behaviors.

Once a treatment plan was in operation and the graph indicated successful progress, a new behavior was selected for modification. Often the new behavior had to be completed following treatment. It was assumed that the parents would have adequate skills by the end of treatment to deal with problems on their own. To achieve autonomous treatment planning, the leader in later meetings began to rely on the members' ideas with gradually increasing frequency as to procedures to be used. As the members developed skill in designing plans for each other in the meetings, the leaders encouraged them to develop entire plans at home and report them to the group.

To maintain the learning developed in the group, various plans were used. In several groups, the buddy system was continued long after the formal training program had been terminated; in two other groups, follow-up meetings were held a month after the end of the program. Two advanced groups were organized. The one for parents of the retarded kept the parents actively working on new behaviors beyond termination of the original group, but a second group of Aid to Families of Dependent Children (AFDC) mothers faded away in the course of the summer. Six parents served as models for subsequent groups, a function that probably enhanced their learning. Although these practices were restricted to just a few groups, there was at least self-report evidence that the major principles of reinforcement still were being maintained.

To help parents in maintaining the children's accomplishments, they were taught some of the principles of maintenance. Groups discussed such principles as shifting reinforcement from material reinforcement, moving from continuous to more intermittent reinforcement schedules, and fading of treatment cues.

Modifying Group Attributes

Not all the leaders' efforts were directed toward facilitating the attainment of individual treatment goals. Because of the group context and the reliance on group discussion as a major means of treatment, the leader had to be concerned with controlling work-related attributes of the group. To deal with such group problems as a dominant participant, too little mutual reinforcement, vague or nontask-oriented interaction, and the absence of good suggestions by parents, observers behind a one-way screen recorded interaction patterns in the group. If one of the above problems was observed, verbal reinforcement of the desired behavior (for example, reinforcement, participation, task-oriented statements) was used by the group leaders. On occasion parents were presented with the charts of their interactive behavior. This was done as a means of explicating interactive problems as well as demonstrating correct monitoring, charting, and verbal reinforcement procedures.

Following is an example of how a leader dealt with a problem of members who did not appear to listen while others were speaking. Instead, they tended to chat with their neighbors. The goal was to reduce subgrouping and increase attending behavior in the group.

> First, the leader made the problem and goal explicit. She also justified the goal in terms of the work efficiency of the group. Second, at the suggestion of the members, a different seating pattern was arranged in which leader and coleader sat among the members rather than together. Third, the leader reinforced members aloud for performance of desirable behavior and cued members for deviation by handing out slips of papers with an indication that they were "subgrouping." In addition to the leaders' activity, the members also reinforced each other for successful attention giving and pointed out in a joking manner those who, it appeared, were going to chat among themselves.
>
> The problem was quickly resolved. From the fifth to the ninth meeting, there was only one incident of subgrouping. Interaction was broadly distributed and participants appeared to listen to each other. Since the parents continued to attend regularly, stay on-task, and achieve treatment goals, there were no apparent deleterious side effects of the program.

To make all the groups as attractive as possible for participants, a food break usually was held in the middle of the meeting during which general and nontask-oriented talk was encouraged. Informal contact among the members occurred at this time and after the meetings. Although no data were collected on a regular basis to ascertain the cohesiveness of the groups, guest observers sitting behind the one-way mirror often commented that in spite of the high degree of task orientation, the groups appeared to be highly attractive and the members appeared to be enjoying themselves. This observation was borne out by the statements of the members. Other indications of high cohesiveness were the regularity of attendance and the punctuality of the parents.

In more recent groups, a brief weekly group evaluation is submitted to the members to ascertain the attraction of the group. Small changes in attitudes of members toward each other, toward the leaders, and toward various aspects of the program can be readily noted and acted upon in the following session.

Treatment and Research Staff

The staff for each group consisted of two group leaders and several observers. The group leaders initially provided parents with information, training in the application of principles, and alternate treatment plans. (Later, as the group members' familiarity with the material increased, they became more autonomous in developing their own treatment plans.) The leadership role gradually changed from that of trainer and planner to that of facilitator of group interaction and of parental treatment planning. From behind a one-way mirror, the observers collected data on the group process and the activities of leadership. Following each session, this material was reviewed by the observers with the parents and the leaders.

Since the method was relatively new, a set of procedures had to be developed to train the staff. The author directly observed and supervised the leaders of the first group. The first leader eventually shared his responsibility with the coleaders and ultimately withdrew completely from leadership as the coleaders assumed complete responsibility. At the end of each meeting, the activities of the leaders were discussed with the entire staff, and plans were made for the next meeting. Coleaders of the first group eventually served as the leaders of subsequent groups. Each in turn gradually delegated leadership responsibilities to a new coleader, who had observed a previous group while demonstrating effectiveness in carrying out limited assignments. By using this method, an increasing number of groups could be led by trained staff members. Parallel to this practical training, a theoretical training program instructed all the leaders and observers on this method of group training.

The methods employed in the training of parents and staff were the same for both the welfare mothers project and for the parents of retarded children. They were different in terms of how parents were recruited, specific behaviors treated, and the outcomes. In the following sections, these aspects of the study will be presented.

PROJECT 1—AFDC AND MIDDLE-CLASS MOTHERS

There is little research to indicate whether welfare mothers can utilize such a program; most research is with middle class parents. Yet the welfare mother has the same problems as others in child rearing. In addition, they are subject to special pressures inherent in poverty. Anecdotal accounts of groups for welfare mothers suggest a relatively high dropout rate. Thus, welfare mothers represent a hard-to-reach and hard-to-maintain group. For these reasons, this project was designed to compare the performance after behavior training of parents receiving Aid to Families of Dependent Children (AFDC) with middle class parents. In a pilot study of a group composed solely of AFDC mothers, only one out of four had used the group effectively, so it was decided to compare groups composed of both middle-class and AFDC parents and those consisting solely of AFDC parents.

Population: Welfare and Nonwelfare Mothers

Most of the welfare mothers were recruited from the Family Living Program of the Family Court Services of Madison, Wisconsin. A newsletter describing the program was sent to all parents connected with the program. After the first few groups had been completed, the trained parents informally recruited members from among their acquaintances. The nonwelfare population was referred primarily from the Family Health Services of the University of Wisconsin, and also from parents in the original group. Some parents also were referred from school social workers throughout the city. Although in most cases only the mother attended the meetings, two fathers attended with their wives and two fathers attended without wives.

The AFDC group focused on the behavior of children ranging from 10 months to 6 years. The middle-class parents dealt with the behavior of children ranging from 3 to 10 years. For problems with children over the age of 10, family treatment rather than parents training was recommended.

The distinction between AFDC and middle-class is not necessarily a sharp one; several of the AFDC parents came from strong middle-class backgrounds, and several non-AFDC families originally came from lower economic backgrounds. In general, the educational level of the non-AFDC parents was considerably higher than the AFDC parents. Two of the middle class parents had Ph.D.s; two were pediatricians; and most of the rest were college graduates or had attended college. Two of the AFDC parents were attending college at the time; two others had some college credit; and most owned high school diplomas. Only four had not completed high school. In no case was there evidence in the mixed groups that the highly educated intimidated the more poorly educated.

As parents applied for the program, they were assigned to available groups. Thus, the composition was not planned. As a result, two groups of AFDC parents were trained, six groups consisting of both AFDC and middle-class parents and three groups solely of middle-class parents. The groups ranged in size from 3 to 8 parents. A total of 29 AFDC and 29 middle-class families participated in the project.

Table 12.1 presents the results of the middle-class and AFDC parents in both mixed and homogeneous groups. Success of the parents was determined in terms of the successful modification of one or more behaviors, a period of correcting monitoring of two or more behaviors, and completion of the course.

Table 12.1 shows two striking differences. AFDC parents do impressively better when put together with middle-class parents than when segregated. And, even if one does not consider the results of the AFDC-only groups, middle class parents appear to be somewhat more effective behavior modifiers than AFDC mothers. The significance of these results will be discussed later.

Many of the 14 unsuccessful parents tended to fall into a category that

Table 12.1. A Comparison of Outcome of AFDC and
Middle-Class Families.

	Successful	Unsuccessful
AFDC families in AFDC-only groups	3	7
AFDC families in mixed groups	14	5
Middle-class families in mixed groups	21	2
Middle-class families in MC-only groups	6	0

Patterson and Cobb (1971) refer to as "diffusion parents." Characteristically, these parents appeared to be unskilled and uncommitted to change. They were only incidentally involved in monitoring and arranging contingencies for their children's behavior. No matter what assignment they agreed to complete, these parents would return the following week with a new behavior to monitor. They would not persist more than a few days at a given task. Since monitoring successfully was a prerequisite for treatment, these parents seldom got to the treatment phase. They would occasionally use unapproved treatment procedures, which would inevitably fail, either because the parents were not yet skilled enough to apply such procedures or because they did not carry out their plan consistently. In eight cases of failure (including two middle-class families), the parents terminated early. In the remaining six cases, the parents stated that they had learned a great deal, and they continued training until the end.

Table 12.2 indicates the behaviors that the parents dealt with while in the group. A behavior was considered as treated if it was at least monitored for a one-week period. Success was ascertained if the behavior increased or decreased in the direction and to the degree desired by the parents. In some cases, no treatment other than monitoring brought about the desired level of behavior.

The 29 middle-class families successfully dealt with 62 behaviors, while failing to effect changes in three—verbal aggression, enuresis (bed-wetting), and compliance. The 29 AFDC mothers successfully handled 33 behaviors, while failing only in enuresis (2 cases) and compliance. The major difference was in the tempo of learning. It usually took longer for the AFDC parents to develop an adequate monitoring and treatment plan; therefore, they were able to treat fewer behaviors (average of 1.2 per family) than the middle-class parents (average of 2.2 behaviors per family).

In the selection of targets of treatment, two differences can be noted. Middle-class parents chose with much greater frequency to deal with picking up toys and clothes and verbal aggression (for example, swearing and name calling) then the AFDC mothers, who emphasized the treatment of physical aggression and toilet training.

Table 12.2. Behaviors Treated by AFDC and Middle-Class Parents.

	AFDC		Middle Class	
	Successful	Unsuccessful	Successful	Unsuccessful
Verbal aggression	2	0	11	1
Physical aggression	7	0	9	0
Temper tantrums	3	0	5	0
Picking up toys/clothes	0	0	10	0
Crying, whining, pouting	3	0	5	0
Toilet training/enuresis	4	2	4	1
Bedtime routines	1	0	4	0
Self-dressing	3	0	6	0
Compliance	3	1	4	1
Other	6	0	4	0
Total	33	3	62	3

In the follow-up interviews with 10 of the middle-class families and 6 of the AFDC mothers, all stated that behaviors learned in the group were still at a desirable frequency. They also stated that as a result of the group, they were positively reinforcing with a much higher frequency and punishing much less. None, however, was doing any systematic counting.

Conclusions

It appears from the findings that by putting AFDC mothers together with middle-class families, they are better motivated than when segregated. The AFDC parents complained that all too often they are put together in parent effectiveness training or in other services with "their own kind." Several stated enthusiastically that "it was nice for a change to see that other people have the same problems as we do." Until contradictory data appear, one can conclude that homogeneity in group structure is *not* a desirable condition of social education programs for AFDC mothers.

Moreover, the presence of AFDC parents in no way seemed to hinder the performance or dampen enthusiasm of the middle-class mothers. To the contrary, they seemed to enjoy helping and being helped by people whom many of the middle-class parents previously had viewed as failures in society.

Although as a group welfare mothers tended to be slightly less effective and to work at a somewhat slower pace than better educated middle-class parents, the data indicate that most welfare mothers successfully can apply systematic procedures for dealing with their children.

PROJECT 2—PARENTS OF RETARDED
CHILDREN

Because of years of frustration in attempting to teach their children even the simplest motoric and verbal skills, parents of the retarded are sometimes discouraged and often set too low standards for their children. Frequently, social problems develop because of siblings' and other children's responses to the retarded child's behavior. A method that promises to make the learning process more efficient and that provides a specific means of improving social relations should be highly valued by the parent of the retarded child.

For the above reasons, this project was designed to provide training for parents of mentally retarded children in a group context to become behavior modifiers of their own children and to evaluate the effectiveness of that training, as evidenced in the modification of their children's behaviors.

Parent Populations: Natural and Foster

One population was recruited by mail from local organizations for parents of mentally retarded children. After the first few groups had been completed, the trained parents informally recruited members of subsequent groups from among their acquaintances. Other parents heard about the groups at various activities for parents of the retarded, where the author or his students were asked to speak. The foster parent population was recruited by social workers attached to an institution for the mentally retarded. Over a period of two years (June 1970 to June 1972), 33 families in groups were trained during 11 training programs (each lasting 7 to 10 weeks). Each group met weekly at one of two major referring agencies.

It should be noted that the children in the families treated ranged in chronological age from 2 to 14 years; all were either moderately or severely retarded. Only two children fell above and one below the 3 to 8-year-old range. One set of parents worked with an 11-year-old boy of normal intelligence, who was a long-term guest in their home because his behaviors were of a higher "nuisance value" than those of their retarded child.

According to criteria of success described earlier (see p. 174), 27 of the 33 families entering the program successfully modified 55 of the 58 behaviors for which monitoring and treatment plans were initiated. Three families terminated the program early, and three others, although having completed the program, failed to modify even one behavior successfully.

Successful behavior modification was determined in each case from the data collected by the parents. If the undesirable behavior was eliminated or reached a level acceptable to the parents, it was classified as successful. If a desirable

Table 12.3. Behavioral Outcomes of Retarded Children.

	Successful	Discontinued	Unsuccessful
Increasing vocabulary	2	0	0
Compliance	7	1	0
Temper tantrums	7	0	0
Aggression to self (hair pulling, hitting self)	2	1	0
Dressing (zipping, undressing)	5	0	0
Enuresis (diurnal and nocturnal) and toilet training	10	0	3
Preparing for bed (remaining in bed)	2	0	0
Aggression to others (hitting others)	6	1	0
Feeding (chewing, utensil usage)	9	1	0
Picking up toys, clothes	2	0	0
Other (cooperative play, getting ready for school, sucking)	3	0	0
	55	4	3

behavior increased to a level acceptable to the parents, it was classified as successful. If the behavior was monitored and the parent discovered that the level was not problematic, or decided not to treat it, the behavior was classified as discontinued.

As Table 12.3 shows, only three cases of enuresis persisted. In a sample follow-up interview (3 to 6 months following treatment of 21 of the parents), all gains (except one of the successful enuretics) were maintained, and most parents claimed that they were still using increased reinforcement procedures and fewer punishment techniques. Several had designed new programs of their own, but none, however, was still monitoring behavior. At the time of the follow-up, one of the unsuccessful families appeared to have become successful in using sophisticated procedures.

In comparing three groups of foster parents with eight groups of natural parents, no significant differences were observed either in terms of parental success or behavioral changes in the children. One of the groups categorized as a natural parent group consisted of two natural parents and one foster parent. For purposes of comparison, the outcome for this foster parent was included in a foster parent data cell in Table 12.4.

In two cases of failure, the parents terminated early. In three other cases, the parents remained until the end and stated that they had learned a great deal. One unsuccessful parent was herself borderline mentally retarded, a fact that may account for her inability to complete or even understand assignments.

Table 12.4. A Comparison of Outcomes of Foster and Natural Parents.

	Foster	Natural	Total
Successful	10	17	27
Unsuccessful	2	4	6
Total	12	21	33

The remaining couple, categorized as unsuccessful, monitored adequately but terminated early when their child was institutionalized.

Conclusions

Based on the findings, one can conclude that training parents of retarded children in groups is a meaningful endeavor. Not only are parents able to learn the necessary skills to modify successfully their children's behavior, but they are able to learn from leaders who have had relatively little training. Because of the high probability of a positive outcome and the ease of observation, training groups also provide an excellent vehicle for training students in the role of group leaders.

Moreover, this approach is useful with persons with a wide range of education. In this study, parents with tenth grade educations were as successful as those with college educations. Differences in social class also appear to be no barrier.

PROBLEMS IN GROUP TRAINING

A number of problems arise in group training that are not commonly found in individual training. The first is a discrepancy among members in tempo of learning. The tempo of the slower learner tends to hold back the tempo of the faster. This may not be a disadvantage, however. The more skilled parents in the groups described in this study were reinforced for helping the slower ones in such capacities as models and buddies. They demonstrated to the slower parents that the skills are applicable by parents as well as group leaders and helped them develop treatment plans. This extra opportunity for the faster parent to practice the basic principles theoretically should result in greater stabilization of the learning gains (see Goldstein, Heller, and Sechrest, 1966, pp. 212–259).

Another potential problem in groups is personal conflict among members, as evidenced by a high frequency of arguments, disagreements, punishing statements, and outbursts of anger. In behavioral practice, this has rarely occurred. The task orientation of the discussion appears to mitigate against aggressive interaction. Moreover, in group training members are not encouraged to state how each feels about one another. They are, instead, given models of persons who praise frequently; observations show that they tend to imitate that model. Disagreements, of course, do occur as to the best strategies of dealing with specific problems, but the concerned parent is always the final judge as to the action to be taken. The outcome provides the criterion for the correctness of the decision.

Does this lead to flat and dull meetings? Although never approaching the emotional peaks (or depths) of an encounter group, parents consistently indicated in response to evaluation questionnaires that they enjoyed the meetings, the contact with the other parents, and the task orientation of the leaders. The more objective evidence was the fact that meetings were attended almost perfectly.

PERSPECTIVES

As a result of these projects, several changes are now in operation or are being considered for new parent groups. In more recent programs, specific contingencies have been attached to the completion of behavioral assignments. This has increased the rate of completion from about 75 percent to 95 percent. Our initial hesitancy to attach contingencies to contract completion wasted an opportunity to model the very principles we were trying to teach.

Because of the size of the program, we did very little in the way of checking the reliability of the parents' observations. On those few occasions where it was convenient or requested that a leader enter the home, the observations of the leader usually overlapped with those of the parent. However, in some few cases the discrepancy was immense. For this reason, in the subsequent series of parent groups, leaders have been advised to include a small sampling of each parent's observations either through the buddy system or through intermittent home visits. As in all other behavioral practices, if the parents are told early in treatment that such reliability checks are a part of the process, they rarely object. The vast majority of parents appear to find the checks reinforcing of their accomplishments.

To find additional estimates of changes in the child, a pre- and posttest also has been included in all groups. Either the Walker (1970) or one of the Devereux checklists (Spivack and Spotts, 1966) is used. Since standardized norms exist for both tests and they have been used extensively in a large number of projects, the results of our groups can be compared to those of others. (In our experience, the Walker seems preferable for less educated parents.)

A series of vignettes of parent-child situations are presented to the parents both before and following training to discover changes in parent behavior. The parents are asked to respond to these situations in the best way possible.

Criteria have been developed to score their responses. Where video apparatus is available, parents are asked to role-play their responses, which are recorded on tape.

One of the major problems in both of the earlier projects was the few behaviors with which each family worked. The average ranged from 1.1 to 2.2 per family per group. In some cases, the behavior worked on was not the most significant to the parent. Yet, because of the brevity of treatment, there was insufficient time to work on additional behaviors. Another problem was that in working with only one or even two behaviors, a given parent was inadequately prepared to deal with the myriad of new problems that might arise in the family after treatment.

To offset this, Baum and Garfinkel (1974) taught the members of their group how to employ a family token economy. That is a situation in which each parent works on several behaviors of several children in their families. All the children receive tokens for such behaviors as the completion of chores or study behaviors. The tokens are cashed in for reinforcers at family meetings, which are held at regular intervals. In some cases, the parents place themselves on the token economy for chores the children expect them to perform more adequately. To train parents, all the models, examples, and exercises were drawn from family token economies. As a result, four of the five families they worked with utilized items that resulted in their modifying an average of 8.1 behaviors per family. It should be pointed out that these were unusually experienced leaders. The leaders of the earlier groups might not have had the skill to develop these more complex plans. However, it appears that the incorporation early in treatment of training for family token economies is a useful development in the parent training approach.

Although there is still much to learn about training parents in groups, the results of these projects suggest that the venture is productive, and they point to specific improvement in programming and teaching. In general, the group approach has been effective and satisfying both to staff and clients, and, as an added feature, is an opportunity for staff training and development.

13 Assertive Training in Groups[1]

LACK of social competence is a problem for a large portion of the population —for many, so severe a difficulty that they must lead isolated and fearful lives. This deficit is often a part of other problems, such as alcoholism, sexual dilemmas, absenteeism from school and work, depression, and loneliness. Because this social deficit has broad relevance for therapy, a program has been derived that is aimed directly at increasing or improving the quality of social skills. Clients are taught to develop conversational skills, the ability to say "no" when appropriate, use the telephone, make social visits, have dates, use facial expressions more effectively, and increase or control the manifestation of appropriate feelings. Some clients may become more socially competent by learning to be less aggressive (see Alberti and Emmons, 1974, for a discussion of the distinctions between assertion and aggression). As a person gains greater social competence and learns to be appropriately assertive, there is evidence that her or his anxiety is reduced (Wolpe, 1973).

Assertive training identifies a therapeutic procedure aimed at increasing a client's ability to engage in socially appropriate and satisfying behaviors. This therapy method refers to a set of procedures for training clients in specific behavioral areas in which they lack social skills. Considerable anecdotal evidence exists for the use of this approach (Bloomfield, 1973; Edwards, 1972; Gittleman, 1965; MacPherson, 1972; Nydegger, 1972; Serber, 1972; Stevenson

[1]This chapter was coauthored with Steven P. Schinke.

182

and Wolpe, 1960). Furthermore, many experiments in recent years have demonstrated the effectiveness of assertive training in treating populations and behaviors such as dating (Curran, 1975; MacDonald, Lindquist, Kramer, McGrath, and Rhyne, 1975; Twentyman and McFall, 1975), sexual offenders (Laws and Serber, 1975), schizophrenics (Hersen, Turner, Edelstein, and Pinkston, 1975; Weinman, Gelbart, Wallace, and Post, 1972), marital interactions (Eisler, Miller, Hersen, and Alford, 1974; Fensterheim, 1972a), mothers in dysfunctional families (Shoemaker and Paulson, 1976), women (Brockway, 1975; Jakubowski-Spector, 1973; Richey, 1974), speech anxious, middle school students (Johnson, Tyler, Thompson, and Jones, 1971), a variety of areas identified as problematic by college students (Friedman, 1971; Galassi, Kostka, and Galassi, 1975; McFall and Twentyman, 1973), and psychiatric inpatient populations (Goldsmith and McFall, 1975; Hersen and Bellack, in press; Hersen, Eisler, and Miller, 1974; Percell, Berwick, and Beigel, 1974).

Specific assertive training techniques, which have been empirically tested and found to be effective, include behavior rehearsal (McFall and Marston, 1970), modeling (Eisler, Hersen, and Miller, 1973), covert modeling (Kazdin, 1975), model reinforcement (Kazdin, 1974b), role-play (Friedman, 1971), practice (Hersen, Eisler, Miller, Johnson, and Pinkston, 1973), coaching (McFall and Lillesand, 1971), verbal reinforcement (Young, Rimm, and Kennedy, 1973), and feedback (Fensterheim, 1972a).

It would seem that deficits in social skills can be treated most effectively in the small group setting. The group can serve as a protected laboratory to practice skills that eventually must be carried out in the community. The group provides clients with a variety of social situations and potential roles that each can play. Moreover, in role-play, modeling, and rehearsal, clients offer each other an assortment of antagonists and protagonists. In the group, members have opportunities to assert themselves as leaders, therapeutic partners, or consultants to other group members.

To treat clients in the group, one by one, as individuals would fail to utilize the group's unique attributes. Therefore, in addition to direct treatment, the therapist initially must strive to: 1) make the group attractive to its members; 2) create group situations requiring members to be socially competent; 3) create a variety of roles that members can play; 4) gradually delegate the responsibilities of leadership; 5) enable members to function as consultants and partners in the therapeutic endeavor; and 6) control overwhelming group conflict so that members are not driven away.

Several studies have partially demonstrated the effectiveness of assertive training in groups. Shoemaker and Paulson (1976) have shown that, after participating in such a program, mothers exhibited significant increases in assertive behaviors and decreases in aggressive ones. Similar results were obtained for their husbands, who had participated only indirectly in the program. Moreover, parents' ratings of their children also improved. Two studies by

Rathus (1972, 1973a) compared group assertion training with either group discussion (1972) or placebo therapy (1973a), and a no-treatment control. Both studies found that assertion subjects reported greater gains on the Rathus Assertiveness Schedule (1973b). Only subjects in the latter study, however, were judged by independent raters as superior on overall assertiveness. Conclusions drawn from these studies are limited because Rathus used college students from his own classes and served as the therapist for all of his groups. Hedquist and Weinhold (1970) compared a behavioral rehearsal group involving role-playing, modeling, and coaching with a social learning theory group involving only modeling, followed by subjects' attempts to carry out assigned tasks in their natural environment. Both of the behavioral groups proved superior to a group discussion control on self-reported assertive verbal responses at the end of therapy. There were no significant differences, however, at a two-week follow-up.

Lomont, Gilner, Spector, and Skinner (1969) compared results of therapy for hospitalized patients through group assertiveness and therapy through group insight. Assertively trained patients showed significant changes in various subscales of the Minnesota Multiphasic Personality Inventory (MMPI) and the Leary Interpersonal Checklist, whereas the insight groups showed no such changes. Wright (1973), in a study of college discussion group participation, conducted treatment in groups and performed assessment in simulated group discussions and actual college group discussion sections. Behavioral training effects were found in the simulated group discussions, but they apparently did not transfer to the "real" discussion sections.

Fensterheim (1972b) describes a "mini-group" model in which three bachelors were given assertive training skills to combat social isolation. Although the program did not employ an experimental design, the results are used to illustrate the efficacy of the small assertive training group as an ancillary treatment procedure. Finally, a study by MacDonald and others (1975) examined the relative effectiveness of four group training conditions: behavior assertion training; behavior assertion training with client contact between sessions; attention placebo; and, a test-retest control condition. A role-play dating interaction rating scheme revealed significant improvements for both of the assertive training conditions when compared to the two control conditions. A six-month follow-up assessment, however, indicated some decay in the magnitude of effects for the two behavioral groups.

The results of these studies, although not conclusive, strongly suggest that assertive training is a legitimate method of group practice and target of clinical research. A question of particular concern to the group therapist is whether this approach can be applied in a variety of social agencies for clients of varying backgrounds with a wide range of problems related to social incompetence. The first project in this chapter addresses that question in a description of the development of a program of assertive training in five different agencies. Specifically, it describes how problems are assessed, data collected, behaviors treated, group attributes modified, and changes maintained following treatment. It also points out the results each group obtained. A second project involves an experiment in which assertive training in groups was compared to a placebo-control condition.

PROJECT 1

Population and Staff

In academic year 1973–74, students in a graduate social work program of a large midwestern university, organized a project (reported upon by Rose, 1975) involving five assertive training groups under the auspices of five different social agencies: a family service clinic, a university family health service clinic, a county mental health clinic, a church-affiliated family service agency, and a clinic at the school of social work. The groups ranged in size from 4 to 8 members each. About one-third of the members were students. The groups also included secretaries, homemakers, nurses, mothers in the AFDC program, an unemployed white collar worker, a machine operator, a teacher, a school principal, and a day care supervisor. Members were equally divided between males and females, and they ranged in age from 16 to 45.

All clients came to the group after reading an advertisement about a program treating social anxiety or an announcement of a social skills workshop, or after being referred through the agencies' normal referral routes. Applicants presented problems such as the lack of conversational skills, anxiety in the face of authority figures or members of the opposite sex, social isolation, imposition by others, and inability to form meaningful friendships. Clients were grouped in the order of the application, and each group held weekly meetings of one-and-a-half to two hours for 8 to 10 weeks.

All therapists in the program were graduate social work students who had had courses in learning theory and behavior modification and a seminar in the behavioral approach to group treatment. Their ongoing field work was in the main behaviorally oriented, and most did their research projects in areas related to behavioral change. Both their fieldwork and their work in the seminar on group treatment were supervised. Among the staff also were observers, most of whom were students in social work or nursing.

Data Collection

A major characteristic of all behavioral approaches is the collection of data from various sources for several purposes. The first purpose is to provide information for the determination of the target behavior. The second is to

provide information about ongoing changes for evaluating the relative influences of session-to-session interventions. The third purpose of the collection
of data is to provide a basis of determining the effectiveness of treatment for
both individuals and groups.

In assertive training groups, several types of data are necessary to meet
these purposes. The major source of data is from self-reported descriptions of
behavior occurring outside of the group. Each member has one or more target
behaviors that he or she continuously monitors until satisfactory levels are
achieved or failure is ascertained. Such behaviors as talking to persons of
authority, having dates, and talking to members of the opposite sex are examples of self-monitored behaviors. In the initial sessions, each member is taught
how to count and record the occurrence of such behaviors between sessions.
Results are reported back to the group.

In one group that used a method originally described by Hedquist and
Weinhold (1970), each member was asked to keep a diary and record all
responses and situations that were identified as distressing. The frequency of
verbal assertive responses was determined by requiring participants to record
daily the place, the date, the time of day, and the person(s) with whom each
made the responses described in the diary. Requiring the subjects to specify
place, time, and person would appear to make the self-reports more valid. In
addition, clients in some groups were asked to record their subjective units of
disturbance (SUDS) on a scale ranging from 0 (perfect calm) to 100 (complete
panic) (Wolpe, 1973). To relate the findings to other conceptual systems, a
number of personality inventories were administered before and after treatment. These included the Rathus Assertiveness Schedule (RAS) (Rathus,
1973b); the California Psychological Inventory (CPI) (Gough, 1957); the Situation Reaction Inventory of Anxiousness (S-R) (Endler, Hunt, and Rosenstein, 1962; Endler and Okada, 1975); and the Willoughby Personality
Inventory (Wolpe, 1973).

Since only the RAS was used in all groups, it alone will be described in this
chapter. This test provides information on the client's perception of situations,
each on a scale that ranges from –3 to +3. A client could receive a total score
ranging from –90 to +90. A negative score indicates less assertiveness and a
positive score more assertiveness. Rathus (1973b) reports a moderate to high
level of test-retest and split-half reliability and a satisfactory level of validity.

Three groups collected data by tape recording the clients' responses to a
number of situations calling for assertiveness. In each group, the client was
presented with nine situations that could elicit assertiveness in four different
categories: conversation skills, positive responses, negative responses, and refusal responses. For example, the client was told "You are wearing some new
clothes and a casual acquaintance remarks, 'You certainly look nice today!'

What would you do?" or, "A clerk in a store waits on the second person who has come in after you, and you are in a hurry. What would you do?"

During both pre- and posttherapy sessions with individuals, the therapist read the same nine situations to each client. Clients were instructed to tape record their characteristic response for each situation, plus their SUDS level. After all responses were recorded, three raters, blind to whether the responses were pre- or posttherapy, were asked to judge subjectively the level of assertiveness for each response, based on a 10-point scale with 1 and 10 representing extreme unassertiveness and extreme assertiveness, respectively. Reliability was determined by Kendall's coefficient of concordance. Another means of data collection involved direct observation of individual behavior and group interactions as they occurred during group meetings. For each session of all groups, observers collected data on the frequency and sequence of verbal interactions. In addition, some groups collected data on the distribution of reinforcement, task content of conversation, assertive responses (both positive and negative), and the behavior of group members with respect to leadership. To prevent rater fatigue, observers would sample behavior every other 10 minutes during a session. Reliability checks also were obtained at random intervals.

Targets of Change

As pointed out earlier, the instruments of data collection provided information about appropriate targets of change. In addition, most of the groups held a pretreatment interview to orient members to the group and discover the relative priority of problems on the instruments of data collection. In the initial sessions, members completed exercises in problem formulation. Written case examples or examples from members were redefined in terms that could be observed and rated. Shortly thereafter, clients were given the assignment of counting specific behaviors that were identified in the pretreatment interview or in the first session as potentially problematic. Finally, data collected on behaviors in the group were used to facilitate the determination of appropriate targets.

As a result of these procedures, all clients determined their own target of change. At the second group session, clients were presented with the data that had been collected, on which basis they could choose any set of behaviors for the start of treatment and could add new behaviors when this was found useful. Group members were encouraged to make suggestions to one another as to which behaviors they thought should be treated.

Once clearly delineated target behaviors were determined, the self-observations provided data for a baseline or pretreatment estimate of the frequency of the problem behavior. After baselines were established, treatment plans were developed for each client.

Treatment Procedures

The major treatment procedures used in training the clients in assertive behaviors were modeling, coaching, behavior rehearsal, covert rehearsal, group feedback, and contingency contracts.

In most groups, members were required to note in their diary all situations calling for assertiveness, and then describe how they responded. Situations that clients considered important, but for which they did not have an adequate response, were selected for modeling and rehearsing in the group. Usually one, two, or three situations were selected in each session for role-playing.

In the initial modeling presentations and in most of the rehearsals, group members and therapists commented on how the performance might be improved. If these comments called for major revisions, rehearsals were repeated, incorporating the suggestions. Some groups issued tokens to shape role-played assertive behaviors during the rehearsals. In this procedure, the therapist distributed a token to any member performing the designated behavior. This token usually served only to provide feedback or information. As the sessions progressed, successively more difficult behaviors were required for obtaining tokens.

During initial rehearsals of a new behavior, one group member often was assigned to provide cues to target clients when they appeared to be at a loss for words. Several groups used covert rehearsal to supplement overt rehearsal. The advantages of covert rehearsal are that it can be used with the entire group at the same time, it allows for multiple trials, and it protects the highly anxious client more than the overt rehearsal does. Moreover, it is a procedure that can be practiced readily at home.

McFall and Lillesand (1971) have provided evidence for the efficacy of the covert rehearsal procedure. After explaining the basic steps and rationale of covert rehearsal, the therapists describe a common problem situation. Members are asked to imagine how they would respond. After a brief discussion of their imagined responses, the leaders make several suggestions. Members are then asked once again to imagine their response, this time incorporating the most suitable suggestions from other group members and leaders.

Negotiated Assignments

At each session three to five different assignments were negotiated with each client. These included observing and self-monitoring, a reading selection, contacting a buddy, performing a task, planning a role-play, joining a club, performing exercises for relaxation, and obtaining new information. Completion of these assignments resulted in tangible and/or social reinforcement, which would be administered by a buddy or partner in the group, a family member, a friend, or the client.

The written document that pertains to the expectation of the behavior to be performed, the type of reinforcement to be received, and the conditions under which the reinforcement is to be delivered is referred to as a "contingency contract" (Homme, Csanyi, Gonzales, and Rechs, 1969). Clients selected their own reinforcers, which consisted of such things as money set aside for use only when earned, the opportunity to eat favorite foods, the right to participate in specified (otherwise not available) activities such as reading, watching television, or remaining longer in bed. When possible, someone in the client's environment monitored both the performance of the target behaviors and the distribution of reinforcers.

In most groups, clients were taught relaxation procedures. Wolpe's (1973) abbreviated instructions for alternating tension with relaxation for large muscle groups were used. Clients were directed to use these procedures before they entered situations calling for assertiveness. Procedures of relaxation were usually practiced at every session, and assignments were given to practice at home to master the techniques.

All procedures thus far discussed could have been carried out either in individual or group treatment. Other procedures, however, could be used only in the group. Group members received feedback through group discussion, showing them how peers perceived their performance. Individuals who had experienced similar problems offered a wide variety of ideas on how to improve performance. The buddy system was used to facilitate monitoring of the performance of extragroup behavior. Clients mutually selected partners with whom to exchange either telephone calls or visits between sessions. During these contacts, they discussed the difficulties they were having with the assignments and ways of resolving the difficulties. This procedure trained individuals in the self-therapy behaviors they would need when the group had terminated. To provide members with different types of partners, buddies in most groups were shifted once during the treatment period.

A set of goals and an agenda for each meeting were established to maintain a task orientation. Initially, the therapist designed the goals. As the clients learned the criteria for goal determination, they increasingly took responsibility for goal formulation. The criteria for the establishment of goals for each meeting were: 1) the session goals be related to the long-range goals of the group; 2) goals could be achieved reasonably before the following meeting; 3) the criteria for the goals' achievement are explicated; and 4) the goals have implications for the majority of group members, in serving either as target persons or as helpers of other persons. For example, one group, at the end of the third session, established the following goals:

By the end of this session, for at least one target behavior, all members will have a monitoring plan that meets the criteria discussed at the first meeting.

By the end of this session, all members who have successfully monitored a target behavior for a period of at least 10 days will have designed treatment plans to alter the frequency of the target behavior.

These plans must meet the criteria established in the modeling and rehearsal presentations.

Once session goals had been established, agenda items were developed to facilitate their attainment. The unfinished items usually were relegated to a subsequent meeting. Most of the group leaders used either *Your Perfect Right*, Alberti and Emmons (1974) or *Self-Directed Behavior*, Watson and Tharp (1972) for weekly reading assignments on the theory and application of behavioral change.

Group Attraction

Many come to an assertive training group to learn how to socialize with others in informal ways. Interaction that is too prescribed may limit the group's attractiveness for members. Therefore, a number of procedures are used to stimulate group attraction. First, since members in previous groups have given role-playing a high rating, role-play demonstrations are used in the first session. In addition, clients interview each other in subgroups as a way to learn names and get acquainted. Having the therapist clearly point out the advantages of the group appears to increase the attraction, as does the use of food. Since active participation by all persons seems to be related to attraction, everyone is encouraged to speak at the first meetings. However, too much pressure to speak may drive unusually taciturn clients away.

The purpose of increasing the attraction in the initial phase is to keep group members in treatment and increase the strength of the therapist and the group as reinforcers. There is some evidence that attraction is related to group effectiveness (Schachter, Ellerston, McBride, and Gregory, 1968).

Deposits offer another way to keep members. All five groups required per person deposits of 5 to 20 dollars above whatever fee was charged for training. The deposit was forfeited for imperfect attendance. The fact that no one dropped out of the five groups after the first session suggests the efficacy of the procedures used to increase attraction and to prevent premature termination. Moreover, the records of attendance and promptness at any given session substantiated group attraction of the previous session. Finally, clients in two groups were asked at the end of every session how attractive each found the group.

The foregoing treatment procedures were designed to facilitate the attainment of individual treatment goals. In most cases this involved increasing assertive behaviors. Because the group impinged on the treatment of each client, group or interactive goals sometimes had to be modified. For example, some persons rarely were able to give help to others or obtain help from them. Occasionally, members tended to communicate with leaders rather than with each other. Frequently, the therapists alone performed the leadership functions, which should have been distributed more broadly. In two groups, the degree of mutual reinforcement among members was so low that the therapists' intervention was required.

When group interaction was the target of change, some groups used token feedback as the major means of intervention. Participants received tokens when the desirable form of interaction occurred. Prior to the use of tokens, members usually were coached in forms of interaction specifically desired, and the rationale for such interaction was discussed. On several occasions the whole group rehearsed desirable patterns following discussion.

Table 13.1. Behaviors Treated in Five Assertive Training Groups.

Behaviors	Number Treated Successfully	Number Treated Unsuccessfully
Conversation with peers	8	1
Conversation with authority persons	3	0
Conversation with opposite sex	3	0
Positive responses or praise	7	0
Stating opinions	4	0
Giving suggestions	2	1
Refusal responses	3	0
Stating disagreements	4	0
Giving criticism	2	0
Speaking up in class	3	0
	39	2

Results

Table 13.1 shows behaviors that clients treated over several weeks, primarily using contingency contracts and rehearsal procedures. The average number of behaviors successfully treated per person was 1.6. All but three persons successfully changed at least one behavior. In addition to these continuously monitored behaviors, most clients successfully dealt with one-shot problem situations that were treated solely with modeling and rehearsal. These included a job interview, a bargaining situation, a situation calling for refusal, and the dressing-down of an inadequate employee. Since these situations were not monitored, no data are available, although their accomplishment is reflected in improvement on the RAS.

As Figure 13.1 indicates, all five groups showed positive changes on the Rathus Assertiveness Schedule. The mean pretherapy score for all clients was −19.1. The mean posttherapy score was +7.9. On a sample of graduate social work students not in therapy, the mean score was +32.5. We are, therefore, confronted with the extreme unassertiveness of the clients coming into therapy. Although these people made drastic gains in their self-reported assertiveness scores, they are still relatively less assertive than their non-therapy-seeking counterparts.

On all other instruments, all but two clients showed changes in the directions predicted. Since no more than two groups used other instruments, and since all the results were consistent with the behavioral and RAS findings, only the latter are reported here. To ascertain global success in the program, changes on the RAS or another inventory, change in one or more behaviors,

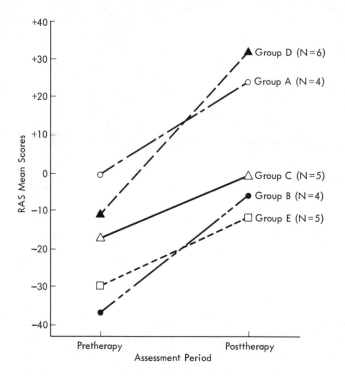

Figure 13.1   Rathus Assertiveness Schedule (RAS) mean scores at pre- and posttherapy for five assertive training groups conducted at separate outpatient clinics.

Table 13.2.   Average Productivity, Attendance, and Promptness in
Five Assertive Training Groups (Percentage).

Group	Productivity	Attendance	Promptness
A	85.0	96.8	93.6
B	77.2	88.5	n.a.[a]
C	90.7	90.0	85.7
D	67.2	96.6	74.1
E	90.0	100.0	88.0

[a]*N.a.: data not available.*

and completion of the program were used as indexes. On the basis of these
criteria, 21 out of the 24 who attended more than the initial session, or 89%,
made successful use of the program.

As mentioned earlier, each client negotiated 3 to 6 different assignments
each week. The average percentage of assignments completed at the beginning
of each session was used as an indication of the productivity of the previous
sessions and the intersessions. Since these data in previous groups were correlated with the number of behaviors changed ($r = .62$), their relevance for
indicating productivity is partially validated.

Attendance and promptness at each session were noted as indicators of
attraction to the group at a given session. Percentage of attendance was based
on the number of persons present divided by the number of persons who were
registered for the group. Percentage of promptness was based on the number
of persons who arrived on time divided by the number of persons attending
the meeting. Table 13.2 shows the percentage of behavioral assignments completed, attendance, and promptness for all meetings of each group. Considering the complexity of the assignment, productivity was extremely high.
Productivity in group D appeared to be skewed by one person who rarely
completed any assignments. The high percentages of attendance and promptness also indicate high attraction.

Several experiments were designed to modify group interactions. Simple
token feedback was shown to be effective in increasing the frequency with
which members talked to each other rather than to the leader. However, token
reinforcement was insufficient by itself to increase the frequency of mutual
reinforcement or positive responses among the members.

Discussion

The results of this program indicate that in 8 to 10 sessions of assertive
training in groups, it is possible to obtain both behavioral and attitudinal
change for most participants. These results may be obtained in a wide variety
of agencies for clients of differing social and educational backgrounds.

Such results do not suggest that the successful clients have lost all their anxiety, or that these clients are appropriately assertive in all situations calling for assertiveness. Some clients, although improved, still have negative RAS scores after treatment, suggesting further training. But for most, initial goals have been achieved—and the possibility of further success either through their own efforts, or with additional assistance is promising.

Not only were individual treatment goals achieved, but the groups also maintained a high level of attraction and productivity from week to week, in spite of their strong task orientation. It was not possible to identify all the factors that went into the success of the program, but the combination of treatment procedures appeared to be a powerful and inexpensive tool for facilitating the therapeutic goals of patients who initially claimed to be unassertive and socially anxious. Thus far, we have assumed that the differences were, the product of treatment. In the absence of a control group, however, one can not reject several alternative hypotheses to the one that treatment produced change. The differences could have been due to systematic learning on the RAS, since the test was given twice. However, others using the RAS have not demonstrated such a learning effect (Rathus, 1973b). Furthermore, Campbell and Stanley (1963) refer to a maturation error in which changes over time are due to the normal development of individuals. Although this is unlikely over a short period of time with adults, the maturation hypothesis cannot be rejected. A more likely alternative is the regression error; that is, the tendency for extreme scores on tests to move toward the mean when the test is repeated. The initial scores for many of the subjects were, indeed, quite far from the mean.

Finally, even in assuming that none of the above account for the significant shift in scores, one still does not know whether the placebo effects of treatment, rather than the behavioral procedures, were the cause of the changes. All of these alternative hypotheses could be eliminated in a control group study. For these reasons, a second study was launched (Schinke and Rose, 1976), which compared a population treated by means of the previously described assertive training package with a population treated by means of behavioral discussion (placebo-control). In addition to using self-report measures of the RAS and California Psychological Inventory, a situation role-play test was employed which evaluated behavioral change.

PROJECT 2

Population and Procedures

Thirty-six clients were recruited, as in the previous study, by means of newspaper ads, posters, and referrals from social agencies, and were randomly assigned to 7 treatment groups with 5 to 6 members in each group. Four groups followed the assertive training format, using primarily behavioral rehearsal and contingency contracting, and three used a behavioral discussion (placebo-control) format. The overall socioeconomic characteristics of the clinical population in this experiment were similar to those in the previous study.

The format of the assertive training package was identical to those described in Project 1. The behavioral discussion format was concerned solely with the analysis and discussion of problematic situations. There also was time allotted to general topics related to clients' social problems. Therapists were restricted from modeling, rehearsing, and verbal or written contracting.

To insure a broad-based evaluation of therapy, three outcome measures were employed. The first was an audio-taped, role-play test similar to instruments used successfully but unsystematically in the previous study. In this project a series of 16 situations requiring assertive responses were constructed from a pool of problematic events identified by the study sample at a pretreatment telephone contact. Clients in the project individually completed the role-play test by responding to 8 of the 16 situations at posttherapy and 8 at follow-up, three months after treatment. The audio-taped responses to these stimulus situations were rated on the following criteria:[2]

1. Affect. The client's speech was scored on a five-point scale for affect, with 1 indicating a very flat unemotional tone of voice and 5 indicating a full and lively intonation appropriate to the situation.

2. Fluency of speech. The fluency of a client's speech for each situation was rated on a five-point scale, with 1 indicating very nonfluent speech and 5 indicating very fluent speech. Long pauses, hesitations, repetitions, and use of ah, oh, uhm, and other expletives were considered nonfluent speech.

3. Positive affective responses. A frequency count was taken on the number of client statements that indicated a personal liking for another's responses, character traits, or behavior. Examples: "I really enjoy talking with you." "That was a great lecture."

4. Negative affective responses. A frequency count was taken on the number of client statements that indicated a personal dislike, irritation, or disagreement with another's verbal and/or nonverbal behaviors. Examples: "I don't like your attitude, Fred." "The radio is so loud I can't concentrate."

5. Refusal responses. A frequency count was taken on the number of client statements that indicated an unwillingness to conform to, or go along with, another person's or group's suggestions, advice, instructions, or demands. Examples: "No, I'd rather go later." "I don't want to join the club."

[2]Criteria 1, 2, 6, 7, 8, and 9 were developed by Eisler, Miller, and Hersen (1973); criteria 3, 4, and 5 were developed by Brockway, Brown, McCormick and Resneck (1972).

6. Compliance content. Compliance of verbal content was rated on a dichotomous occurrence or nonoccurrence basis for each situation. Compliance was scored if the client did not resist the stimulus model's position (for example, if the client agreed to loan out important lecture notes before a final exam).

7. Content requesting new behavior. Verbal content with respect to requesting new behavior also was scored on an occurrence or nonoccurrence basis for each situation. Responses scored in this category required more than mere noncompliance. The client had to show evidence that he or she wanted a change in someone else's behavior (for example, the client had to indicate that he or she wanted a friend to return a borrowed $5 within a specified period).

8. Duration of response. Length of time the client responded to the stimulus situation was recorded for each scene. Speech pauses of greater than three seconds terminated timing until the person began speaking again.

9. Overall assertiveness. After rating all of the previous behavioral categories, judges were asked to rate the audio-taped responses for assertiveness on a five-point scale, with 1 indicating very unassertive and 5 indicating very assertive. Since clients gave idiosyncratic patterns of responses to each of the above behavioral categories, the overall assertiveness criteria was considered most important in assessing assertive behavioral change. Rating the above eight categories was necessary, however, as preparation for the raters in determining overall assertiveness.

Group members' tape-recorded responses to the role-play situations were transcribed to other audio tapes for retroactive ratings of response quality. Posttreatment and follow-up responses for each of the 36 clients were placed on the tapes and labeled such that the responses appeared to be from situations 1 to 18. Thus, at no time did any rater know if he or she was rating a posttreatment or a follow-up response. Situations one and two were transcribed onto tapes 17 and 18 to obtain a measure of between-rater pairs reliability. Four undergraduate students served as raters after learning the scoring system. The raters were given approximately 20 hours of training by the use of descriptions of assertiveness as found in Alberti and Emmons (1974) and Wolpe (1973), and audio-taped practice role-plays. The four raters were then assigned to a predetermined rating schedule, which required all permutations of rater pairs to rate an equal number of response tapes. As a result, each rater worked individually with every other rater, and each pair rated three response tapes.

An index of interrater reliability (Pearson product moment correlation coefficient, r) was calculated for all pairs of raters across all nine audio-tape response criteria. The mean reliability coefficient across all pairs of raters for the nine response quality criteria ranged from .858 to .998. Between-rater pairs reliability was computed for situations one and two, which were re-rated by a different rating pair, as situations 17 and 18. Between-rater pairs reliability coefficients were, therefore, computed from scores assigned by two different rating teams listening to the same set of responses. A range of .887 to .988 suggests that rating pairs were highly reliable in their ratings of identical responses.

Scores assigned by these raters were summed across the eight posttreatment and eight follow-up role-play situations for each of the nine response quality criteria. Means and standard deviations for the two treatment conditions were computed from these ratings.

The second assessment instrument used in this project was the California Psychological Inventory (CPI) (Gough, 1957). Specifically, the Class I Scales were given, which are designed to measure personality characteristics of poise, ascendancy, self-assurance, and interpersonal adequacy. Each client's completed CPI, Class I Scales, administered at pre-, posttherapy, and at the three-month follow-up, were scored according to the *CPI Manual* (Gough, 1957). This scoring resulted in numerical values for six individual subscores: dominance, capacity for status, sociability, social presence, self-acceptance, and sense of well-being, and a total score for Class I Scales. Pre- to posttherapy and pretherapy to follow-up change scores were computed for each of these seven scoring categories.

The third assessment instrument used in this project was the Rathus Assertiveness Schedule (RAS), identical to that used in Project 1. All completed RASs, given at pre-, posttherapy, and three-month follow-up, were scored according to the procedures developed by Rathus (1973b). Pre- to posttherapy and pretherapy to follow-up change scores were computed for each client.

Results

Two-sample, independent t tests performed on all posttreatment measures revealed no significant differences between the two treatment conditions prior to beginning the program. In this study, four female and three male therapists of similar backgrounds and professional disciplines were trained in the use of one of the two therapies employed. One-way analyses of variance performed on all assessment instruments described previously indicated no significant differences due to therapist on any measure.

To test the hypothesis that there would be beneficial changes as a result of treatment, two sample, independent t tests were conducted on raw scores for those assessment techniques administered at posttreatment and follow-up only, and on change scores for those instruments administered pre-, post-therapy, and follow-up. Group means rather than individual group members' scores were used as the unit of analysis since the study had a hierarchical design (Winer, 1971, pp. 359–366). Two-tailed tests were used in all data analysis to allow for serendipitous findings.

AUDIO-TAPED, BEHAVIORAL, ROLE-PLAY RATINGS

Analysis of posttherapy and follow-up mean scores of the responses indicates significant differences in favor of the assertive training package on the overall assertiveness rating at posttreatment, $t(5) = 22.11$, $p < .001$, and at follow-up, $t(5) = 6.90$, $p < .001$. Ratings of affect at posttreatment show group differences in favor of the assertive training condition, $t(5) = 3.10$, $p < .05$, as do negative affective responses ratings at follow-up, $t(5) = 2.71$, $p < .05$. Relatively greater improvement is suggested, but not statistically significant, for the assertive training condition on refusal responses at posttreatment, and content requesting new behavior at follow-up. Group means for the two conditions revealed higher scores for the assertive training condition on all nine response quality criteria at posttreatment and eight of the nine criteria at follow-up. Duration of response at follow-up is the only criterion on which the behavioral discussion condition scored higher than the assertive training condition. These results give strong evidence that the clients receiving the assertive training package were rated as being significantly more assertive than the clients in the behavioral discussion condition. A comparison of mean scores for the two assessment periods indicates a parallel upward movement for both groups, posttreatment to follow-up, on the components of affect, fluency of speech, refusal responses, and content requesting new behavior. A downward posttreatment to follow-up trend, which is difficult to interpret, is displayed by both groups on positive affective responses and compliance content. The group means given for negative affective responses reveal much greater upward movement for the assertive training condition.

CALIFORNIA PSYCHOLOGICAL INVENTORY SCORES

Independent t-test analyses of the CPI Class I scales revealed no significant differences between the two treatment conditions at either posttreatment or follow-up. A comparison of mean change scores for pre- to posttreatment and pretreatment to follow-up shows a fairly consistent trend of upward movement across all assessment periods for both treatment groups.

RATHUS ASSERTIVENESS SCHEDULE SCORES

Independent t-test analyses of the RAS scores revealed no significant differences between the two treatment conditions at either posttherapy or follow-up.

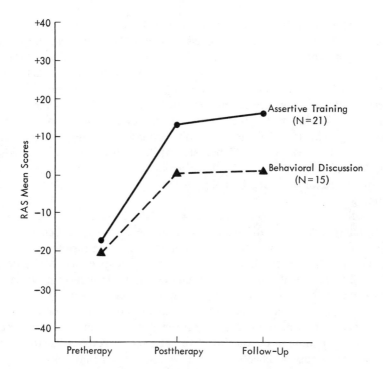

Figure 13.2. Rathus Assertiveness Schedule (RAS) mean scores at pre-, posttherapy, and a three-month follow-up for assertive training (experimental) and behavioral discussion (placebo control) conditions.

Although differences between the two groups are nonsignificant, examination of Figure 13.2 reveals impressive pre- to posttherapy change scores for both conditions, with the assertive training condition achieving higher gains at pretreatment to follow-up than the behavioral discussion condition.

Discussion

Results of Project 2 provide support for the use of an assertive training package in the group treatment of a clinical sample. Data analyses indicate significantly more improvement for the assertive training (experimental) clients on components of the role-play test, as compared to clients receiving the behavioral discussion (placebo-control) condition. The experimental group also achieved higher mean change scores on a number of other measurements that did now show statistically significant differences between the two conditions. Thus, the conclusion of greater improvement for the assertive training clients is based primarily upon the results of the behavioral role-play test.

Since the major thrust of interpersonal skill training in groups is the manifestation of new social behaviors, assessment instruments that measure observed performance in a role-play situation are more likely to predict behavioral patterns in the "real world" than self-report instruments that assess one's perception of change. Because the audio-taped, behavioral role-plays were developed from actual problematic situations given by the treatment sample, and blind rated, they provide a useful approximation of actually measuring behavioral change. Therefore, as many other investigators (Eisler, Hersen, and Agras, 1973a, 1974b; Eisler, Miller, and Hersen, 1973; Goldsmith and McFall, 1975; Serber, 1972) have concluded, this assessment technique is ideally suited for the evaluation of programs using the components of assertive training.

Results of posttreatment and follow-up data analyses show strong significant differences in overall assertiveness, on the audio-taped, behavioral role-plays, for the assertive training condition. This group also was rated significantly higher on the indices of affect at posttreatment and negative affective responses at follow-up. All nine rating dimensions at posttreatment, and eight of the nine at follow-up, show the assertive training condition as attaining higher mean scores than the behavioral discussion condition on the instrument. These findings suggest that the assertive training clients were able to learn and maintain the learning of verbal assertive responses better than the behavioral discussion clients. It must be emphasized that neither treatment group was taught specifically to respond to the explicit criteria of the rating system. Rather, the assertive training clients rehearsed and contracted for the performance of specific interpersonal behaviors, which they had identified as problematic in their environments, while the behavioral discussion clients only discussed these behaviors. Assuming that verbal responses in a simulated situation measure an important component of assertive behavior, it is possible to conclude that the assertive training clients did, indeed, learn to behave in a more appropriately assertive manner than those not receiving the specific training package. It could be argued, however, that the significant differences on the audio-taped responses are more of an artifact of the assertive training clients being taught how to role-play, and therefore performing well on a role-play instrument, than a reflection of learned assertive behaviors. Because this project used a treatment package, including behavioral rehearsal and role-play, the specific components of treatment that account for the posttreatment and follow-up differences cannot be determined. Perhaps a placebo-control role-play group would have shown significant gains on the role-plays when compared to a nonrole-play group.

Analyses of the Rathus Assertiveness Schedule and California Psychological Inventory data give a picture of strong changes within the two treatment conditions, but no differences between them. Since the Rathus Assertive Schedule is a self-report scale of assertive behavior, it was the most reactive of the two instruments administered at pre-, posttreatment, and follow-up. California Psychological Inventory results reaffirm the notion that clients in both conditions perceived their respective treatments as equally helpful.

The findings of all three assessment instruments raise some interesting issues about the manifestations of change due to assertive training in groups. One interpretation of the data suggests that a behavioral discussion group can bring about the same magnitude of self-perceived behavioral change as an assertive training group, but only the latter training gives clients the skills of actual assertive behaviors. Equal satisfaction of clients across the groups is confirmed by session evaluations and anecdotal data, which indicate the behavioral discussion groups were consistently rated as highly as the assertive training groups. Clearly, all group members had good relationships with their leaders, regardless of the treatment intervention used. Under these conditions, the "hello-goodbye" phenomena (Hathaway, 1948; Lang, Lazovik, and Reynolds, 1966), could account for the lack of significant differences between conditions on self-report instruments.

An additional explanation of the similar results for both conditions on the two self-report instruments is the learning due to repeated testing. This is quite possible since the self-report tests were given at pretherapy, six weeks later at posttherapy, and three months later at follow-up. Results obtained on assessment instruments used in this project warrant the conclusion that ratings of behavioral response components and a long-term follow-up represent important tools and procedures in the assessment of assertive training.

In summary, the findings identified by the present authors, and results of other investigators, provide an empirically tested model of assertive training suitable for a clinical population. An assertive training program that employs a package of specific treatment components, delivered in the small group context, appears to be a beneficial, efficient, and economical approach to therapy with clients presenting social deficit problems. Moreover, the clinician can draw from a wide variety of experimental literature for the development of responsible treatment interventions for specific problems and homogeneous populations. In addition to the empirical literature, there is a growing body of self-help manuals written expressly for the lay public interested in acquiring appropriately assertive skills (see, for example, Alberti and Emmons, 1974; Fensterheim and Baer, 1975; Osborn and Harris, 1975; Phelps and Austin, 1975). It seems safe to conclude that the therapeutic method known as assertive training now represents a well-defined and tested set of principles available to clinicians and clinical populations at nearly every level of sophistication.

14 Behavioral Group Therapy in the Institution

"APATHETIC," "withdrawn," "unresponsive" are all words that have been used to describe institutionalized patients. They are allowed to make few decisions on their own and are usually entirely dependent on the hospital staff for the most minimal needs. As a result, they have or take little responsibility for their own lives. Often afraid of other people, they seem to avoid them, and, when they are active, are frequently perceived as troublesome and/or bizarre (Maley, 1974).

A few institutions have turned to token economies for increasing activity, social interaction, and responsibility (see Allyon and Azrin, 1968). Although differing from institution to institution as to specific characteristics, these token economies can be identified by three major attributes. First, the targets for change are specific behaviors (related to the general categories mentioned above), which are to be increased, decreased, or maintained. Second, a medium of exchange, usually tokens, is distributed by the staff to the patients either when desired behaviors are performed or undesirable ones are omitted. Third, the tokens can be exchanged at regular intervals for desirable objects or privileges. The token economy is usually in effect on at least one entire ward and is sometimes used throughout the entire institution. Even though they have demonstrated major benefits for the patients, Maley suggests that it may be necessary to go beyond the narrow confines of the strict operant model and use a wide variety of empirically validated treatment procedures to provide more subtle training in social skills. One such means may be the small group used either in addition to or instead of the token economy as a vehicle for social skill training.

TYPES OF INSTITUTIONAL GROUPS

The purpose of this chapter is to describe groups with a behavioral focus commonly found in institutions and to detail previous research and personal experience in this area. A number of different kinds of institutional groups can be identified, although there is considerable overlapping among them.

The first type is the task and decision-making group, whose goals are to increase decision-making and self-governing skills, sense of responsibility, and ultimately the self-respect of the patients. In such groups, patients eventually are given major responsibilities for their own treatment and that of their peers. (Patient self-government groups also belong to this category.) The second type is known as the minimal social skills training group, for those patients with extremely low intellectual functioning levels and with virtually no social responsiveness. The major goals in these groups are to extend the limited repertoire of behaviors so that the patients can make maximum use of, and increase satisfaction with, their present situation. (This type of group probably would not be necessary in a ward with a functioning token economy.)

The third type of group is the transitional group, which focuses on preparing the patient for return to the community. Such groups are especially relevant for patients with acute problems. However, as more of the chronic patients are moving into foster homes, day care facilities, halfway houses, or back to their own homes, this type of group becomes increasingly important to them as well. The Group Therapy and Research Project has been concerned primarily with the last two types; however, because of the widespread use of task groups in institutions, this category also has been included.

Task Groups

Task and decision-making groups enjoy a positive reaction from many professional staffs in institutions, and a few research projects have explored the efficacy of this approach. Among these, the most complete project was carried out by Fairweather (1964). He describes an extensive project in a mental hospital in which small task-oriented groups run by the patients were set up to increase their social skills. The research staff divided the patients in one ward into four groups; they met four days a week by themselves with a psychologist available for consultation. On the fifth weekday, each group would recommend to the staff any treatment plans for each of its members, concerning passes to be issued, money to be received, privileges to be withdrawn, problems to be dealt with, and so forth. On a matched control ward, the staff performed these functions.

In the experimental groups, each person received funds and privileges in proportion to the step level attained. Each subsequent step level required increasingly high responsibility for self-control and planning for oneself and others in the group. At the highest level, patients were assisted by the group in planning for their discharge and future employment.

The experiment lasted 27 weeks, with a follow-up six months after each patient left the hospital. Assessment and observation took place throughout the project. Some of the results have major implications for a small group approach in which patients are maximally involved in their own treatment. For one thing, the small group members spent significantly fewer days in the hospital, stayed out longer, and achieved better employment records than the control group. They also took less medication daily. The recidivism rate, however, was not improved by the small group—a possible explanation is the abrupt termination of both treatment and therapeutic contacts in the small group.

The effectiveness of task-oriented groups in a mental hospital also was explored by Olson and Greenberg (1973). The authors randomly assigned 74 institutionalized male mental patients in one of three treatment conditions for a four-month period. Patients in all three conditions received the customary hospital treatment—medication, daily work assignments, recreation therapy, weekly group therapy with nursing personnel, weekly ward meetings, and other activities associated with the typical hospital milieux program.

The interaction condition received, in addition, two more hourly meetings in small groups, focusing on problems that prevented the patients from being discharged and on how the patients could help each other overcome these problems. In the incentive condition, the patients also received two hours of additional therapy plus response contingent management of their behavior. In this condition, group therapy consisted of the members planning and administering their own treatment. At each meeting the concrete target was a progress report on one of the members, selected by the group, and included recommendations as to a specific course of action for the target person's treatment in the hospital. Examples of recommendations were changed in work assignments, roommates, discharge privileges or town passes, plans for foster homes or other living arrangements, the nature of privileges to be received, or limits to be set. Recommendations were discussed by staff, who had ultimate authority to accept or reject them but who were obligated to explain their decisions. To train the members in the decision-making process, staff members initially served as leaders, providing models for the members, but gradually their role was faded. After two months the group met alone, and a group member chairman, elected by the members, served each of the following months as discussion leader.

The patients in the incentive small group condition were significantly different from the patients in the other two conditions on four of the five outcome measures—the number of days spent out, number of town passes, percentage of attendance at details, and on the Social Adjustment Behavior Rating Scale. The first three point to the greater effectiveness of the incentive condition both at termination and four months following the end of the program. The fourth condition, the rating scale filled in by the nurses, indicated that the behavior of the incentive system had deteriorated. This is consistent with the findings of Maley (1974), who discovered that as patients get better in terms of objectively improved behaviors, they are rated as more belligerent by the nurses or ward attendants. This may indicate that as patients learn to be more independent and assertive, they cause more trouble to the nurses and attendants and consequently are rated as more poorly adapted.

Unfortunately, in the crucial area of increased decision-making, no data were collected by Olson and Greenberg (1973). If hard evidence eventually shows that these skills do indeed increase as a result of the decision-making groups, it will provide stronger support for the use of these groups in institutions. In the absence of better evidence, however, the experiences of Fairweather and of Olson and Greenberg suggest that decision-making groups are worth further exploration.

Minimal Skill Training Groups

There have been several experiments demonstrating the efficacy of operant procedures in training psychiatric patients in minimal communication skills required to function in group therapy. Heckel, Wiggins, and Salzberg (1962) used an unpleasant auditory stimulus after each 10 seconds of silence in group therapy to condition participation and reduce the number and duration of silences. Hauserman, Zweback, and Plotkin (1972) successfully used concrete reinforcement to facilitate verbal initiations by adolescent inpatients in group therapy. Dinoff, Horner, Kurpiewski, Rickard, and Timmons (1960) used both eliciting and reinforcement techniques to increase verbal behavior of schizophrenics in "group therapylike" situations. Similar success in manipulation of verbal statements was found by Wagner (1966) and Williams and Blanton (1968). However, no generalization to other situations was observed in any of these studies. For this reason, in attempting to develop minimal skills, we have emphasized a wide package of procedures, in addition to reinforcement and eliciting techniques, to enhance the transfer of change from the group therapy situation to other situations in the hospital.

A program of minimal skill training in small groups in a psychiatric hospital was carried out by Gutride and others (1972). The purpose was to train patients in such interpersonal skills as starting and carrying on a conversation. In groups of 6 to 8 patients with 2 therapists, about half of the 87 hospital patients in the study underwent a 12-hour training program, 3 hours a week. The program consisted of presenting four modeling tapes, one each week, that depicted several types of responses to others. The therapists pointed out the general principles and provided numerous role-plays. In comparison to an equivalent control sample, the trainees did better on a large number of behavioral measures not only in contrived role-play situations but also when observed at mealtimes.

In another example, Pierce and Drasgow (1969) used tokens in small groups to facilitate more effective communication of feeling. They selected seven male psychiatric inpatients at random from a group of 14 patients who had not been assigned to individual or group therapy. Although they began with what they called an integrated didactic and experiential approach, they soon modified it to emphasize shaping of verbal behavior to reconstruct the communication process gradually. Patients were given a list of common feelings such as anger, depression, and joy. They were then given a sentence by one of the trainers or another patient. When the patients were successfully using one-word descriptions, they were expected to build their responses into sentences such as "You feel sad." Through differential reinforcement, the trainees gradually shaped two- and three-sentence responses until patients could interact for periods of 15 to 20 minutes.

The results of the study indicate that in terms of empathy, positive regard, genuineness, and concreteness, the shaping group, after only 20 hours, improved far more than a control-control group, a medicine control group, an individual therapy group, and a group therapy control. As the authors conclude, "The major implication for traditional therapy is that progress in improving interpersonal relations must be taught directly."

A detailed ancedotal account of a minimal skill training package in the Group Therapy and Research Project was described by Frank (1974),[1] who organized a group of four chronic mental patients, ages ranging from 53 to 62. The four had limited intellectual capacities, minimal physical capacities, minimal social skills, and long histories of institutionalization. Using tokens, modeling, rehearsal, and out-of-the-hospital trips, Frank focused primarily on increasing the number of interactions, positive responses, and total responses in only eight sessions. He describes the development of the group and the individuals in the following paragraphs:

> The meetings themselves seemed to change appreciably. At first there was almost no inter-member interaction; the only responses were to the questions of the leaders. There appeared to be little observable enthusiasm or enjoyment even of the recreational activities, which originally constituted the main portion of the agenda. The members expressed

[1] A similar example of the kind of data obtained and the research design utilized in this study is found on p. 71.

no opinions, feelings, or preferences. As the shaping program was instituted first for increasing member-initiated responses, a definite increase was observed in the members speaking without the use of prompts or questions. Though most of the reactions were still observed as being directed toward the leaders, the atmosphere appeared more spontaneous, with increased attention to the conversations of others; even smiles and occasional jokes were observed. As reinforcement was then applied to member-member interactions, members began to speak to each other, considered each other more in their conversations and tended to speak more frequently. The time spent in recreational activities dropped as everyone appeared to be enjoying talking to each other as much. The frequency of members stating their ideas and opinions also increased as preferences for the next meeting's agenda were being discussed. Enthusiasm seemed even higher as positive statements were added to the treatment program. Much more talking, joking, story telling, and relating of past experiences were noted as the activity portion of the program was dropped completely. Members helped plan future meetings, as compared to their total failure to respond during the first meeting. When planning for termination, the discussion of personal feelings was also observed, which had been non-existent just a few weeks prior. Assertive behavior in meetings and in the wards also appeared to be higher for the group as a whole. Specific changes were noted for each of the four participants.

During the first meetings, Mr. H made only statements which were clearly unrelated to the subject under discussion. Near the end of the group, all of his responses seemed much more appropriate. Instead of being short and blunt, and often ignoring the statements and requests of other patients, he eagerly engaged others in conversations, even making attempts with those less likely to respond. His assertiveness appeared to increase as well as his consideration of others. On the ward, he was observed to be sitting with others more frequently and also initiating more conversations. He seemed less seclusive and more active physically.

The most dramatic changes seemed to appear in Mr. K. Rather than just quietly sitting in one place in the hospital, he was observed walking all over the hospital and its grounds, usually in the presence of another with whom he would be eagerly attempting to converse. On a couple of occasions, he even ran down the hall of the hospital to eagerly greet this leader and began a long barrage of questions. "I like . . ." is now a major portion of his verbal repertoire, since group treatment focused on positive statements. His intellectual capacity seems to hinder him from being a good conversationalist; however now, whether on the ward or in the group, he seems to try the hardest of all to get conversations going.

Originally, Ms. O appeared suspicious and reserved in the group. Toward the end both in the group and on the ward, she became more helpful toward others, initiated more conversations, and generally appeared more at ease around people. Rather than spending all of her time secluded in her room, she is now observed most frequently out in the open lounge area around others. Her mood also seems warmer and more friendly. She is now being considered for a position at a transitional workshop center in the community.

Ms. S also seemed to improve appreciably in the group. Instead of sitting quietly, infrequently responding or appearing to attend the meeting, she began to respond more and with longer sentences. She began smiling and laughing when others were joking, which had never been observed by the therapists previously. She began to walk around the hospital, and its grounds occasionally, in contrast to her previous custom of sitting in her one favorite place, and she was also observed several times initiating conversations. However, it appeared that she had again become quiet and reserved since the group had ended. Being the least proficient of all the members, she probably needed a more intensive program. A longer time period with much more practice may also be one of the requirements for stabilizing the changes she showed in treatment.

Minimal skill training may be quite useful to the clients involved, as well as facilitating the attainment of agency goals. In a group consisting of five male nursing home residents, Sistler (1975) successfully used the group to get isolated residents out of their rooms and involved in other agency activities. The group members were referred to the group by the activity director and the director of nurses because the patients seldom interacted with each other, rarely attended nursing home activities, and spent most of their time isolated in their rooms. The members ranged in age from 62 to 91. All of them had minimal self-help skills and could get to the meeting themselves. Of the six who were referred originally, all attended voluntarily to see what the group was about, except one, who broke his hip and could not attend. The group varied in interests, education, socioeconomic class, and degree of participation in the home.

To evaluate the attractiveness of the group, the promptness of the members was observed, comments from patients to staff were solicited, and the members were asked at the end of each meeting to rate their satisfaction. Except for the first meeting when the average was 4 minutes late per member, members arrived on the average from 3 to 9 minutes early each meeting. Satisfaction ranged from 4 to 5 on a scale from 1 to 5, where highest satisfaction was 5. And nurses commented that all they were told about the group was positive.

To evaluate the effectiveness of the group in facilitating participation in outside activities, their participation was recorded before and after the program was completed. To evaluate member participation with each other, the rate with which they communicated with each other, as opposed to the rate they communicated solely with the leader, was recorded.

Basically, the program consisted of a discussion of topics in which the members had expressed interest. This included such things as the planting of roses, a trip to Hong Kong, and the idiosyncrasies of the stock market. The discussion was, however, primarily a vehicle to increase their interactive skills and social relationships. The therapist attempted to reinforce discussion with each other, since in the initial discussion all comments were directed toward her. At one meeting tokens were used to reinforce member-to-member interaction, but the group indicated that they preferred not to use them. Behavioral assignments were used, however, to continue discussions outside of the group with other persons and to participate in other activities.

A procedure that they evaluated highly was the use of the members as discussion leaders. The members agreed to the procedures at the third session, and one member volunteered for each subsequent session. One of the members who expressed some concern with the idea of leading a group was instructed in leadership skills by the therapist by means of modeling and rehearsal, and as a result his leadership was as effective as that of the others.

Modeling and rehearsal also were used to train the members in approach responses to other residents and the techniques that were needed to carry out a conversation. In contrast to most groups, this group did not evaluate role-playing procedures highly, so they were used minimally.

The therapist also shaped the members to assume responsibility for meetings. First she planned the meeting herself and had the members evaluate her plan. Later she had the group select agenda items from a limited list that she proposed. And, finally, members developed their own agenda with consultation from the leader.

Several group problems arose in the course of the eight meetings. One member was particularly loquacious and off-task. The members complained about this on the evaluations. The therapist handled the situation by giving the individual the leadership task of praising other members and entered into a contract with him of their both speaking less to help others to speak more. The first assignments were not carried out with any enthusiasm or completeness. When the therapist involved the members more in negotiating the contracts, the rate of completion increased dramatically.

The results of the eight-week hourly meetings were positive but modest. All of the members except one increased their activities in the institution. The one member who did not increase his activities had an extremely short memory and did not remember any assignments that were given. One member was encouraged to make plans to leave the institution and to set up in a semi-independent living arrangement. During the meetings, he talked about what he was going to do when he left and how he had to prepare for leaving. The member-to-member interaction in the group increased from an average rate of .75 per minute to a rate of 4.3 per minute. The leader-to-member interaction decreased from 4.9 to 1.1 per minute. This change was parallel to a change in increase in time spent in more therapeutic discussion, such as preparing for and evaluating behavioral assignments. An interesting side effect was that the therapist's profession, social work, was evaluated more positively by the nursing staff. They felt that the social worker had made their job easier, as well as facilitated the clients to attain important personal goals.

Considering the nature of the topics discussed, most of the members demonstrated a moderate to high level of intellectual functioning. The group served to channel the members from the isolation of their rooms into the institutional community, and in one case into the outside world. The expanded repertoire of activities and interest of members were demonstrated clearly as a product of the group. This was achieved without threatening the custodial staff, who historically have been opposed to therapeutic interventions (see, for example, Perrow, 1965). The therapist felt that more demanding goals could be achieved in subsequent meetings. Since the group agreed to a series of follow-up sessions, these would shift from a minimal skills group focusing on improving the quality of interaction to helping patients who were physically competent to return to the community (this was compatible with recent institutional policy). Thus, the new group would become a transitional group.

Transitional Groups

Transitional groups facilitate change from one community, usually an institution, to another, usually a foster home, independent placement, or halfway house. Most institutions train their patients in behaviors that have little use in the outside world. For this reason, the patients are less prepared for living in the world than they were when they entered the institution. Even those institutions that focus on teaching skills needed in the community have little time to prepare the patient for the immediate problems he or she faces on leaving the institution. To fill this gap in treatment, transitional groups have been developed in a number of institutions.

Rose, Flanagan, and Brierton (1971) described a group set up in a correctional school where the problems of readjustment to the community are comparable to those facing other institutional residents. This program was established for those who had demonstrated by their behavior in the institution that they were ready to return home. The focus of the members' activities in this group was on planning to use their furloughs to reintegrate themselves into the community. Individual treatment plans were developed by the group members for each participant, emphasizing the specific behaviors each needed to work on, such as staying out of fights, obtaining a job, talking to a probation officer, future employer, teacher or parent, and self-maintenance skills in the home. Behavioral assignments were given by the group members to perform while on furlough. The meetings focused on planning for and monitoring the results of these assignments. Extensive use was made of social reinforcement, modeling, and contracts.

Fairweather (1964), in the project mentioned earlier in this chapter, describes a transitional group with a behavior focus that served as an employment committee for other patients. As soon as patients demonstrated that they were functioning well enough to seek employment, they were referred to the patient committee for a personal interview and an evaluation of their applications. If, for instance, a man was found ready by staff, the committee provided him with information and helped him to prepare for the interviews. When necessary, his way was paved further by telephone calls by committee members or visits on his behalf. Although not dealing with all aspects of transition, this unique program appeared to be a highly useful treatment procedure. There was a great deal of enthusiasm about the program from the patients and staff, and even from some of the prospective employers.

A unique transition group consisting of five deaf persons was organized by Vest (1974). Three were institutional residents and two were living in the community. All were selected by staff members as needing involvement in community and educational activities away from the hospital and sheltered situations (and, once referred, all of them participated voluntarily).

The expressed goals of the group were that each member would become involved in (attend regularly) one community social recreational activity or one educational activity not housed in the institution. More specific goals pertained to the acquisition of those skills each would need to achieve the more general goals. For example, one member had to improve his eye contact with others. As a lip reader, he could not communicate with others if eye contact remained poor. All but one of the members needed to learn to participate in group discussion since they had little experience in this area.

The chief means of communication in the group was sign language, which slowed the rate of communication compared to other populations. Also, some concepts were difficult to explain in sign. In spite of these limitations, the procedures used were the same as all other groups. However, a total of 15 meetings were required to meet even approximation of the treatment goals.

Data collection on intragroup behaviors such as eye contact and participation was carried out by observers. For the extragroup behaviors, self-report validated by telephone calls to the community agencies concerned was used. The treatment methods included modeling, rehearsal, contingency contracting, verbal and token reinforcement, and group contingencies.

The results of the group were for the most part successful. Although one member dropped out early, the rest continued not only for the originally agreed-upon nine sessions but for four additional sessions following termination. All of the clients are now living in the community. Of four who continued the group, two became actively involved in community groups. One became a regular member of a swimming and weight lifting group at the local Y. The second had joined a sewing class. The youngest member, a high school student, began to attend basketball games and other school functions, which she never had done before. The fourth member became active with a small circle of friends and was saving money for a bowling tournament upstate.

All four improved in the specific behaviors they were working on in the group, which facilitated their more general improvement in social interaction. This was especially important for their group decision skills, which improved dramatically in the course of the meetings. Thus, all four were socially activated by the program and were helped to become more independent and involved in the community.

ORGANIZATIONAL REQUISITES FOR GROUP TREATMENT

In the Sistler study concerned with male nursing home residents, the group existed in part only because of the cooperation of the nursing staff. Its future also lies in the hands of this staff. Within the institution, the group is always embedded in a web of formal and informal staff expectations, organizational goals, personal needs, and limited resources. One often hears complaints of communication problems, unclear goals, staff conflicts, authoritarian administration, and resistance to innovation (see, for example, Perrow, 1965).

Behaviorally oriented groups in institutions make several specific demands on the organizational policies. First, a more liberal policy of out-of-hospital visits and furloughs are extremely important. Resources to be used as reinforcers, especially in the initial phases of treatment, also must be made available. Auxiliary staff must be trained to reinforce the same behaviors that the therapists are reinforcing, or at the very least discontinue punishing them. It would appear that the nurses were not appropriately involved in the Maley (1974) project discussed in the section on task groups. If these and other similar considerations are not taken care of prior to the initiation of a treatment group, the group will never be able to realize its potential.

Most group therapists in hospitals or nursing homes have to fulfill three roles—therapist, public relations specialist, and informal staff trainer. In the latter two roles, the therapist has to spend a great deal of time with staff at various levels discussing the program, pointing out advantages as well as costs of the new program. He or she has to provide the staff with feedback on patients with whom they have been working. And often the therapist has to defend his or her theoretical position in a number of situations, such as in staffings, staff meetings, and the coffee room. Although line staff has been interested in a technology that spells out clearly what one is to do, the group therapist who does not perform other organizational duties still will fail to gain organizational support. Several kinds of specific support needed for groups to survive can be identified (see Peal, 1965). First, meeting times must be relatively well protected. If patients are pulled out for medicine, occupational training, or psychological tests, the meetings will be attended irregularly, and the result will be low attraction and still lower productivity. The attendance of members at meetings must be supported by the administration. Second, the administration formally must make time for the group therapists to prepare as well as to lead the group. Peal also suggests that the administration be willing to allow for failure or only moderate success in a new program. Within a reasonable time period, however, a program must be able to stand on its results.

Where the institution is already being run with a token economy, some of the organizational demands have already been taken care of. However, at each change in the structure of the program, a renewed effort must be made to mobilize organizational resources and support on behalf of the endeavor.

The use of small groups as the context of treatment in institutions appears to be increasing. However, it behooves the therapist to spend as much time on his or her organizational housekeeping as on preparation for treatment, if a group therapy program is to be permitted to flourish.

15 Weight Control Through Group Therapy

OBESITY is one of the major health problems in the United States. In 1964 over 52 million Americans were either dieting or were concerned about their weight (Stuart and Davis, 1972). Besides being a health problem, overweight is often a personal handicap. Employers seem to prefer normal weight employees, fat children are teased, and overweight people are less likely to find mates (Dublin, 1953). Given the high incidence of excessive overweight and its close association with high blood pressure, diabetes, and heart disease, and, given the psychological problems often associated with being overweight, its treatment is of major importance.

Self-reinforcing behaviors such as overeating are among the most difficult to change, and respondent methods have not been successful (Stuart and Davis, 1972, p. 71). It seems, therefore, that the most desirable technique would be the use of operant methods for strengthening or weakening the existing responses associated with eating.

The prototype of operant methods applied to obesity was an experiment by Ferster, Nurnberger, and Levitt (1962). They instructed dieters to keep records of food eaten, to schedule activities incompatible with eating at problem times, and to schedule regular hours for eating.

This method has been further developed by Stuart and Davis (1972), who recommend a three-pronged approach that includes managing the environment as it relates to eating and exercise. Management of the environment would be exemplified by learning to purchase low calorie foods, by minimizing contact with excessive food, by slowing the pace of eating, by making acceptable foods as attractive as possible, and so on. By stressing nutritional management, both health and weight loss more likely are to be maintained in comparison with eating eccentric foods, fasting, or using dietary aids (Stuart and Davis, 1972, p. 30). By also stressing moderate exercise, it is less necessary to reduce food intake radically since exercise burns up calories. A moderate program of dieting and exercise should be easier to maintain than an extreme program in either category.

The purpose of this chapter is to describe the application of such a self-management behavioral approach in a group setting. There have been a number of studies in recent years on the treatment of obesity that have attempted to compare behavioral approaches in groups to other theoretical approaches and/or to a control group (Harmatz and Lapuc, 1968; Wollersheim, 1970; Penick, Filion, Fox, and Stunkard, 1971; Hagen, 1974; and Abrahms and Allen, 1974). The results tend to support the efficacy of group treatment in weight reduction when compared to control and/or placebo groups, but not always at a more effective rate than other theoretical approaches or other contexts. In most of these studies, however, there has been little direct manipulation of the group attributes as an added tool in the training process. We will review these studies first and then outline the model that has evolved from these as well as from the author's experience with overweight persons in groups.

Harmatz and Lapuc (1968) compared three groups of overweight psychiatric patients. Treatment techniques were contingent positive reinforcement (money) and response cost (loss of money) for the behavior modification group. The second group was a diet-only control, and the third was a group therapy treatment group (social reinforcement and pressure). Both the group therapy and the behavior modification groups were significantly different from the diet-only group during treatment, but at a four-week follow-up, only the behavior modification group continued to lose weight. The fact that the patients in the group therapy condition lost weight only during the time that the group was in session supports the idea that the group serves as a control on behavior and highlights the importance of regular attendance at group meetings.

Penick, Filion, Fox, and Stunkard (1971) randomly assigned 32 obese patients to four groups. Two groups received training in behavior modification; the two others received conventional group psychotherapy. The therapy in each group session lasted two hours once weekly over a period of three months. The therapy group received supportive treatment, instruction about dieting and nutrition, and, upon demand, appetite suppressants. The behavioral group therapy involved description of the behavior to be controlled, modification and control of the discriminatory stimuli governing eating, and prompt reinforcement of behaviors that delay or control eating. The authors describe specific use of the groups only "when a patient had lost his entire fat bag." At this point the group as a whole presented him or her with a book, cosmetics, or other concrete reinforcers along with lavish praise. In the behavioral groups, 27 percent lost more than 40 pounds and 53 percent lost more than 20 pounds.

Wollersheim (1970) compared behavioral group therapy in the treatment of overweight to two other types of therapies and a control group. The behavior therapy involved both the shaping of new behavioral eating patterns and the learning of relaxation to reduce tension. The alternatives were the use of positive expectation and social pressure and a nonspecific therapy oriented toward developing insight into unconscious motives for eating. Although all three groups evidenced significant weight reduction in contrast to the control group at both posttreatment and at the follow-up period, the behavioral approach was superior in the reduction of certain types of eating behavior and in the amount of weight loss. There also was no evidence of a therapist effect as an alternate explanation to the outcome, nor was there any evidence of symptom substitution, which is a commonly held hypothesis in regard to weight loss.

Hagen (1974) compared treatment of obesity with 89 coeds in three conditions—a behavioral group therapy, a bibliotherapy group (use of a written manual), and group therapy and bibliotherapy combined. Wollersheim's behavioral treatment program discussed above was the basis of the weight reduction manual and the group therapy. In the group situation, personal contact, as well as emphasis on learning principles, was emphasized. Although treatment was followed by significantly greater losses than control groups, no significant differences occurred across treatment conditions.

The purpose of the Abrahms and Allen (1974) study was to examine the utility of the Stuart and Davis self-instructional program in conjunction with social pressure factors and monetary payoffs for weight loss. The context for examining these questions was the group. Forty-nine female student subjects, varying from 19 to 139 percent overweight, were assigned randomly to four treatment conditions: a no-treatment control, a social reinforcement condition, a behavioral programming with social reinforcement, and a behavioral programming with monetary remuneration condition. All treatments lasted 10 weeks, with a follow-up weigh-in six weeks after termination.

In the social reinforcement condition, each subject weighed in before the group and announced her weight and weight change from the previous week. The group members and therapists praised the subject when she lost weight and expressed mild disapproval when she gained. The group also spent time discussing topics such as caloric intake of various foods and recipes. In addition, subjects in the behavioral programming and social reinforcement condition were taught nutritional, exercise, eating management, and recording procedures of Stuart and Davis (1972). Subjects in the behavioral programming plus monetary remuneration condition, in addition to the procedures for the above two conditions, also were paid money for losing weight.

Results indicated that behavioral programming conditions were more effective than either the social reinforcement or the control group. There were no significant differences between the two behavior programming conditions. Moreover, the gains were maintained at the follow-up period for the two behavioral programming groups.

This study provides support for the efficacy of behavioral programming training in groups for overweight patients. What part social reinforcement plays, however, is not clear. Used alone, it does not appear sufficient to bring about weight loss. But since it was present in both of the other treatment conditions, there is some question whether behavioral programming without social reinforcement would be effective.

In all of these experiments, the behavioral approaches in groups fared as well or better than alternative approaches. They did better than the control groups in all cases. Such research provides an excellent basis for the development of the clinical model presented below. Organization, assessment, individual and group change, as well as the results and discussion of results of the clinical program for the treatment of the overweight, will be discussed in detail.

CLINICAL PROGRAM FOR TREATMENT OF
THE OVERWEIGHT

Organization for Group Therapy

All four groups reported on in this project were organized under the auspices of the Family Health Services in cooperation with the Group Therapy and Research Project of the University of Wisconsin. In all of the groups, members were referred by friends, a dietician, or a physician, or they came on their own initiative. In addition, the members in two groups also were recruited by advertising. Prior to participation, clients provided evidence that they recently had had a physical examination and that there were no known limitations to moderate dieting and exercise. All participants were at least 20 percent (by their own personal estimates) above what they perceived to be an adequate weight, and all had previously tried other methods unsuccessfully. The actual weights ranged from 135 to 235 pounds, with more than half of the patients over 150 pounds.

The members in the first two groups were in a behavioral group for the first time. In the third group, four of the six were continuing for the second time, and in the fourth group one of three was continuing for the second time.

There were 8 to 10 sessions in each group, each lasting two hours and usually divided by a 10-minute break for diet soda and coffee. All members were required to sign a contract indicating their willingness to participate regularly and to pay a deposit, which was refunded contingent on regular attendance.

All groups were conducted by advanced social workers with training in both behavior modification and group treatment. In one of the first groups, a dietician also was used as a coleader. (In subsequent groups she served as a guest expert.) Nursing and social work students were observers for each group.

Assessment and Monitoring

Once the group has been organized, it was necessary to determine the locus of the problem. Although achieving and maintaining weight loss were the goals of all the members, it was important to find out what situations seemed to be related to excessive eating, the nutritional value of present eating patterns, and the frequency of exercise. In this way, it was possible to obtain a picture of general life-style and how it affected the individual's eating patterns. To achieve this varied picture as quickly as possible, all clients filled in a behavioral checklist, a baseline eating monitoring form, and a weight watchers questionnaire, and they weighed themselves at each meeting. The behavioral checklist is given below.

The behavioral checklist is an extension of the one developed by Stuart and Davis (1972) and focuses on the client's perception of what eating situations are problematic to him or her. Each client indicates whether a problem is problematic (P) or whether he or she should take a look at it by monitoring (M) it. In the first group meeting, the members review all their P and M items and spell them out in enough detail so that a monitoring plan can be developed. The modeling effect of old members spelling out problems in behavioral specific terms appears to speed the process of problem identification for new members. At the first meeting, the members are instructed to fill in the baseline

WEIGHT LOSS GROUP BEHAVIORAL CHECKLIST

P = definite problem   O = no problem   M = requires observation and monitoring

1. Arranging to eat only in one room. _____
2. Arranging to eat in only one place in that room. _____
3. When you eat, only eating, avoiding other activities. _____
4. Buying nonfattening foods. _____
5. If you buy problem foods, keeping them out of reach. _____
6. If you eat problem foods, making sure they need preparation. _____
7. Always shopping from a list and buying only foods on your list. _____
8. Doing your shopping after you have eaten. _____

9. Taking into the store only enough money to buy items on your list. _____

10. Looking for times of your own weakness and taking steps to change them. _____

11. Training others to help you curb your eating. _____

12. Making small portions of food appear large. _____

13. When you eat, measuring all portions. _____

14. Making second helpings hard to get. _____

15. Taking steps to avoid boredom, loneliness, depression, anger, fatigue, and hunger. _____

16. Always eating three regular meals (planned) every day. _____

17. Always keeping handy: a list of friends to call, hobbies, interesting reading material, housework. _____

18. Looking for ways to prevent anger/express anger in least costly way. _____

19. Sleeping regular hours and getting enough sleep to keep you going comfortably. _____

20. Keeping on hand a variety of safe foods for snacks. _____

21. Keeping track of how much you have eaten and how much you have left. _____

22. Eating slowly at the beginning of the meal and throughout the meal. _____

23. Keeping graphs of calories, weight, and exercise. _____

24. Eating sitting down. _____

25. Setting the table before eating, the more elaborate the better. _____

26. Preparing and freezing portions in advance if possible. _____

27. Eating from a plate and putting all servings on your plate at once. _____

28. Eating your favorite high calorie food only as a reward for doing well on your diet each day; making sure it fits within your calorie list. _____

29. Setting a time for yourself that you must wait after having something to eat until you can have something more. _____

30. Planning exercise into each day. _____

31. Knowing and using refusal lines to turn down food. _____

32. Taking only one helping of food. _____

33. Avoid snacking while cooking. _____

34. Arranging your eating schedule so that you have a meal just before a situation in which the tendency to eat is especially strong. _____

eating form, which they turn in at each subsequent week of treatment. On this form, also developed by Stuart and Davis, the client records the amount and type of food eaten, whether the food is a snack or part of a meal, the social conditions of eating, and the mood associated with eating. At the second meeting, these forms are discussed in the group meeting, and, when necessary, additional training is given on how to formulate the answers.

These data, together with the weight and exercise information, provide the basis for establishing the individualized targets for each person. In most groups, however, several targets are worked toward in common. All members in this project worked on increasing exercise and reducing caloric intake. Most members worked on eliminating snacking between meals and in the evening, eating while preparing food, or eating while doing housework. Others worked on reducing the frequency of eating while reading, refusing high caloric snacks when offered, reducing the speed of eating, and increasing the number of bites per mouthful.

For purpose of assessment, one meeting in the weight loss group is devoted to a potluck dinner in which each person brings one item. An informal discussion takes place during this dinner, as observers note speed of eating, number of times utensils are set down, and so on. The dinner serves two purposes: to obtain an in vivo, baseline data on the above problems and to increase the attractiveness of the group. As has often been noted, eating together is an excellent way to develop firm relationships.

In addition to the individual data, information is collected on the interactional pattern of each member in the group to determine whether each is sufficiently involved in the group and is able to play a helping as well as a help-seeking role. Is also is possible to use these data to determine whether group leaders or particular members are dominating the interaction. Finally, subjective data on satisfaction with and attraction to the group are derived from the weekly evaluation to determine whether the group is progressing satisfactorily.

Treatment Procedures

The major *individual* treatment procedure used in this approach is contingency contracting. Modeling and rehearsal also are used occasionally. The *group* procedures most commonly used are the buddy system, group problem-solving, and group feedback. Some didactic procedures, such as the use of required readings from Stuart and Davis and discussion of these selections, are used as well.

Contingency contracts are written every week by each member of the group. These contracts consist of a specification of the behaviors to be monitored, the buddy to be contacted, the chapter to be read, behaviors to be self-reinforced, the exercise to be completed, and so on. It also includes contingencies if all the items and agreements are met. (These contingencies in most cases are money, which is often held by another person.) The contracts are the focus of most meetings in that each week all contracts from the previous week are reviewed and those for the subsequent week developed. They also provide practice in behavioral specificity and correct goal formulation. The contracts are reviewed at first by the leader and later by one's buddy to see whether they are correct and complete.

Following is a typical example of a contract developed by one of the members during the fourth session.

CONTINGENCY CONTRACT

From_____To_____

I, E. B., agree to the following:

I will perform the following behaviors:	If and only if successful:
I will eat three meals a day.	I will put 30¢ into the kitty.
I will keep under 1,200 calories a day.	Each day successful I will put 50¢ in the kitty.
I will record snacks.	Each day I will put 10¢ in the kitty.
I will perform the equivalent of 100 calories of exercise and record what I did.	Each day I will put 30¢ in the kitty.
I will call my buddy every day and tell him how well I did.	Every time I call I will put 10¢ in the kitty.

At the end of the week, movies and all paid recreational activities are contingent on having enough money in the kitty. If not, tough luck, E. B.!!!

Date	Signed	Witness
1/6	E. B.	K. R.

As part of developing contingency planning, one session is devoted to developing a list of reinforcers. Some of the reinforcers brought up in these project groups were crocheting, knitting, volunteer work, horseback riding, walking, swimming, sex, rock climbing, ping pong, shopping, dancing, concerts, and movies. More active reinforcers are encouraged for two purposes: they reinforce appropriate eating habits and they increase the number of calories used in exercise.

Refusing to eat when pressured by others is one of the most difficult procedures to master and a common reason for breakdown in diets. The following skit is used as a means of modeling what one can do when pressured by others.

The chocolate cake in this skit may be replaced by ice cream, alcohol, or whatever food appeals to the given target person. To make it more realistic, the food or drink is brought to the meeting and the other members (in spite of their diets) should pretend to be eating (drinking) it.

> G:"Have a piece of chocolate cake."
>
> V:"No, thanks, I'm on a diet."
>
> G:"Oh, go ahead, I made it myself. It's really good."
>
> V:"I really would like to, but if I do, I really mess up the diet. I promised myself I wouldn't eat between meals, especially things like cake."
>
> G:"Of course, if you don't want it."
>
> V:"Oh, I really do want it. That's the real test, you know."
>
> G:"Then, take just a small piece."
>
> V:"For me cake is like peanuts, once I start, I just go all the way. I guess I'm a food-olic."
>
> G:"I think you're being too hard on yourself."
>
> V:"Maybe you're right, but nothing else works."
>
> G:"Listen, if you stop doing things that are worthwhile, just for a few ounces, it's hardly worth it."
>
> V:"It's worth it to me. I've got to lose weight. The pain of being too heavy is worth the loss, even of a delicious cake."
>
> G:"Well, it's your life."
>
> V:"Darn right (laugh). But maybe I'd better get out of this room with all the food."

Following the modeling demonstration, each member of the group who has a problem with refusal rehearses the procedure with his or her particular weakness. The specific content is determined by the significant others, and the pressure is gradually increased.

Group problem-solving is used when a member brings a problem into the group, which he or she doesn't know how to solve alone. Rather than answer the question him- or herself, the leader throws the question to the group, first asking them if they have any questions and answers. The members brainstorm any suggestions that come to mind. Finally, the individual with the problem selects and evaluates with the group those solutions which he or she thinks might work.

How to get back on the diet program once you have "slipped," and how to avoid eating candy when you work next to the candy machine are examples of the type of situation dealt with within these groups. The group suggested restructuring the environment for a few days to make dieting easier. Scheduling activities at times when overeating usually occurs, using more powerful reinforcers, getting rid of all problem foods in the house (in this case, soliciting the help of a roommate), and having low-calorie meals prepared so that one could eat them when one came home "too tired to eat but not too tired to munch" were ideas to solve the first problem. Suggestions for the second problem included carrying no money to work for the candy machine and having pieces of fruit and vegetables to eat.

The buddy system is used throughout the group, starting at the first meeting. Part of every weekly contract is "calling your buddy" to check on treatment progress and to solicit support and/or suggestions for dealing with real or anticipated diet problems. Members occasionally are reminded that calling their buddies is not the time to emphasize other personal problems or to seek sympathy, because this only serves to reinforce complaining behavior. The focus during these contacts is a discussion of what each had achieved to date, of technical problems that arose, and of possible solutions to those problems. If both agree that no solution is possible, the leader is called. In all four groups in this project, this occurred only twice. Role-playing also is used to model the content of a talk with one's buddy.

A variation of the buddy system—subgrouping into pairs during meetings —is used to increase client responsibility for each other's programs. Rather than the group as a whole listening to the design of a new program, the dyads discuss each other's plans in the subgroup and make suggestions for improvement. When the plans are developed, each member reports his or her partner's plan to the whole group. This procedure was used only in the groups of four or larger.

Group contingencies were used in working on increasing the frequency of member-to-member interaction in proportion to member-to-leader interaction. Also used as contingencies were longer breaks and rebates on the fee for the session. In both cases the contingencies were eliminated several meetings prior to termination.

In summary, a complex package of individual and group procedures were used to facilitate behavioral changes leading to weight loss. The degree of success of the package is discussed in the following section.

Results

The results in all four groups were not as satisfactory as originally expected or as reported on in the literature. In almost every group, one or two persons dropped out after the first session because the approach was not what they had expected. In all four groups, one person did not lose weight, and the remaining persons lost an average of 3/4 of a pound a week, which is somewhat less than what Stuart and Davis suggest is adequate continuous loss.

For those persons for whom follow-up data was available, most of those who did not continue in another program regained the lost weight. Those who continued in a program continued to lose or to maintain their weight.

One member, after two groups of eight weeks each, organized her own group with two other members. She wrote out weekly agendas and continued contingency contracting, daily telephone calls for mutual support, and even role-playing. She lost a total of 35 pounds over a year and maintained that loss.

It should be pointed out that most of the patients were clinical referrals. They had a history of rapid weight gain and loss. Many had a multitude of other social problems that prevented them from carrying out agreed-upon instructions. Moreover, they had been heavy for many years.

In another study (Rose and others, 1970) primarily with students as clients, the results were somewhat better. The purpose of this study was to test the implication of group composition on the effectiveness of control groups. It was our assumption that groups working on more than one type of self-control problem, such as weight loss and cigarette smoking, would be more effective than groups that consisted only of one type of self-control problem.

To test our hypothesis, a total of 36 persons were assigned to six groups: two smoking groups, two weight loss groups, and two, mixed, weight loss–smoking groups. Assignment for the overweight clients was random to the two overweight conditions, and for the smokers, random to the two smoking conditions. The population was recruited among students in the university during the summer session. Announcements of the program were made in several large undergraduate classes and several posters were placed around the campus. All clients signed a contract agreeing to attend all six sessions. A deposit of $10 was charged, to be refunded on completion of the program. For our purposes, we will discuss here only the weight loss clients and weight loss methods.

The methods used in this study were similar to those described earlier, except that clients were allowed to select from a list of procedures whatever ones they thought would work best for them. The meetings were used to train them in their desired behaviors.

The results are shown in Table 15.1.

In general, although there are differences among groups, there are no differences between conditions. It is interesting to note that one person dropped out of each group and forfeited the deposit (three of the four dropouts did provide final data).

During the 6-week period, 4 persons lost 12 or more pounds, 14 persons lost 6 or more pounds, and only 4 persons lost less than 6 pounds.

The question may be raised why these four groups did better than the clinical groups reported earlier. The population in this study were students, in contrast with the four case studies in which the clients were clinical referrals. The students may represent a more disciplined population insofar as carrying out instructions and using daily techniques. Although there is no systematic follow-up in the Rose and others (1970) study, the few persons with whom contact was maintained for six or more months regained much of the weight

Table 15.1. Weight Watchers—Individual Data.

Group	% Lost	Absolute lb. Diff.
M 1	−6.6%	−13
M 1	−10.1%	−14
M 1*	—	− 0
M 2*	−5.6	− 7
M 2	−6.1	−10
M 2	−1.6	− 2
W 1	−8.7	−13
W 1	−5.8	− 8
W 1	−4.9	− 7
W 1	−7.5	−10
W 1	−5.7	− 7
W 1*	+ .6%	+ 1
W 2	−4.0%	− 6
W 2	−6.6%	− 9
W 2	−14.0%	−18
W 2	−7.0%	− 9
W 2	−11.6%	−15
W 2*	−5.8%	− 8
W 2	−3.0%	− 4

lost in the group. Thus, if this is representative of the population, the differences may be equalized over time.

One could tentatively conclude that, at least with college students, the group procedures used do have at least a short-term effect on weight loss. However, whether a group is composed solely of weight loss or combined with other self-control problems does not appear to effect outcomes.

Conclusion

The findings suggest that although 6 to 10 sessions are sufficient to obtain moderate weight loss for most patients, and a great deal for a few, for the majority of seriously overweight people, it is not a long enough treatment period to obtain significant weight loss and/or to maintain the loss they have achieved.

A second series, then, is essential to carry out maintenance of change procedures. At that point, further experience still would be necessary to ascertain whether the second series of meetings would be adequate to maintain the new life-style acquired by the patient.

The role of the patient in the second course, in addition to participant, would be as model or coleader of the group with new patients and/or as an aide to the group leader. They would be obliged to learn the principles sufficiently well to teach them to others. At the same time, the period of the external monitoring of their dieting, exercising, and environmental control of their eating would be extended another three months. The role shift also would make the group less boring. Furthermore, 8 to 10 weeks is, for some patients, insufficient to learn even the necessary behaviors to control the several aspects of their environment that is required for adequate weight control. However, 16 to 20 weeks, should be adequate to work on a large number of behaviors.

It may be possible to work on more behaviors from the behavioral checklist the first eight weeks by following the Stuart and Davis program more rigidly. Less choice is given to the patient in what is to be monitored and what is to be treated, and, therefore, less time is spent in group discussion obtaining appropriate targets for all the members. Initial experience with a more directive approach, in fact, led to more rapid selection of relevant targets.

It is quite clear that to follow this program the patients either must be highly organized individuals who readily can follow fairly complex instructions or must be people who can be taught to do so. Most, but not all, of our patients were middle-class with at least a high school background. As a rule, they were not well organized, and the instructions had to be tailored to their individual learning tempo. We found that too many demands placed too soon upon some clients resulted in their leaving the group. It is doubtful whether this approach would be useful at all with highly disorganized individuals.

In summary, although success in losing weight was high for students with a divergent clinical population suffering from a high level of overweight, group treatment promises only mixed results. If the clients are sufficiently well interested to remain in the group for a period of 16 or more weeks, they may be more likely to lose at a moderate or low rate and to maintain that loss. Only future research can ascertain who will remain and who will not. But, based on experience, one guess is that those who are well organized will do the best with this approach, as well as those for whom social reinforcement is as powerful as food.

16 Communication Skills Workshop[1]

MAINTAINING an enduring, mutually satisfying relationship is a difficult, often unsuccessful task for many couples. Increasing divorce rates and a steady proliferation of marriage manuals and books on alternative relationships attest to these difficulties. A substantial contributing factor appears to be in the area of communication. In 1973 the American Psychiatric Association reported that communication problems were evident in 85 percent of marriages judged dysfunctional. Similarly Beck and Jones (1973) note, "The areas of the marital relationship most frequently reported as problematic by help-seeking couples are communication and sex" (p. 148). Although sexual problems in recent years have been subject to considerable investigation resulting in relatively effective treatment programs (Masters and Johnson, 1970; Lobitz and LoPiccolo, 1972), surprisingly little is known about couple communication and how to increase its effectiveness.

In this chapter we develop a social learning framework in which the relationship between various attributes of communication and marital satisfaction are defined. This framework provides the context of a training program for couples called the Communication Skills Workshop (CSW), an educational program designed to teach couples general communication and problem-solving skills believed necessary for the maintenance of harmonious relationships.

[1]This chapter was coauthored by Stanley Witkin and Sheldon Rose and is based on a paper, "The Communication Skills Workshop," presented at the 15th annual meeting of the Council on Social Work Education, February 1976, in Philadelphia, Pennsylvania.

Although the extensive evaluation project of the CSW has not been completed at this writing, some descriptive data on case examples are available. These preliminary reports constituted part of the pilot testing and program development stage of the project. The workshop description in this chapter is based partly on information collected during this initial phase.

COUPLE COMMUNICATION

A widely accepted definition of communication has not been easy to formulate. The difficulties in achieving consensus are illustrated by the many articles written with the sole purpose of defining communication or clarifying existing definitions (Miller, 1966; Gerbner, 1966; Minter, 1968; Dance, 1970; Thayer, 1963). The abundance of literature on the subject has prompted one author (Dittman, 1972) to suggest that the task of definition in itself almost has become a subfield of communication!

Recognizing the difficulties that do exist, a "working definition" of this term is offered to provide a common framework within which the following discussion and workshop may be understood. In this case, our concern is with dyadic interpersonal communication within the context of marital relationships. Communication from this perspective is conceived of as a process whereby each partner assigns meaning to (interprets) stimuli he or she perceives as originating from his or her partner. Communication, therefore, is not viewed as the transmission of messages (although transmission may be attempted); instead, it results from the active interpretation of stimuli into meaningful symbols. The process aspect of this definition emphasizes the interrelatedness of messages. Each message unit interpreted can function as a stimulus for subsequent messages, a response to previous ones, or both. Furthermore, this view supports the contention of communication as an active, two-way process. Responsibility for communication effectiveness therefore rests with *both* persons involved in the communication process.

It follows from this description that communication need not be verbal, nor the product of conscious intent on an individual's part. In addition, manner and style in which messages are expressed will be influenced by the situational context in which they occur and the responses that may be elicited. For example, the physical setting, the number and relationships of others nearby, and previous encounters are some of the factors that can exert a modifying influence upon what one attempts to communicate, how one communicates, and how it is interpreted.

Communication per se is inevitable between dyadic partners (see Watzlawick, Beaven, and Jackson, 1967). Consistent with the above definition, the processing of stimuli into meaningful information is all that is necessary for communication to occur. Our concern then (and presumably the concern of couples) is with the quality, or "effectiveness," of communication. This effectiveness can be inferred largely from the result of a message, that is, the behavior exhibited by the interpreter as a result of the processing of stimuli (see Hartman, 1963). Effective communication can be conceived of as a consistency between the intentions of one partner (message source) and the behavior of the other partner (message interpreter). Pace and Boren (1972) note that this conceptualization includes any message the interpreter reports (verbally or nonverbally) as consistent with the source's intent, even if the interpreter does not behave in the intended manner. For example, if an individual requests a glass of water from his/her partner and the partner replies that he/she is too busy to honor the request, communication still is effective. If, on the other hand, the interpreter begins to mop the floor after the same request, we would assume either that the message was not perceived at all or that the interpretation differed markedly from the intention of the source.

Consistency between intention and interpretation is related to communication accuracy. Although the need for some amount of accuracy is intuitively obvious, it is not sufficient as the sole criterion of communication effectiveness in couples. Two limitations of the accuracy criterion are evident: it does not account for messages in which the source reports little or no awareness of intent; and there is some evidence to suggest that as one's feelings towards a communication source grows stronger, there is a tendency to distort one's interpretation of the message (see Mehrabian and Reed, 1968). Thus one would not expect the happiest couple to be more accurate in their communication than the unhappiest, although the distortion would be in a positive direction for the happy couple and a negative direction for the unhappy one.

Awareness of intent is also important to how reasonableness of a communication explanation of marital distress is. If distressed couples attempt to express messages that their partners will evaluate negatively, they may in fact be communicating effectively. In contrast, if their intentions are as positive as are those of couples from nondistressed marriages, this would support the notion of ineffective communication in these relationships. Unfortunately, little research has been conducted on this topic. In an unpublished study, Gottman (1975) found that couples from distressed and nondistressed marriages did not differ in their communication intent but that distressed couples were not interpreted as positively as they intended.

Two additional factors related to effective couple communication may account for these apparent difficulties: openness and quality. Communication openness refers to the use and acceptance of feedback by a couple. Feedback is a process by which a couple receives information about their communication and its effect upon each other. This information may be utilized as a stimulus for changing behavior or as a means of counteracting change and maintaining the status quo (Watzlawick and others, 1967). Although all couples probably exchange feedback to some extent, *how* it is expressed will likely affect its interpretation, which in turn will influence how it is utilized.

The process of how feedback—or more generally—messages, are communicated is termed communication quality, the third criterion. The most important factor appears to be the positive and negative quality of messages exchanged. This phenomenon seems to be related closely to the amounts of satisfaction that couples experience in their relationship, and it greatly influences their use of other communication procedures (for example, feedback) believed necessary for effective communication. It should be noted that our three criteria of effective couple communication—accuracy, openness, and quality—in practice are not discrete but closely interrelated. For example, it has been demonstrated that communication accuracy is correlated with the availability of feedback to the source (see Mehrabran and Reed, 1968). Similarly, the manner in which messages are expressed will affect the willingness of couples to permit direct feedback. Elaboration of the importance of positive and negative messages in the communicative behavior of couples will be the concern of much of this chapter. The emphasis upon these messages stems from their central role in the maintenance of mutually satisfying dyadic relationships. Before investigating this relationship, the concept of marital satisfaction should be examined.

MARITAL SATISFACTION

Marital satisfaction is a complex, multidimensional concept that (like communication) has been viewed from many different perspectives (Burr, 1973). Although use of such terms as "marital satisfaction" and "marital happiness" has been criticized severely (Hicks and Platt, 1971; Barry, 1970), investigation of this relationship factor seems warranted, given the multitude of couples experiencing problems and seeking assistance in these areas (Knox, 1972; Greene, 1970; Renne, 1970; Landis, 1963).

Research from various sources has indicated that aside from the difficulties engendered by divorce and separation, a critical problem exists with those intact households characterized by unhappy or dissatisfied mates. Unfortunately, children often are hurt most by such relationships. Reviewing the literature concerning the effects of divorce on children, Udry (1971) concludes "that children from happy marriages are better adjusted than children from divorced marriages, but those from divorced parents are better adjusted than those from parents whose marriages are intact but unhappy" (p. 458). Other research has reinforced the idea that the quality of a relationship is a more crucial contributory factor to the problems of children than the completeness of the family unit (Tait and Hodges, 1962; Rutter, 1972). Children, however, are not the only casualties of discordant marriages. Admissions of adults to mental hospitals and the occurrence of alcoholism are two manifestations of problems produced in part by marital stresses (Beisser and Glasser, 1968; Gerard and Saenger, 1966; Cahalan, Cusin, and Crossley, 1969). Perhaps the most promising approach to understanding marital satisfaction is exemplified in the research by Wills, Weiss, and Patterson (1974) in their study of behavioral determinants of global ratings of marital satisfaction. Seven married couples made daily recordings for two weeks of instrumental and affectional behaviors and how pleasing or displeasing these behaviors were. Instrumental behaviors are "those necessary for the marriage to survive as a social and economic unit" (p. 803)—for example, "spouse cleaned the bedroom." Behaviors serving to maintain interpersonal attraction between mates "by conveying acceptance, affection, and approval" are defined as affectional (p. 803)—for example, "spouse said I looked nice." In addition to the behavioral recordings, couples completed global ratings of satisfaction each day. The results suggested that negative behaviors had the greatest influence on global satisfaction ratings, especially negative instrumental behaviors. Pleasurable behaviors interacted with sex differences; affectional behaviors were more important to wives and instrumental behaviors to husbands. Another important conclusion was that pleasurable and displeasurable behaviors were independent of each other. These results have important implications for training, in view of the almost exclusive focus on increasing positive behaviors in most behavioral counseling methods (Stuart, 1969; Weiss and others, 1973; Wieman, Shoulders, and Farr, 1974).

Communication Effectiveness and Marital Satisfaction

The importance of effective communication to the maintenance of harmonious relationships is widely held by clinicians and researchers alike (Satir, 1964, 1972; Haley, 1963; Stuart, 1974; Lederer and Jackson, 1968; Udry, 1971; Raush, Barry, Hertel, and Swain, 1974). Despite this consensus on the critical role of communication processes, it has yet to be demonstrated whether communication difficulties are the cause or result of relationship problems. It does appear, however, that a strong relationship between measures of communication effectiveness and marital satisfaction does exist. Studies by Navran (1967), Murphy and Mendelson (1973), and Kind (1968) indicate significantly high correlations between self-report measures of effective communication and marital satisfaction. A similar relationship was found by Kahn (1970) between observed nonverbal communication and marital satisfaction.

The specific behavioral components of dyadic communication corresponding to reports of marital satisfaction have not yet been isolated and identified. Promising research, however, has been reported in the general area of communication quality, particularly the positive and aversive properties of message exchanges. This research, although from diverse sources, consistently suggests that marital satisfaction is closely related to the use of positive forms of communication. Some of these studies are noted below.

Levinger and Senn (1967) in a study of 32 couples—15 in counseling and 17 not known to have serious problems—found that marital satisfaction was more strongly associated with a higher proportion of pleasant than unpleasant disclosures. Navran (1967) studied the responses of 24 happy and 24 unhappy couples recruited from a retail clerks' union to two self-report inventories: The Locke Marital Relationship Inventory and the Primary Communication Inventory. Of those items capable of discriminating between the two groups, the most powerful was the higher frequency (among happily married couples) of discussions regarding pleasant experiences during the day. In an investigation of the communication patterns associated with high and low marital adjustment, Mendelson (1970) found that highly adjusted couples, although more rigid in their emotional communication than those less adjusted, expressed this rigidity in terms of positive emotional messages. Couples in the highly adjusted group also had significantly smaller differences in their positive emotional exchanges; the lower adjusted couples revealed a higher frequency of one spouse being more negative.

Further support of the importance of positive and negative messages in marital satisfaction comes from a study by Thomas, Walter, and O'Flaherty (1974), in which they used a verbal problem checklist to assess the difficulties of couples complaining of problems in communication. These couples were characterized, among other things, by too frequent negative evaluations, excessive disagreements, and too infrequent positive talk. Finally, Birchler, Weiss, and Vincent (1975) analyzed the rate of positive and negative messages exchanged between spouses judged distressed and nondistressed. Couples' interactions were analyzed by collecting behavioral data in both the laboratory and home environment. In the laboratory setting, couples were observed in free conversation and a problem-solving task. Their interactions were coded through a 29-category coding system defining positive and negative message units and problem-solving behaviors. Results revealed distressed couples to exchange significantly greater negative messages and fewer positive ones than the nondistressed couples. Similar results were found in the home environment where distressed spouses reported a significantly lower proposition of pleasing to displeasing behaviors.

Taken together, these studies (although not without methodological shortcomings) provide some support for the contention that positive and negative message exchange is an important component of couple communication related to marital satisfaction. These findings can be integrated readily into a social learning framework of communication training, which provides the basis for the Communication Skills Workshop.

SOCIAL LEARNING THEORY AND
COMMUNICATION

Dyadic communication, like other behaviors, is viewed as a learned skill, subject to modification by various contingencies that may impinge upon it. Among the most important of these contingencies is the communicative behavior of one's partner (Skinner, 1957). The amount, quality, and interpretation of messages within the marital dyad is believed influenced to a marked degree by the consequences—real or anticipated—associated with various messages. Also, it is affected by the association of messages with emotional and evaluative responses.

Language is a powerful agent of behavior change, capable of functioning both as conditioned stimuli eliciting emotional responses and as reinforcing stimuli following responses (Staats, 1972). From a social learning perspective, communication between spouses provides an exchange of stimuli that is interpreted in light of one's learning history, especially with one's partner. Through their association (direct or vicarious) with various consequences, words take on the property of discriminative stimuli for affective and instrumental behaviors (Hartman, 1963; Staats, 1972). The consequences associated with spousal interactions provide both information for future interactions and incentive to engage or not to engage in them. How messages are expressed—what words and gestures are used—therefore can have important implications for the response of the interpreter. The reinforcing or aversive quality of message exchanges in a relationship can, therefore, result over time in characteristic patterns of responding between partners (Birchler and others, 1975). Attempts to control or change one's partner will tend to reflect these patterns.

Two common interaction patterns have been identified by Patterson and Reid (1970) and Patterson and Hops (1972) as reciprocity and coercion. In reciprocity, there is generally an equitable exchange of social reinforcers between partners. Coercive patterns are characterized by the use of aversive stimuli to control or change each other's behavior. This latter pattern is assumed to arise in marital relationships when spouses demand immediate change in some behavior of their partners. Although the use of positive (reinforcing) change procedures might reduce the probability of conflict in this situation, these are not often applied. Instead, according to Patterson and Hops, partners tend to rely on aversive behaviors (shouting, nagging), which are reinforced through eventual compliance. In addition, partners often learn that sending delaying or avoidance messages ("I'll fix it later") results in the cessation of the aversive stimuli. This consequent negative reinforcement maintains such responses. The reciprocal reinforcement experienced by both partners increases the probability of similar interactions reoccurring when they are confronted with other problematic situations.

In conclusion, communication is viewed as learned behavior, which to a large extent regulates and directs the interaction of the dyad. Messages exchanged by partners may take on various stimulus and response properties, evoking cognitive, emotional, and overt behavioral reactions. These message exchanges provide guidelines and incentive for future interactions. Since many couples rely on aversive control techniques in eliciting change from their partners, a useful strategy might be to train couples in positive message exchange. Combining these procedures with various problem-solving techniques provides the strategy for the reduction and successful negotiation of conflicts.

Contribution of Behavioral Treatment to the CSW

Successful modification of marital interaction through the use of behavioral methodology (Liberman, 1970; Rappaport and Harrell, 1972; Stuart, 1969; Azrin, Naster, and Jones, 1973; Weiss and others, 1973) has been described frequently. Most of these approaches are based upon increasing positive behaviors exchanged between the spouses. To this end, couples often are taught negotiating skills to help arrive at equitable behavior exchanges and contracting skills to help maintain the agreed-upon changes.

Innovative writings of Gerald Patterson, Robert Weiss, their associates at the University of Oregon, and Richard Stuart have been influential in the development of the Communication Skills Workshop. These authors have recognized the necessity of treating the communicative behaviors of couples and have incorporated communication training into their marital treatment programs.

One characteristic of communication emphasized in behavioral approaches is that of specificity. This entails describing events and behaviors in observable terms and operationalizing global or vague messages. Weiss and others (1973) point out that using behaviorally specific messages enables couples to determine expectations that—due to their vagueness—may be impossible to fulfill (for example, the expectation of being a "considerate" husband). Specificity also helps to clarify the utilitarian value of a behavior. Furthermore, they note that specificity can help eliminate "mind-reading" statements in which one partner claims to "know" what the other is thinking or feeling.

Negotiating skills are useful in mutual behavior exchanges. Stuart (1974) has presented procedures for helping couples to examine their decision-making processes and how power is distributed in their relationship. Most authors agree that specificity and positive phrasing of change requests are crucial features to the negotiating process. Helpful procedures for problem-solving have been advanced by D'Zurilla and Goldfried (1971). These authors reviewed the literature related to problem solving and suggested procedures to facilitate this process based upon the empirical evidence. Many of these procedures (for example, generating alternatives) are intimately tied to the communicative skills utilized in a relationship. Contracting utilizes written communication to help couples implement behavior change agreements. Besides holding each partner accountable for his or her messages, contracting helps couples to avoid the ambiguities, forgetfulness, and misunderstandings that often characterize verbal agreements (see Weiss, Birchler, and Vincent, 1974 for an excellent discussion of different types of contracts and their various uses).

Feedback is utilized throughout the negotiating process as a means of ascertaining progress. In the CSW, the use of both verbal and nonverbal feedback is taught and its interrelationship with specificity and positive messages stressed. Specifically, the value of feedback is limited when used in isolation from skills related to positive message formation and specificity.

COMMUNICATION SKILLS WORKSHOP

The CSW is an educational, group training program for couples. It emphasizes the teaching of a general set of skills to improve communication, rather than focusing on the resolution of specific problems. In this sense, the CSW has a preventive orientation, although couples may use the skills learned to ameliorate present difficulties. The three basic communication skills taught in training are positive message exchange, behavioral specificity, and feedback. These lay the groundwork for effective problem solving and conflict resolution. Didactic and modeling presentations by the workshop leaders and structured exercises performed by the participants provide opportunities for extensive learning and practice in these skills.

Groups of three to five couples are trained for six sessions (each two hours long) by male and female coleaders. Three methods guide the presentation of concepts and skills to the group: short didactic discussions, modeling by the leaders, and role-play practice by the group. Situations employed for communication practice include those developed by the authors and utilized in all workshops and those developed by the couples from their own experiences.

The group context provides participants with additional sources of potential learning. Couples serve as models for the acquisition of new skills and provide positive and corrective feedback to each other. The use of models is particularly important for learning in training programs of short duration. Bandura (1974) states that "even in instances where it is possible to establish new response patterns through other means, the process of acquisition can be considerably shortened by providing appropriate models" (p. 3). Additional research has suggested that modeling plus instruction may be more effective in increasing group verbal behavior than either of these techniques used alone (Whalen, 1969).

Group feedback is "shaped" by the instructors throughout the program.

Members gradually are required to provide behaviorally specific feedback on the skills of other couples. In the early sessions, the leaders structure the feedback so that it is mostly positive. This helps to promote group attractiveness and provides added incentive to practice the skills taught. During the latter half of the workshop, critical feedback also is encouraged, with the stipulation that it be accompanied by a constructive alternative. Encouraging feedback of this type helps members to increase their observation skills and provides valuable practice in a useful communication procedure. Homework assignments structure additional practice for the couples and are an important means of transferring skills learned in the workshop to each couple's natural environment. All assignments are monitored by the couple on "discussion sheets" handed out at the sessions, and all sessions begin with couple demonstrations of the skills assigned for practice at home.

Shaping procedures are evidenced both within and across the sessions. Each session follows in a logical sequence from the preceding one, adding to its content and teaching more complex applications of skills. For example, the beginning sessions are devoted to teaching various prerequisites for effective communication and such basic skills as specificity. Later sessions focus upon the application of those skills to problematic situations. This same type of logical progression is followed within each session as well. Skills taught in the early part of the session typically are those more likely to be present within a couple's behavioral repertoire. Gradually, more structured, complex procedures are introduced. Similarly, role-play situations, initially of low conflict potential, are subsequently replaced by more "serious" relationship issues.

Transfer and maintenance procedures are used, in addition to those already described. Group cohesiveness, deliberately fostered in the initial sessions, is curtailed by the couple focus of the group exercises and the increasingly personal nature of the topics. Role-plays and rehearsals range across a wide variety of situations, providing couples with diverse practice opportunities. Situations planned by the coleaders introduce to the couples unpredictability, thus simulating their extragroup interactions. In later sessions, couples are required to provide more of their own situations, thereby giving them increased responsibility for their training. Finally, repeated practice trials and the teaching of general principles underlying the skills further serve to increase the probability of transfer and maintenance of learning (for a review of these and other principles, see pp. 154–163).

Program Description

The first workshop session serves as a general orientation to the rest of the program and an introduction to the concept of effective communication as applied to couples. Content relates to prerequisite behaviors for effective communication beginning with attending procedures. Session two continues with preliminary concepts, focusing on increasing message clarity and accurate interpretations. The latter half of the session is devoted to methods for developing and increasing positive communication. Session three further develops the theme of positive messages and a variety of procedures for couples to practice is introduced. Session four begins to apply the skills and concepts learned in the first three sessions to areas of decision-making and conflict. To this end, negotiation training is introduced. Session five continues the negotiation process with additional training in contracting procedures. Nonverbal communication is the focus of the rest of the session. Session six provides couples with additional practice of their skills in more difficult situations. Selected topics, such as communication avoidance around certain subjects, are discussed and dealt with. Finally, procedures for maintaining skills over time are taught and practiced. A more detailed description of the procedures in each of these follows.

SESSION ONE

Procedures are taught to elicit and maintain attention, ranging from common everyday types of behavior—for example, eye contact—to more highly structured techniques—for example, talk times. The main procedures are as follows.

1. Asking for a response. By requiring a response from the intended message recipient, the probability of his/her attention is increased (Hartman, 1963). Phrasing messages in a manner requiring responses, as, for example, through questions, is discussed and practiced by the couples.

2. Paraphrasing—restating a message in one's own words—is a useful attending behavior especially for important topics. Couples are given a few minutes to discuss experiences occurring to them during the day. Each practices paraphrasing after the speaker indicates the expression of a complete thought.

3. "Talk times" (Stuart, 1974) are presented as a method of structuring a "communication only" time period. This prearranged time interval is devoted to discussion of a particular topic without outside distractions. Emotionally charged issues, conflicts, and topics requiring lengthy discussions are particularly well suited for this procedure. Talk times are used in the session assignments as a way of devoting a specified amount of time to skill practice.

SESSION TWO

Ambiguous messages and their role in misunderstandings are discussed. Methods of rendering messages specific are modeled, and couples are given practice in changing general statements to specific ones ("Stop being so lazy" becomes "I'd like you to mow the lawn"). Paraphrasing and questioning are then reintroduced and briefly practiced from the perspective of clarifying messages.

A special case of specificity used in response to an expectation—for example, "I'd like you to change your attitude"—is operationalizing (Weiss and others, 1973). Involved here is an attempt to describe exactly how an expectation can be met. Once the expectation is "put into operation," the initial message sender evelutes his/her partner's response.

A role-reversal procedure is taught as a message clarification technique especially with emotionally tinged, unclear messages. The basic sequence followed is: 1) an individual describes some situation and attendant emotions; 2) message recipient takes first person's role and "replays" original message as he/she perceived it; and 3) original message source provides feedback on interpretation. Couples are encouraged actually to try to "be" the other person when switching roles. Accordingly, they are instructed to speak in the first person and utilize perceived nonverbal cues.

The focus of the workshop shifts slightly at this point toward analyzing negative communication patterns, decreasing their occurrence, and increasing positive interactions. A "coercive" interaction is modeled by the leaders, and its various features (demand for immediate change, mutual reinforcement of aversive behaviors) and consequences (likelihood of negative change efforts being repeated, original issue unresolved) are pointed out. A second interaction, based upon positive message exchanges, is again modeled, and the procedures followed above are repeated.

To increase their repertoire and use of positive messages, members are asked to list on cards all the ways in which their partner communicates that make them feel good, loved, and so on. Categories of positive messages (appreciation, understanding, compliment, positive feelings) assist couples in formulating their "pleasure list." It is requested that these lists be placed in a prominent place in the home (for example, on the door of the refrigerator) and added to periodically.

SESSION THREE

This session begins with a role-reversal exercise for changing unpleasant communication patterns into positive ones. Group members identify communication patterns that they find unpleasant. They use role-reversal to illustrate this pattern to their partner. After some feedback, the role is replayed, however, this time demonstrating how the individual would *like* his or her partner to communicate in the same type of situation. If the partner positively evaluates this new method of communicating, he/she then rehearses it with his/her partner.

Even with all the previous emphasis on positive messages, it is certain that couples occasionally will use negative messages in their interactions. The following procedures were designed to teach responses to negative messages that would decrease the probability of a reciprocal negative exchange sequence.

What, how, why—couples are taught to view requests or demands for change from a "what" (specificity) and "how" (operationalizing) perspective, rather than from a "why" point of view. Various problems leading from an insistence on knowing why a behavior occurred are explained and illustrated. For example, each "why" may lead to another, as in many instances the reasons for a person's behavior are unknowable.

Responding to content—in some instances, aversive interchanges can be avoided by responding only to the content of a message. Naturally, this depends upon the clarity and intensity of the feelings expressed and the importance of the message. Role-playing exercises allow couples to practice this procedure.

Positive Statement Procedure (PSP)—Azrin, Naster, and Jones (1973) devised this as a part of their reciprocity training package for distressed couples. Couples are taught to use nonresponse to a negative message as a cue to their partners to either add a positive message to the negative statement ("You did a lousy job on the dishes" becomes "You usually do such a good job cleaning up that I was surprised to see some of these dishes not clean"); or rephrase the message in a positive way ("The dishes seem to need additional washing").

Selective communication—Stuart (1974) suggests partners ask themselves three questions before disclosing potentially unpleasant information to their partners: Is it true? Is it timely? Is it constructive? These three criteria are broken down further into message problems associated with each. Examples include improper use of the verb "to be," always or never classifications, and labeling. Couples are given practice in recognizing these communication problems by observing each other's interactions. Supervised discussions of various topics provide opportunities for communication without these pitfalls, and subsequent reinforcement from the leaders and group.

SESSION FOUR

Couples are taught to apply the skills learned in the first half of the workshop to areas of decision-making and conflict. Identification of actual or potential trouble spots in the relationship is aided through the use of a small chart, which each partner completes. The chart indicates various areas of potential conflict, for example, finances, sex, and whether decisions in each are made equally, unequally by agreement, or unequally without agreement (see Stuart, 1974). Another section allows couples to rate negotiations around a particular area, thus serving as a measure of progress.

Once problematic areas have been defined, guidelines for negotiation of problems are taught and rehearsed. A five-step structured negotiation procedure is presented (two steps in this session).

Information gathering. The first part of the negotiation process involves the gathering of sufficient information about the problem. This is further broken down into five main components: a) recognition of the problem; b) description of the nature of the problem; c) speculation of causes; d) possible effects upon the relationship; and e) future implications for the relationship.

Generation of alternatives. This step, extrapolated from the problem-solving literature (for example, see D'Zurilla and Goldfried, 1973), is based on the idea that quantity (of alternatives) breeds quality. Couples are encouraged to be creative and suspend all judgment while formulating a written list of possible solutions.

SESSION FIVE

The remaining three steps of the negotiation process are presented and practiced.

Evaluation of alternatives. Short- and long-range consequences of alternatives are considered within a framework of compromise. Termination of a conflict is proposed as a desired end, rather than one partner getting his/her way.

Planning. In this stage, couples begin to formulate tentative plans for carrying out the alternatives they decided upon. Use of operationalizing is stressed, with attention to specifying details of the proposed plan.

Formalization of the final plan is presented in terms of a contract (initially written). Various forms of contracts are presented, and advantages and disadvantages discussed. Contracts help couples to specify the reward/cost ratio for their individual behaviors in the plan, and appropriate compensation for their efforts then can be agreed upon. For example, a plan for handling finances might include one partner paying all the monthly bills. Performance of this task may "earn" a backrub from his or her partner. As can be seen from this example, couples are encouraged to exchange positive behaviors for completing their agreed-upon tasks.

Two types of contracts are discussed with the group: those in which the problem centers on behaviors of each other (for example, lack of affection, more time together); and those viewed as mutual problems by the couple (for example, finances, relatives). Finally, renegotiation and evaluation clauses are presented as essential to every contract (see pp. 92–95 for more detailed discussion of contracts).

Evaluation of the plan. The importance of specifying *observable* changes desired from the couple's plan is crucial to this final negotiation stage. Couples practice formulating specific criteria for successful fulfillment of their contracts.

Nonverbal communication exercises focusing on the problem of "mixed messages" follows the presentation of the negotiation process. Mixed messages are those in which there is incongruity between the verbal and nonverbal aspects of the message, for example, saying "I'm not angry" through gritted teeth. Various techniques for dealing with these messages include: 1) attending only to the verbal content (if positive); 2) interpreting ambiguous messages positively; for example, a smile is interpreted as happiness rather than sarcasm; 3) checking with message source for further clarification; and 4) using role-reversal techniques.

SESSION SIX

The last session continues to teach couples how to apply their skills to problematic areas of their relationship. Methods and practice geared toward maintenance and transfer of skills are emphasized.

Taboo areas are defined as high-anxiety topics usually involving implicit contracts between the partners to *not* discuss a particular topic. These areas remain sources of ambiguous messages and conflicts, since they are not made explicit and discussed. Procedures for "neutralizing" a taboo area include: 1) recognition of a taboo area (as through the previously discussed chart in session four) and breaking of avoidance contracts—this step is accomplished by addressing one's anxieties, utilizing communication skills *intra*personally, and proceeding in small steps (shaping); 2) setting up a "talk time" to discuss the taboo area, following an agreed-upon agenda to help stay on task; 3) approaching the area slowly and, as above, in small steps through a series of talk times; 4) recognition of taboo "traps" (e.g., "mind reading") and avoidance of these traps by behavioral specificity and other procedures to increase understanding previously learned.

Relationship rules to help keep conflicts at manageable levels and to foster the use of learned skills are presented. Such stimulus control techniques as limiting arguments to specific times and/or places are suggested, as well as the creation of certain rooms ("love rooms") where *only* positive interactions can occur.

Stuart (1974) has discussed three levels of conflict representing increasing levels of deterioration: the issue-specific level, the personal level, and the relationship level. Couples practice keeping arguments on the issue-specific level and learn to recognize movement to the other levels.

The final exercise provides practice in dealing with new areas of conflicts. Structured role plays, in which each partner receives potentially conflictual information from his or her partner, are performed by the couples. This procedure simulates the occurrence of conflicts in each couple's actual extra-group interaction and provides useful practice in utilizing skills learned in the workshop.

Case Example

A group consisting of three couples provides an illustration of the possible effects of the workshop. Social work graduate students trained in the program served as group leaders. Couples were recruited locally and reflected the high educational level typically found in a university community.

Couples were evaluated a week prior to beginning training and again one week and six weeks after training. Two self-report measures, the Marital Communication Inventory (Bienvenu, 1970) and the Locke Marital Adjustment Questionnaire (Locke, 1951), were used to assess the general areas of communication effectiveness and marital satisfaction respectively. In addition, behavioral data based upon each couple's interaction in two conflict situations were obtained utilizing the Marital Interaction Coding System (Hops, Wills, Patterson, and Weiss, 1972). The MICS records interactive behaviors in the areas of positive and aversive messages and problem-solving behaviors.[2]

In addition to the measures mentioned above, couples completed a participant evaluation form immediately after the last training session. Results of these three questionnaires are described below.

MCI

All three couples made overall gains on the MCI at the posttest (see Table 16.1). At the follow-up session two of the three still maintained increases over

Table 16.1. Marital Communication Inventory Scores.

Couple	Test	Male	Female	Mean	Mean Differences*
1	pre	113	121	117	
	post	121	120	120.5	+ 3.5
	follow-up	117	115	116	− 1.0
2	pre	101	81	91	
	post	103	93	98	+ 7.0
	follow-up	109	94	101.5	+10.5
3	pre	101	88	94.5	
	post	111	103	107	+12.5
	follow-up	105	95	100	+ 5.5
Group Mean	pre	100.8			
	post	108.5			+ 7.7
	follow-up	105.5			+ 4.7

*Refers to pre-post and pre-follow-up differences.

[2]Unfortunately, problems with the audiovisual equipment rendered the tapes uncodable.

their preworkshop scores, and one couple remained at approximately the same level. Of interest is that this latter couple scored high on the inventory *before* any training, suggesting a possible "ceiling effect" on their scores. Couples 2 and 3 showed gains of 10.5 and 5.5 at follow-up, indicating some positive change in aspects of their communication. Examination of male and female scores separately shows an almost identical gain at follow-up, although males were a little more than eight points higher initially.

LOCKE

Changes in marital satisfaction were substantial (see Table 16.2). Interestingly, although two of the three couples showed only a slight gain at posttesting, all couples gained at least eight points by follow-up. This increase in scores six weeks after training was predicted on the belief that the effects of the skills learned would not translate immediately into higher global satisfaction ratings. Experience has shown that familiar patterns of communication are not modified easily. Assimilation into daily interactions of the skills learned therefore would not be unlikely to occur immediately after training.

EVALUATIONS

Evaluation forms were completed anonymously by all participants at the end of session six. These forms provided ratings for specific procedures as well as general comments on the value of the workshop. In general, couples evalu-

Table 16.2. Locke Marital Questionnaire Scores.

Couple	Test	Male	Female	Mean	Mean Differences*
1	pre	105	107	106	
	post	110	103	106.5	+ 0.5
	follow-up	114	114	114	+ 8.0
2	pre	93	101	97	
	post	101	111	106	+ 9.0
	follow-up	109	122	115.5	+18.5
3	pre	107	99	103	
	post	107	100	103.5	+ 0.5
	follow-up	122	119	120.5	+17.5
Group Means	pre	102			
	post	105.3			+ 3.3
	follow-up	116.6			+14.6

Refers to pre-post and pre-follow-up differences.

ated the workshop as a useful learning experience. The use of specificity and positive messages were viewed as particularly important. Teaching by modeling, role-playing, and at-home assignments also were evaluated favorably.

Discussion

Preliminary findings suggest that the CSW might be a useful training program for couples wishing to enhance their communication and conflict-resolution skills. Presumably, the acquisition and use of these skills help reduce the number of conflicts between partners and help keep those that do emerge at a manageable level. Of course, the data presented here are meager and continued research is necessary. An extensive evaluation program currently is being undertaken to determine the program's effectiveness compared to other methods of training and with couples of various educational and occupational levels. Once accomplished, investigations of isolated program components can be tested for effectiveness.

The CSW is not a therapeutic program for highly distressed couples. Early experience revealed that couples experiencing serious discord had difficulty with many of the exercises and homework assignments. This in turn detracted from the learning of other group members.

As an educational program the CSW has the potential of reaching a wider population than mental health services usually do. The general nature of the skills taught makes it suitable for use in educational as well as in community service agencies. The CSW is prevention oriented, since it attempts to train couples prior to the onset of serious relationship difficulties. Training focuses on enhancing the positive qualities of a relationship while providing skills to prevent serious conflicts and to deal effectively with those that do occur.

Couples of limited educational backgrounds might have difficulty with some of the concepts and terminology of the CSW. In these situations, the instructors must simplify the language and spend additional time on such key concepts as specificity. Such modifications might require the addition of an extra session or longer sessions.

Another difficulty occasionally encountered involves hesitancy on the part of a couple or couples to engage in role-plays (see pp. 117–118). Some methods of overcoming such "resistance" are to reemphasize the importance of role-plays for learning, additional modeling by the leaders, modeling by a couple who are not hesitant to role-play and praise by the leaders. Alleviation of a couple's anxiety over role-playing can be accomplished by having a leader initially play the part of one partner or having the couple role-play privately.

It must be stressed that this chapter, although providing some background information on the program, is not intended to prepare workshop instructors. Knowledge is presumed of at least elementary concepts of social learning and interpersonal communication models. Leaders of past groups found it necessary to devote approximately 20 to 30 hours to training, of which approximately half was supervised by a trained instructor. Video tapes of past groups and role plays of the various procedures were helpful in training. Finally, it is our current belief that at least one "apprentice" group must be conducted before a trainer is qualified to teach these skills.

17 Behavioral Supervision in Groups

WHETHER an individual learns social skills or professional skills, the laws of learning are the same. For these reasons, a model of supervision has been developed that is quite similar to the one used in the various treatment groups thus far covered. In this chapter we will discuss the format of teaching professional skills in groups and the results of some of the author's initial experiences.

The purpose of supervision in clinical settings is primarily to assist professionals in improving their own therapeutic skills and helping them to resolve immediate and long-range problems with clients. A number of models have been proposed as to how supervision should be carried out both with individuals and in the context of the small group, but few have suggested a method by which the effectiveness of the supervisory approach can be determined. The establishment of explicit learning goals for those supervised would provide a basis for estimating whether or not a given individual has achieved those goals. The overall approach can be evaluated if most participants achieve the learning goals that they and their supervisors have determined are relevant targets of change. Because of its specificity, a behavioral approach lends itself to explicit goal formulation. Procedures can be evaluated in terms of their effectiveness in facilitating goal attainment. Furthermore, a behavioral approach offers the supervisor and the practitioner a wide variety of ongoing data-gathering procedures, which provide information for evaluating the effectiveness of the training as it progresses.

A behavioral approach, moreover, gives the supervisor behavioral procedures derived from learning theory for the training of the supervisee. Such procedures as reinforcement, contingency contracting, discrimination training, shaping, modeling, behavior rehearsal, and desensitization add tested learning procedures to the supervisor's repertoire of didactic and cognitive skills.

If the behavioral approach to supervision is carried out in groups, several additional factors may facilitate goal achievement. Since no supervisor has a monopoly on all ideas as to how a person should function in clinical settings, a multiperson unit provides a multisource of suggestions and experiences upon which each person in the group can draw for client assessment or treatment planning. The supervisory group serves as an exemplary model, which can be used as a point-of-departure for the supervisees in their own groups. The supervisory group offers varied role-players in modeling and behavior rehearsal situations. And, finally, it gives each participant the possibility of sharing in the planning for a large number of situations far beyond the limited scope of any one person's immediate experience.

The purpose of this chapter is to describe a behavioral approach to group supervision, the major principles involved in carrying it out, the major problems encountered, the major data-collection procedures used to evaluate its effectiveness, and the preliminary results of several projects in the application of the approach. The chapter is designed for the staffs of social and therapeutic agencies and institutions serving clients with behavior problems. It suggests a format for supervision in mental health and child guidance clinics; in schools for social workers, counselors, and psychologists; for staff of social service departments of hospitals; for counseling personnel in universities; for the staff of resident treatment centers; for institutional staff who work with the mentally retarded; and for supervisors of student units in schools of social work and departments of psychology and counseling. To be applicable immediately, the organizations should be making use of behavioral methods with their clients or patients. However, where this is not the major orientation, this chapter may provide a basis for comparison.

Experience with many different types of supervisory groups serves as background for the discussion of this approach. These groups include the author's own student units, six groups of experienced practitioners who participate in a supervisory group as part of courses in behavior modification, and two simulated supervisory groups that were part of a course in group treatment. Also discussed will be the results of a pilot study with six of the short-term groups for experienced practitioners.

Before describing the content of the approach, we will first deal with organizational questions concerning group formation, group size, staff ratio, number of meetings, and so forth, which must be resolved prior to the first meeting of the group.

ORGANIZATION FOR GROUP SUPERVISION

In the groups under discussion (those organized by the author), all partici-pants either had already been trained in behavior modification or were follow-ing a course concurrent with the supervisory program. Some theoretical training is necessary to give the members a common background and to avoid extended theoretical discussions. Similarity in task and formal agency role does not appear necessary.

The size of the groups ranged from 5 to 9 participants. The largest groups could not allow each person to discuss at least one problem of his or her own every session. However, if the sessions had been frequent enough, this would not have been a problem. The groups met once a week to once a month. However, it is clear that to have sufficient time in the beginning to identify relevant problems, meetings as often as once or twice a week are preferable. Meetings can be less frequent as members gain competence in assessment, in raising relevant questions, and in treatment planning. The meetings usually last two hours, although, because of their intensity, the periods are too long without a break. It seems necessary to have such a long meeting in the early sessions because of the vast quantity of work to be performed. Later, shorter sessions may be sufficient.

The staff usually consists of one supervisor, although it is possible to use a cosupervisor, especially as a training procedure in which the cosupervisor is phased into the leadership of the program. The staff also may include one or more observers, who function as the collectors of interactional data in the group. Where observation is part of a supervisory training program, observers may be promoted to coleadership. The supervisor does not necessarily con-tinue to chair all the meetings; often this task is distributed among the mem-bers (see p. 145 for a discussion of this procedure).

When such a group is part of an agency structure, it probably is a continu-ous group. However, the projects on which this chapter is based lasted only between five and six sessions. In each case, it was clear that additional sessions would have been useful, as evidenced by responses on the final evaluation and the desired behavioral changes that the members had not yet completely achieved.

THE BEHAVIORAL APPROACH

Structure of the Program

Basically, the program is designed to facilitate problem-solving skills, to find solutions to specific problems that the participants are having in their groups or with individual clients, to develop specific therapist skills, and to eliminate those patterns of behavior that impede the attainment of treatment goals. To attain these general purposes, the initial meetings are highly structured. Goals for each meeting are developed initially by the supervisor in consultation with the group members; an agenda, which facilitates the attainment of those goals, is designed, and evaluation by the participants, observers, and the supervisor takes place each session. Two types of problems usually are considered at each session. The first is situational problems that require assistance from the supervisor and group members for dealing with a unique configuration of circumstances in one situation. Often the given person is provided with information, advice, encouragement, and clarification of the problem, on the basis of which he or she decides what to do. This is usually dealt with only in one session and monitored by the group at a subsequent session to see what happened. The second type of problem is concerned with a leadership or therapist behavior that each participant decides he or she must learn to increase or decrease in frequency to facilitate the attainment of the clients' treatment goals. Since the identification, monitoring, and training program for modification of this problem occurs over several meetings, it is referred to as a "long-range target." Initial experience with supervisory groups leads to the conclusion that time must be spent at each meeting for dealing with both types of problems. The first assists the participants in day-to-day, clinical activities, which are of immediate concern to them. The second involves them in the development of their professional skills. Moreover, dealing with such problems provides training in a subordinate learner's role, to which every patient or client must submit. In spite of its importance, the long-range problem will be easily neglected if it is not included as a requirement of the program. It demands that participants make themselves vulnerable to criticism to a greater degree than in one-shot problem-solving situations.

At the end of each session, the program is briefly evaluated in writing, usually using a checklist with additional space for comments. At the beginning of the subsequent session, the evaluation results are reviewed, as well as the data collected by the observers, and these are briefly discussed. Their relationship to the new session goals are usually pointed out or better related goals are developed. If any group or leadership problems are noted, a plan may be developed with the members for dealing with them.

Immediately prior to the evaluation, all participants write out a set of expectations as to what they will do for the period between sessions. Although contingency contracts are used in some groups, in others participants have indicated that they are not necessary. If the statement of expectations results in almost perfect completion of all items, contingencies indeed are not required. At the beginning of each session, the expectations or contract items from the previous sessions are reviewed and the percentage of completions for each person recorded.

In subsequent sections of the contract, the various components of the program are discussed in detail. Prior to all other steps, learning goals must be established.

Establishing Learning Goals

To evaluate whether training is effective, learning goals must be established for each member of the supervisory group. Some goals are long-range; others can be achieved in one or two sessions. Some goals are established early in training, but most develop as the members observe what can be learned by their peers in the training process. Thus, there is a continuous process of goal setting, developing plans and procedures for achieving those goals, and evaluating the degree to which goals are being achieved.

Goal setting is not always an easy process. Prior to goal setting, one must determine whether a given frequency of a behavior presents a relevant problem. To determine this, each member (ideally) hypothesizes what he or she suspects may be a target behavior and then monitors it. If the frequency is indeed too high or too low or too undifferentiated, he or she selects the given behavior as a target of change.

Often, however, members do not have adequate skills or experience to select behaviors relevant to them. These are skills that can be learned in their interaction with others. For this reason, it often is useful early in training to assign the members a set of behaviors to be monitored. This does not result in all these behaviors becoming targets of behavior change procedures, but it provides initial training in monitoring and in the use of data for determining relevant targets.

For example, in the supervision of social workers who recently had been introduced to behavior therapy and who had been treating clients with social anxiety, the supervisor assigned the task of monitoring the number of contingency contracts they drew up with their clients and the number of behavior rehearsals they carried out per interview hour. For two of the members, the frequency was quite high in both of these activities, but the frequency for the others was below what each of them decided was an adequate number. On this basis, several were able to select a relevant target of change. As the group progressed in increasing the frequency and quality of the use of these two procedures, the therapists began to discover other areas in their practice that warranted change. Thus, the initial assignment resulted in their learning the selection criteria and in selecting appropriate targets.

Another procedure commonly used to facilitate problem identification is a behavior checklist.[1] Each member rates approximately 30 behaviors on a five-point scale ranging from "needing no improvement" to "needing very much improvement." The results are then discussed in the group.

[1]Obtainable from the author upon request.

As mentioned earlier, two types of targets exist for every session; situational and long-range. Most sessions are involved in achieving both kinds.

Situational Targets

As an example of a situational target, a participant did not know where to refer a client who complained of a medical problem but did not have the resources to deal with it. The supervisor and group members made suggestions as to what he could do, where he could go, and whom he might ask for further information. At a subsequent meeting, the members would ask the therapist how he finally handled the situation. Another example was that of a participant whose adult clients in group treatment were having difficulties in determining what was reinforcing to them. The supervisory group provided some alternatives from their own experiences and suggested some additional reading in the area of contingencies for adults. A third example was introduced by a participant who was having difficulty defining the problem of a client. The group interrogated the therapist, and on the basis of his answers suggested that he might seek additional information in certain areas, and also suggested some possible ways of monitoring that might lead to a useful and accurate determination of the problem.

In these examples, the only data that could be collected on the participants' behavior was whether or not they followed up on the plan of action decided upon in the group. Usually, the participants will include what it is they are going to do between sessions in their between-session contracts and indicate at the following meeting whether the conditions of the contract were met.

In addition to being limited to one or two situations about which the participant has a question, the situational target should be one that is relevant to the other group members either in their roles as teacher or learner; that is, they can, by virtue of previous experience, help the given participant to find an answer to his or her problem or they can, in observing the suggestions of others, learn how to handle similar situational problems of their own.

Usually, extensive assessment is not required for situational targets. The content of the questions asked and the nature of the follow-up often suggest material relevant to the assessment of the long-range targets. In general with all situational targets, such procedures as modeling, rehearsal, and contracts are used to facilitate the carrying out of the suggestions made in the group. One usually attempts to attain the target in one step; successive approximations are rarely used. As situational targets begin to require extensive training, they begin to approximate long-range targets, for which complex training procedures often are introduced to teach the participant the desired behavior. Where the problem is especially complex, shaping the target behavior or, in some cases, backward chaining may be necessary.

Long-Range Targets

Because the learning of complex therapist behaviors contributes to the long-range effectiveness of the participants, these are essential targets in a behavioral approach. There are two major types of long-range problems. The first is concerned with personal organization, such as promptness in getting to work and getting one's work started, completion of recordings and other administrative tasks, ordering one's materials, and planning for conferences with clients. A second area relates to one's interactive behavior with clients, such as excessive advice giving or confrontation, too little positive reinforcement or other treatment procedure, limited interviewing skills, and keeping one's self and one's client on-task. Often as an initial choice of target, participants will select one of the personal organization behaviors. Only after some initial success are they willing to work on an interactive behavior. In long-term groups, this presents no problem. In time-limited groups, this may result in foregoing the opportunity to complete an interactive behavior, and hence in improving their direct clinical skills. In short-term groups, however, less time is spent on situational problems so that a person may take as a target both a personal organization and interactive behavior.

The major criteria for a useful target behavior in either category are: 1) the behavior is sufficiently specific to be monitored, 2) the behavior is important to the participant, and 3) the group can be of use in clarifying the problem and developing a training plan for correcting it. For example, a member of the group decided that he rambled too often in his work with clients, but he had difficulty in defining exactly what that rambling was. The members suggested that he bring a tape of 10 minutes of his worst rambling and 10 minutes of his least rambling to the group meeting. After listening to the tapes, it was clear that his rambling consisted of incomplete or repeated sentences. At the next conference with his clients, the therapist had the clients count his repeated and incomplete sentences. He also taped the meeting to check their reliability. At a subsequent group supervisory session, the group members helped him to develop a plan for decreasing rambling. In group supervisory session, he rehearsed what he would say—whenever an incomplete sentence was stated he was given a red token; a repetition received a white token. Feedback, he hypothesized, was sufficient to reduce the frequency. The data confirmed this hypothesis. He then used the same procedure in the treatment situation with equally successful results and with the side effect that he could model for his client a useful treatment procedure, as well as his openness in dealing with a behavior of his own.

An example of a behavior that developed into a relevant long-range target was presented by a member who wanted to decrease her participation (as therapist) in her treatment group. Initially, she merely identified the problem in the group and was able without any change plan to decrease the behavior.

The group members then encouraged her to select a more differentiated aspect of her participation to delimit. Her second behavior involved limiting all communication except requests for information and clarification, and reinforcement of the contribution of group members. The group helped her to clarify exactly how this was to be measured and identified. In a subsequent meeting, they gave suggestions as to how she might develop a plan for increasing the desired behaviors, since she had no difficulty in decreasing the undesired ones.

Many behaviors that require no other plan than explication may require at least a monitoring plan. Even if participants can do this on their own, they may need help in identifying the problem in the first place. And should they clearly identify their own problems, it may be useful for them to have the group monitor them in carrying out the various plans. In all of these to determine whether a behavior requires further treatment, data must be collected.

Data-Collection Procedures

Data are used for a number of purposes in this approach. First, data are collected to facilitate the assessment of the long-range targets toward which the participants might work. Second, they are used to evaluate the effectiveness of each session as a means of facilitating the learning of the individuals of the group. Third, they are used to assess the existence of group problems and to monitor ongoing changes in them. Some sources of data are recordings of patient contacts, which the participants give to the supervisor and other members prior to meetings; tape recordings of meetings; direct observations by other participants or by the supervisor; data collected by observers at the meetings; subjective evaluations by the participants and the supervisor; and, finally, such data as attendance, completion of behavior assignments, and actual behavior changes.

Summaries of parts or all of the meeting may be written by the therapist or by an observer, or sometimes even by a client. They are highly subjective and tend to include only selectively perceived observations. Nevertheless, they do provide some indication of how the participant works with his or her clients and suggest problems that might be worked on. They are time-consuming to write and to read, especially if everyone in the group submits recordings of all their client encounters. For this reason, if recordings are used, a sample is submitted from each person or all the recordings are submitted from one or two persons, which will be read prior to the session by the supervisor and usually by all the participants. Once a problem area has been determined, only select subjects will be recorded. For example, if most of the group participants are dealing with the use of simulation training, only their experiences in this area are recorded for the group. Further analysis of the recordings with more exact counting procedures are used rarely, although it is conceivable that some form of content analysis might, indeed, yield criteria for the evaluation of participant progress.

Tape recordings are much less subjective and, as such, provide for the group a realistic picture of a participant's interaction with clients. Because tapes are so time-consuming, only brief time samples actually can be played in a given meeting. At a meeting, members are asked to select 5 to 10 minutes of tape related to any topic which concerns them. These will be played at a subsequent meeting. In a two-hour period no more than four or five 10-minute samples can be played and discussed. The more each sample is related to a central topic, the more samples that can be played at a given session. Since tape recordings are subject to lack of technical clarity, the samples chosen should be fairly understandable. If not, they should be typed out for the participants or at least summarized in advance. Despite the time involved, meetings in which tapes were used were evaluated extremely well by the participants. Tape recordings lend themselves to more objective content analysis, but it rarely has been done because of the heavy time demand in preparing such an instrument.

Direct observations by group members of other members in their therapist roles have been a useful technique for obtaining objective data on leadership performance. Observers have sat in the same room or behind a one-way mirror. In any case, the members are aware that they are being observed. Usually, the observers and the given participant develop an observational schedule for specific dimensions along which the participant is observed. A leadership checklist covering many areas also may be used, and at a subsequent meeting those items rated low may be counted more systematically. In the supervisory group meeting, either the participant or the observer report on the findings of the observations. An observer who codes observations as he or she goes along saves time over either written reports or tape recordings. If the members serve as observers to each other, this also gives a reliability check on the perception of each member in the group.

Where tape recordings or direct observation are unfeasible, role-playing difficult situations may provide highly relevant data as to what a clinician is or is not doing that is impeding his or her effectiveness. For example, a participant claimed that he had difficulty in setting limits in his children groups. When asked by his peers what he did, his description seemed effective enough. But when he role-played the situation, it was apparent that his pleading tone of voice needed to be exchanged for a clear and unequivocal tone, which he went on to learn in the group.

The group lends itself to feedback from or confrontation by the other group members as to behavior patterns each uses in the group. Because of the side effects of confrontative methods, they are used only where there is consistent evidence that a pattern of behavior exists that clearly reduces the effectiveness of the participant. Moreover, they are used after other procedures have failed to produce a relevant target.

Behavioral data are the major source of data to evaluate whether or not weekly goals are being achieved. The percentage of weekly assignments being completed indicates the effectiveness of the previous meeting. The actual changes in professional behaviors indicate the success of the training program for each individual. All of the process in the group must be evaluated in terms of whether they lead to increased completion of behavior assignments and changes in the target behaviors. Attendance and promptness give a behavioral indication of the attractiveness of the group and its relevance to the members.

To get the members' subjective impressions of what in the process is contributing to outcome, an evaluation is filled out at the end of every session. Members indicate which goals were achieved, the relevance of the goals, the usefulness of the various program aspects, the supervisor's comments, and the group discussion. Supervisors have found it useful to fill in similar evaluations to discover whether their perception of the meeting is at variance with others in the group. Evaluations are distributed less frequently in later sessions, usually as soon as there is little variance among items and members.

Once targets have been established and baseline data collected, a training plan is established, which consists of one or more training procedures.

Training Procedures

Many training procedures are used in the behavioral approach. The basic ones, however, are reinforcement, modeling, rehearsal, coaching, assignments, and contingency contracting. In addition, such group procedures as group feedback and rotation of the chairperson are employed.

REINFORCEMENT

The most common forms of immediate reinforcement in groups are praise, information, and tokens or other mediating reinforcers. A major difference between behavioral and nonbehavioral groups is the use in the former of praise on a planned contingent basis; one of the concerns of supervisors in the contingent use of praise has been that the members quickly would be satiated by its use or would find it unreal or unspontaneous, and, hence, it would lose its reinforcing potency. This has not been the case. Even when the members explicitly were made aware of what the supervisor was doing, the behaviors that had been praised systematically usually increased in frequency. Moreover, on evaluations of groups no statement of too much praise has ever occurred, whereas too little praise has been the subject of criticism. Few questions were raised; at first every time members of the group asked questions in the early phase of training the supervisor praised the questioner. This increased the question level to a point that made it possible to deal with selected questions. At that point, to shape a more useful quality of questions, the therapist used praise for only those questions that were related directly to practice problems. Praise could be regarded as a particular form of giving information or feedback to an individual. However, one also may use lights, tokens, nods, and evaluations. For example, a supervisor was dissatisfied with the frequency of his own participation in the group. To increase it, a simple apparatus was constructed in which an observer, on noting a comment by the supervisor, could press a button, which turned on a small bulb visible only to the supervisor. The light provided him with immediate information about the occurrence of his comments. Had he wanted to decrease the frequency of his participation, the light would have had a different message. In this case, information can serve either as a positive reinforcer or an aversive stimulus.

Information may be given more globally or at greater intervals by means of feedback sheets, which the members fill in to describe their perceptions of individual or group behavior. Although usually filled in only at the end of each session, they may be used as often as once every five minutes if they are extremely brief. For example, the members were having difficulty attending to each other at the 3:30 Friday afternoon meeting. A kitchen timer was set for random periods between 3 and 10 minutes. When the timer went off, each person was required to indicate whether or not he or she was attending to the speaker. To validate the "yes" answers, the leader randomly asked one question to one person about the content of the immediately preceding statement.

Information about one's performance is most useful if it is immediate. For this reason, tokens have been used for giving information. For example, in a group in which mutual criticism was regarded as being very high, the members were instructed to throw a token into a can in the middle of the table every time they felt that they were being unfairly criticized. As a result, the critics received information as to the frequency of what others perceived to be unfair criticism, and the criticized received feedback as to their sensitivity to criticism.

Most often, positive feedback is used because of the side effects of criticism, which for most persons functions as punishment. However, when feedback is about an objective behavior, the punishing aspects of it seem to diminish. Therefore, in behavioral groups every effort is made to keep feedback as objective, as frequent, and in as small units as possible, and to hold judgments about global characteristics to a minimum.

When tokens are used, one may attach more concrete reinforcement to their informational aspect. That is, the earning of a certain number of tokens will result in a given reward for the individual. Or the earning of a certain number of tokens by all the members will result in some common or group reward. Although used rarely in past years in supervisory groups, the use of tokens as reinforcement has been increasing with no apparant side effects. Practitioners have evaluated the specific use of tokens as either "helpful" or "extremely helpful" on the scaled evaluation question at the session's end in recent groups.

MODELING AND DEMONSTRATION

In supervision, models may be presented through role-played demonstrations, tapes of how others have performed, case studies of other therapists, or the behavior of the supervisor or other members of the group in group interaction. The purpose of modeling is to provide alternatives from which the supervisor can choose ways of more effectively dealing with his or her problems. Although in this section, we discuss two forms in particular—role-played modeling and the supervisor as model in his or her role as supervisor—the other types of modeling are also useful.

Because of the difference in status between the supervisor and the supervisees, the latter often indicate that they feel as if they are forced to select a behavior to work on. This perception often results in the selection of an irrelevant behavior that has little or no learning potential for the member. One way to overcome this is for the group supervisor to demonstrate the selection and self-treatment procedure by choosing a behavior for him- or herself to work on throughout therapy. It is important that the supervisor select a behavior that meets the criteria, which was described earlier, for a relevant behavior if he or she expects the members to do likewise. Support for this procedure has been found in the evaluations. Whenever a supervisor has worked on his or her own behavior, a large percentage of the participants indicated that they found this form of participation extremely useful. In several cases where the supervisor selected a rather innocuous behavior, the evaluations reflected resentment.

Some of the behaviors selected by the supervisor were ones that the members themselves could observe and deal with within the structure of the supervisory group. For example, the supervisor aimed at delegating more responsibility to the members over time. The members indicated the kinds of functions they thought they eventually could perform, and these were recorded in terms of what they were and who performed them. Since most of these functions were performed by the supervisor, the group designed a plan in which members who performed a given function were rewarded with group approval in the form of a "positive" token, and the supervisor was given a "negative" token for performing the same activity. The plan not only resulted in a rapid delegation of responsibility to the members and increased enthusiasm of the group for the general approach, but it provided a model for the selection of the members' own target behaviors and the design of their own treatment plans. If the supervisor gets help from others, the likelihood that others will do the same is vastly increased.

In another supervisory group, a participant said that he did not know how to deal with a problem of handling depressive remarks by his client. Although several suggestions were made, the participant claimed to be somewhat at a loss as to how he actually would carry them out. The supervisor suggested that the situation be role-played by the members who had the original ideas. In the modeling session, the member playing the therapist merely ignored the depressive talk and responded to life-oriented talk. He initially pointed out that he would do this because if he showed interest, it always would result in an increased rather than decreased depression. The role-play was repeated several times with slightly different tactics until the participant with the problem indicated that he had the general idea and the words needed to try it out. At that point, he played his own role and practiced the newly learned behaviors. This practice is a form of behavior rehearsal, which is discussed below.

BEHAVIOR REHEARSAL

Rehearsals have been used in group supervision to practice such diverse behaviors as helping the supervisee to limit children in a group, to use time out from reinforcement appropriately, to introduce new members whom the other clients dislike, to terminate a client, and to make a referral. Because it immediately prepares a person for what he or she is to do, it is one of the most frequently used procedures. Furthermore, it is a skill that the members in their roles as clinicians must acquire. Thus, its use in a group provides additional training for its direct use in clinical practice.

Behavioral rehearsal and other simulation procedures have a major impact on the group in terms of increasing interpersonal liking, satisfaction with the group, and satisfaction with the supervisor. In situations where there is a wide discrepancy in participation, often the introduction of simulation procedures results in greater and more equal participation by all members. For these reasons, simulation procedures should be introduced early in the training program.

Once a behavior is adequately reinforced, it has to be put into action in the clinical setting. The participant assigns him- or herself the task of trying out the behavior prior to the next session. This assignment, in writing and with a contingency attached to its completion, is, as mentioned earlier, referred to as a contingency contract.

CONTINGENCY CONTRACTING

Contingency contracting is one of the major procedures used to facilitate the completion of between-session assignments. Although in some groups only expectations are stated as to what the person will do prior to the next session, in contingency contracting consequences are established both for the completion and noncompletion of each item on the contract. Each person determines his or her own consequences and the frequency with which they are to be delivered. Commonly used in behavior treatment, this procedure serves as a model for practice as well as for increasing the probability of carrying out the assignments.

Assignments for activities with clients are essential to transfer learning from the supervisory to the clinical situation. By agreeing to an assignment, the individual obligates him- or herself to carry out that assignment in practice. The contingency, if relevant to the individual, adds further pressure for its completion. It should be pointed out that the participant should be urged to refrain from agreeing to a condition of a contract that he or she does not feel able to complete. Otherwise, failure is built into the program, not only for a given assignment but eventually for the entire approach. On the other hand, the condition should be sufficiently difficult to push the member to new learning.

An example of a contingency contract used in supervision is the following: "Next week, I agree to: 1) write specific goals prior to every conference with my clients; 2) increase my use of rehearsal procedures to an average of one-half per client seen; 3) write a summary of each client contact; 4) read the literature on modeling in Bandura; and 5) clean my desk before leaving the office each day. On completion of all of these terms to the satisfaction of my colleague, I will permit myself to read 100 pages of science fiction. If I complete three of the items, I will be able to read 50 pages. If I complete less than three, I shall forego the right to read science fiction for the entire week."

In this example, assignments can be found in the following categories: reading, writing goals, personal organization, and techniques of treatment. All of these assignments are related to goals established for each learner early in training.

Group Procedures

Group procedures are those techniques used to modify the behavior of more than one person at a time. Some of the procedures already described could have been either individual or group. One models for the entire group or for one person in the group. Rehearsals are useful not only to the person rehearsing but for persons observing. In contingency contracting, usually individual contingencies are established, but in some cases group contingencies may be utilized.

BUDDY SYSTEM

Some procedures are solely group procedures. For example, the buddy system, by pairing two or more persons to serve as monitors and supervisors for each other, provides each member with supervisory experience. It may even provide him or her with a readily monitorable situation in which he or she can increase or try out new training procedures. As with others, it provides a model for a group procedure that can be used in group treatment.

In most groups, buddies usually check between sessions to see whether their buddy has completed the assignments. If he or she is having difficulty, the buddy may help to carry out the assignment. Buddies may help buddies between sessions to define situational targets worthy of considering in the group. They may help each other directly with their clients. Sometimes assignments are given to buddies rather than to individuals. They may observe each other in their contacts with clients. Buddies usually are not permanent. To give each the opportunity to work with a wide number of persons, buddies are usually rotated every several meetings. However, this may not be advisable in short-term groups.

In a few groups, the buddy system was not effective, as evidenced by the fact that assignments to call the buddy were the *only* assignments not completed. Moreover, in these groups the buddy system was rated low on the session evaluations. The breakdown in the system may be due to the fact that the members do not know the behaviors necessary to carry out the contact between buddies. It is necessary not merely to assign buddies, but to discuss and even to model the nature of how the buddy system is to be used. If, in spite of adequate preparation, the group does not find the system useful, and if all other assignments are being completed regularly, it should be dropped.

LEADERSHIP

The buddy system not only extends the effect of the group; in most groups, it also is used to increase leadership activities by all members. But it is not the only procedure that gives participants the opportunity to practice leadership behavior; another is the rotation of the one serving as discussion leader. The success of the rotation depends on adequate modeling during the first several sessions by the supervisor, careful planning together with the chairperson for each meeting, immediate feedback from the members, careful analysis of all data related to the given session, and an evaluation of the session by the chairperson of what was done well and what needs to be improved.

A great deal of data is available to the discussion leader each session, such as the completion of assignments made at the session and the subjective evaluation of peers. It also would be useful if data were collected on the frequency of participation so that the distribution of communication could be evaluated. The leader may elect to have specific leadership functions monitored also.

Because of the accumulation of data on one's leadership, ideally each person should be allowed to lead the group at least twice to improve upon the initial performance. When there is not time for everyone to be leader or if some of the members are hesitant to be put into the job, it is possible to provide the opportunity for members on a voluntary basis.

MODIFYING COMMUNICATION PATTERNS

It has been observed in groups that certain communication patterns are more effective than others for the attainment of goals. For example, in behavioral groups the communication should be oriented more on-task than off-task. It should be as much among members as between leaders and members; the communication should be shared by all members, and discrepancies, although necessary, should not be too great. The tasks of leadership should be shared between the supervisor and the group members, and to a certain degree among the group members. Members should attend to each other and to the leader. The number of reinforcements or praise should be much higher than the amount of criticism or verbal punishment. The amount of talk about feelings should be lower than the amount of talk about behavior to be performed. On the other hand, if there were no feeling talk, this also could be a group problem. Each of these and similar attributes lend themselves to observation and monitoring procedures, so that it is possible to evaluate at any point how the group is progressing along any of these dimensions. Usually, only a few at any one time will be observed systematically.

In most groups, once a group problem is subjectively indicated either by the supervisor or one of the members, a monitoring plan is developed to check the validity of the subjective judgments. For example, in one group the members did not appear to be talking to one another but only to the supervisor. As a result, they seemed to attend only when the supervisor spoke. The session evaluations indicated that group discussion was seen as the lowest of all procedures. Moreover, the productivity of the group was at its lowest point. At the next meeting, one member volunteered to record the sequence of communication in terms of whether the supervisor spoke or a member spoke. More than 80 percent of the members' communication followed a statement by the supervisor. When the group viewed the statistics, they agreed to develop a plan for dealing with the problem. First, they made up a skit to demonstrate a situation in which member-to-member interaction was more intense than supervisor-member interaction. They then assigned one member to signal approval whenever a member followed another, and disapproval whenever a member followed the supervisor or the supervisor followed a member.

The group was initially amused by the procedure; in addition, the plan worked so well that the supervisor was excluded verbally. It then became necessary to adjust the plan to allow for approved supervisory activity. The evidence for success was found in the communication data, the evaluation, and increased productivity. Most plans for dealing with such group problems include modeling and a rehearsal procedure, and reinforcement. Sometimes, however, confrontation with the baseline data is sufficient to change the behavior. At other times, group procedures are necessary to obtain the desired changes or to prevent certain of the above problems from occurring in the first place.

PRELIMINARY RESULTS

In six short-term supervisory groups, systematically observed and data-recorded by the author and colleagues, the results have been tentatively supportive of the efficacy of this approach. In these groups of 42 participants, which met from 5 to 6 sessions lasting two hours, 36 modified successfully at least one behavior and 18 modified two or more. One group clearly could be considered a failure. Of the six participants, three changed no behaviors. This group also had low productivity and low satisfaction.

In three of the groups a crisis arose at the third session, primarily due to the overloaded agenda but also to the lack of clarity of expectations. When the overload was reduced, the expectations clarified, the frequency of reinforcement increased, and simulation procedures added to the program, the crisis disappeared.

The model differed in these groups from the one proposed in this chapter only insofar as the members only occasionally worked toward situational targets. They primarily oriented themselves toward longer range problems. A few who had no clinical practice worked on problems of personal or household management or of self-control. Because the groups were brief, the termination phase was never reached. Although there was a transfer of responsibilities to the group, there were insufficient sessions to go through a systematic maintenance of change program.

Participants served both as participants and observers. In the role of observer, they recorded the supervisor-member sequence of interaction and the frequency of interaction of each of the participants. This double task was dropped at the third session. Most members felt that the data would have revealed an increase in member-member interaction and, in two groups, observations were resumed in the last two sessions.

The productivity of five of the six groups was moderately high. They each averaged 80 percent completion of all assignments at each of the sessions in which assignments were monitored. One group, however, averaged only 25 percent completion. The evaluations gradually increased on a five-point scale from an average of 2.8 to an average of 1.2 per item (one is the desirable end of the continuum). The low productivity group averaged 4-2.2 per item.

BEYOND ROUTINE

In the initial sessions of group supervision, there is a great deal of work to be accomplished and often too little time to accomplish it. It often requires a great deal of extragroup preparation on the part of both the participants and the supervisor, as well as discipline in the meeting, to get through the agenda.

But, as basic assumptions are learned and as members gain skill in the varied procedures required in the group, the pressure is diminished. After several months, if the program is too unvaried or the problems dealt with too simple, members become bored, attend irregularly, fail to perform assignments, and give other indications that something must be changed.

At the first signs, the group supervisor should begin to introduce new problems, more sophisticated procedures, and other challenging activities. Even before such behaviors occur, the supervisor continually should increase responsibility to members for the direction the group takes, the situational and long-range targets to be dealt with, and the group problems to be considered. Although providing the initial format for supervision, the supervisor uses it only as a point of departure. The only criteria he or she holds to are that all members give demonstrable indications that they are dealing with problematic situations and increasing their skills.

As the participants gain experience in solving various problems, the problem-solving process itself is conceptualized to provide a paradigm for solving future problems. Small experiments sometimes are set up to compare different approaches to dealing with similar problems. Participants may be encouraged to include internal research controls into their practice, to develop a program of follow-up interviews with all their clients, and other means of more systematically evaluating their personal practice and program. Professional reading programs may be added to the tasks of the participants. One of the major problems of practitioners is insufficient time keeping up with current professional literature. If the literature is divided, the group may facilitate an exchange of current ideas and practice. Finally, based on the data they collected, the staff may write a paper criticizing, supplementing, or even rejecting in part the proposals suggested in this chapter.

The cost of supervision is not negligible. A group of five, meeting once a week, and a supervisor costs the agency at least the equivalent of six client contacts per week. To reduce the cost to the agency, the context of supervision shifts to training the participants to function independently or with occasional consultation.

This is a gradual process. As participants demonstrate their skills in a wide variety of procedures, they are encouraged to perform leadership functions in the group. They serve as extragroup tutors for beginning staff members; they are called upon to analyze problems; they serve as consultants to the less experienced members. In this phase, they are trained in leadership and supervisory skills. Although most practitioners will move to more independent status, some eventually will move to supervisory slots as openings are available.

There are still many problems in this approach. It demands inordinate amounts of preparation, especially in the initial phases. It requires a large body of highly specific skills or extensive skill training. The technology is only beginning to become sufficiently sophisticated to deal with complex cognitive targets. But, in the final analysis, a behavioral approach to supervision offers a set of procedures the results of which are vulnerable to criticism and, hence, to change and development.

18 Conclusion

THE behavioral approach to group therapy is described in this book as it appears at one point in its development. New organizational structures constantly are being considered. New themes for groups are being tried out. Innovative ideas are being incorporated in the approach. The opportunity for data collection inherent in the approach provides a concrete basis for minor revision and major change. In this final chapter, we will explore some of those proposals for change now being considered, and will recommend selected areas of research necessary for the further development of the approach.

FUTURE PERSPECTIVES

The most drastic revision being considered is the organization for treatment and the labeling of programs. One proposal is for therapy groups to be organized like an adult education program. This idea is similar to the Adult Development Program of the University of Washington.

A number of courses with small enrollments (6 to 10) would be organized into a set of curricula. These courses would include beginning and advanced sections of parent training, assertive training, communication skills workshop, relaxation training, fear reduction training, mood change training, weight loss course, smoking clinic, and so on.

Prior to entry into the regular curriculum, an assessment course will be required in which members not only learn the skills of self-assessment, but apply these skills to assessing their own problems and those of their peers. Based on the findings of this first course, clients assign themselves to one of the above courses.

Each applicant also will have an advisor, who will help him or her to develop an appropriate program and to assess periodically whether treatment goals are being achieved. In this way, evaluation readily can be built into the program. The advisor also can determine where individual tutoring would be required.

As part of the program, advanced students could assist in groups as aides, models, observers, or, if sufficiently skilled, as coinstructors, as a prerequisite to "graduation." The use of trained volunteer assistants derived from the client body would reduce the cost of the training.

An important advantage of an educational orientation is that it reduces the stigma attached to the label of therapy. Potential clients would enter such a program more readily than therapy. The program should appeal primarily to those persons who are seeking concrete training for and solutions to problems and to those with a practical orientation to personal problem-solving. Of course, those clients seeking psychotherapy in particular would tend to go elsewhere.

Other advantages of the course approach to treatment would be the creation of large-scale programs providing the possibility for experimentation with a variety of groups and group structures. It also could provide a large and well organized field for the training of students.

A more specific organizational change being considered in the structure of group treatment is the spacing of meetings. As pointed out in Chapter 2, most group therapy programs meet once a week and a few as often as twice a week. Consideration is now being given to groups that meet as intensely as 6 to 12 hours per day for a weekend or even work week. Such a program would be faded rapidly to once a week and even once a month. This high intensity of meetings is useful primarily in programs that involve large numbers of simulation procedures such as role-playing. Systematic desensitization and all forms of cognitive training also could be done under these conditions. Where the focus of the group is on preparation for behavioral home assignments and the monitoring of these assignments, the mass training approach would be less desirable because it prevents an opportunity to practice in the real world. The value of back-to-back meetings is in the high frequency of practice for each person in a very short time. Small errors can be dealt with and corrected readily. At this point, there is no reason or research to suggest that mass trials do not produce any less learning per hour than spaced trials. If this be the case, the motivation of the clients should increase as they observe themselves learning new behaviors in a very short time period. For purposes of transferring change, weekly and monthly meetings may be used following the mass training. Or even better, a program could consist of three or four weekends in a row, which would leave the work week for practice in the real world.

New types of groups can be expected to develop. One that bears particular examination is a maintenance of change group, which has as its major purpose the extension of changes brought about in the group into other settings and into the future. Chapter 11 suggested a number of ways of maintaining and transferring change achieved within the treatment group. Since most groups are time-limited, often clients barely achieve treatment goals before the group is terminated. For some clients, re-enrolling in a similar group is one answer to this problem. Other clients might contract for additional numbers of sessions. But for others, not only former group clients but also clients from individual therapy, a group program (maintenance groups) could be developed that is oriented solely toward the maintenance of levels of behavior achieved in therapy.

Most of the characteristics of maintenance groups have been suggested in Chapter 11. They hold infrequent meetings, usually once a month. These meetings may in part be organized by the clients, monitored by them, and even led by them. The therapist serves more as organizer and consultant than as group leader. The membership is quite fluid. Members leave as they demonstrate to themselves and group members their ability to function without the group. The content of meetings is variable. Some are well organized like therapy groups, others may approximate a social recreational or interest group. Although there is concern for evidence of behavior accomplishments, procedures other than counting, such as diaries or self-report, are used. Emphasis is usually placed on self-monitoring, which is the form of monitoring the members might continue after they leave the group. Treatment plans are made for extended periods—at least a month, but as long as four months. Each client need not report on progress at every meeting. Members are encouraged to bring friends to the meetings. There is no attempt to make the group too attractive, since it rarely meets more than six or seven times. On the other hand, membership in alternative social groups is strongly encouraged, both concurrent with maintenance groups and following them.

One topic often selected by members is strategies of independent functioning. How does one live in the community and use one's natural resources for dealing with the inevitable stresses that occur, or the new behavior problems that may arise, or a return of the previous problem? Clients are encouraged to remain in the group until they have been through such a discussion, made such a plan, and carried it out successfully.

In addition, members of some groups are interested in learning how to use other sources of help, such as social agencies, schools, counseling services, and health services. Where appropriate, speakers from these services are invited to discuss what their agencies have to offer. Still other topics would depend on the requests of the clients.

Another kind of maintenance group with a different structure is the refresher course. This is a yearly set of group meetings. In each set, consisting of 2 to 6 meetings, former clients are invited to go over their present progress or status. Often an entire Saturday or weekend may be invested by the clients. The theme is the same as that of the maintenance group, but new treatment procedures may be introduced and lectures and discussions of subjects of interest are included. The members are often polled by telephone prior to the meeting to determine topics of common interest.

This type of group meeting also provides follow-up data. Where the response is heavy, the meetings are broken into subgroups based on topics of interest. For example, when 32 people from previous groups responded to such a course, four subgroups of eight each were organized around the themes of relaxation and breathing, feedback sessions, role-playing new situations, and living without therapy.

Of course, the best maintenance groups may be those organized to support a particular client group (for example, Alcoholics Anonymous, Weight Watchers, Synanon). Before a large investment is made in maintenance groups, a review of the communities' self-help groups might provide a better organized and less costly supplement or replacement of a given clinic's program.

The Group Therapy and Research Project is developing a model for multifamily groups. The purpose is to train parents and their adolescent and preadolescent children to negotiate decisions of common concern, to talk to each other more positively, and to solve common problems. Multifamily groups have the advantage of families being able to demonstrate to other families different patterns of interaction. Moreover, they permit interaction between parents in one family with children in another, which makes trying out new patterns of interaction much easier. Of course, if both families have complex and serious communication problems, no models are available. In that case, an individual family treatment format probably would be preferable.

Multifamily groups present problems not commonly found in other groups. Family roles are sometimes rigidly determined, which often delimits the participation of some members. In the beginning, adolescents may refuse to come to the group, which adds one more point of contention with their parents. As a result, there is a high initial dropout rate (33 percent). Some families do not want to share their problems with other families and prefer to have family treatment alone.

A preliminary program has been developed for multifamily groups. Following an assessment program in which each family member (without interference from other members) is encouraged to describe what he or she sees as the major family problem, the family is trained in concrete formulations of the problems. Then they are taught to negotiate changes in the family interaction pattern. Negotiation training consists of exercises around an artificial problem given by the therapist. Later, the members practice negotiation around what each person should work on while in the group.

In one group, the leader experimented with separating the children from the parents during therapy sessions and then bringing them together for increasingly long periods. In their respective groups, parents and children role-played how to negotiate an agreed-upon situation. They were then brought together to carry it out. One therapist sat behind a child, another behind the parent. They served as coaches to both parties to facilitate a successful experience. On one occasion, parents practiced with the child of the other set of parents before actually negotiating with their own children.

Although negotiation training is initially around one situation, the parties later negotiate changes in behavior that are annoying to the other. The process of determining the behavior to be targeted is not easy. Parents are disinclined to view any of their own behaviors as dysfunctional, although parents might agree that some of the things they do might indeed be annoying to their children. Often innocuous or irrelevant behaviors are suggested; however, the presence of the other party serves as a control. The therapist insists that behavior be relevant and important to both parties before initiating monitoring or treatment programs.

In addition to negotiation training, the program stresses exercises in reciprocal praise. Praise statements are monitored both in and out of the group. Moreover, parents are taught to improve the quality of their praise (for example, by not pairing it with criticism, not following praise with "but . . . ," by using appropriate affect).

Finally, the program aims at dealing with rather than ignoring family problems. The families are given exercises in problem recognition and problem-solving and are encouraged to bring in examples of problems on which they could practice in the group. As yet no systematic observations have been made in these groups. As experience accrues, the model will be evaluated and revised and, hopefully, presented in detail to the field.

SELF MANAGEMENT GROUPS

Chapter XV was concerned with weight loss groups, but these are not the only kinds of groups oriented toward self-management. Clinics and agencies are requesting a large number of groups for smokers, alcoholics, and drug addicts. In universities and high schools, study skill groups also are established. All of these groups are similar in many respects to weight loss groups. Group members are trained in new skills as well as behaviors incompatible with their maladaptive ones. They are trained in specific self-management procedures, such as problem-solving and covert self-reinforcement. They use the broad spectrum of procedures of modeling, coaching, rehearsal, group feedback, the buddy system, behavioral assignments, and contracts. In the immediate future, agencies may be expected to develop a wide range of these kinds of programs, which ultimately may provide a broad data base for the evaluation of their relative effectiveness.

The organizational or thematic structures presented in the preceding chapters in detail, and the ones suggested in the conclusion, might be considered as the tip of the iceberg. Hopefully, new and more effective models will evolve. This can occur only if extensive clinical and analogue research runs parallel to clinical practice development. In particular, a few questions demand early investigation.

RESEARCH QUESTIONS

Throughout the previous chapters, a number of research issues have been suggested for which answers are necessary if this approach is to continue to develop. One of the most crucial questions is concerned with identifying the conditions under which group therapy and training are more and less effective than individual therapy. Unfortunately, there is little research comparing group and individual operant and modeling approaches. Although group approaches at least would appear less costly, even this assumption has not been tested. One of the chief reasons for using the group is the assumption that behaviors learned in the group will be maintained longer than those learned in individual therapy. This proposition, too, requires empirical support.

Perhaps even more relevant is the question concerning the effectiveness of behavioral group approaches compared to nonbehavioral group approaches. A few such projects have been reported (for example, Paul, 1966; and DiLoreto, 1971). In spite of significant findings in favor of the behavioral approaches, the scope of these studies is limited.

In addition to the crucial issues of whether the group is more effective than individual treatment or whether behavioral group approaches are more effective than nonbehavioral ones, a large number of other research issues are of major concern. For example, it is assumed that favorable outcomes are due solely to the treatment package applied during and between group sessions. Certainly there are ample analogue studies to support the efficacy of various procedures used in group treatment. However, little attention has been given in behavioral research to relational factors that may impinge on outcome, in spite of some evidence in support of this contention (Truax and Carkhuff, 1967). Such factors as therapist genuineness, warmth, and empathy have been identified, and scales have been developed to operationalize them. Rather than discount their effects, behavioral researchers might add these dimensions to procedural variations to determine the independent and interactive effects of procedures and relational qualities on outcome.

Not all clients are able to make successful use of behavioral group therapy programs. Yet, thus far, no data is available on the characteristics of those who do not achieve treatment goals. The systematic collection of demographic and behavioral data on all participants in group programs, and a subsequent comparison of those who fail to those who succeed, would provide a profile for determining who should enter such a program. Although there is no certainty that differences will be found, such a question must be examined to give potential clients an empirical basis for deciding whether or not to participate in a group program. Such data also might provide a rational basis for changing the program to meet the needs of those who are presently unsuccessful.

An increasing number of procedures are being borrowed from other theoretical orientations or approaches. Thus far, this has been done in a haphazard manner according to the interests of the individual therapist. There have not been systematic evaluations of the use of these procedures, and the purpose of their use has not been always specified. If group therapists generally are to have ready access to these procedures, a systematic review of the techniques of other group technologies should be carried out; criteria should be established for evaluating the procedures; and experiments should be set up to try them out in comparison with techniques already in use. Although it may be difficult to ascertain the contribution of these procedures to positive outcome in a clinical experiment, it may be possible to examine them in analogue studies.

As the reader may have observed, most of the therapists involved in the Group Therapy and Research Project have been highly trained. This has occurred first to protect the clients and second to insure a positive and successful initial learning experience for the therapist. The question must be raised whether such a level of training is, in fact, required to obtain results comparable to those obtained in this project. To reduce the cost of therapy as much as possible, would it be better to assign the trained therapists to supervisory and planning roles, and to use the lesser trained individuals or even clients as direct therapists? Such a delegation of responsibility first would require a comparison study between groups using extensively and moderately well-trained therapists. Moreover, one could not generalize readily from one type of a group to another. It would be necessary to repeat the research project in many types of groups before one could conclude that degree of training did, in fact, influence the rate of positive outcomes in a wide range of groups.

Although some of the laws of interaction are known as they apply to analogue groups in laboratory group experiments, research on group process in clinical situations has barely begun. Yet some major observational tools are available to the clinician as well as the researcher for examining the types of group interaction and their relation to the achievement of individual behavioral change. Moreover, the small sample designs lend themselves to studying the interaction in groups as time-series designs. Through replication of small sample designs, interactive patterns may become predictable under a wide range of conditions.

Often the group therapist is hampered by the limited choice of process and outcome measures available when evaluating his or her program. Observational systems such as the one used by Linsk and others (1975) should be tested. To be most useful, measures must tap relevant aspects of the interactive process; observers must be readily trainable in the system; and they should be sufficiently efficient and economical that the group therapist, as well as researchers, can afford to use them.

The behavioral role-play test following the model proposed by Goldfried and D'Zurilla (1969) has been demonstrated to be an effective measure of behavioral change with diverse populations (delinquents, psychiatric inpatients, social work students, women, and the elderly). However, further tests of its validity are essential before one can safely assume that the changes are not merely changes in role-play behavior. In the case of institutionalized clients, observation of actual interactions in the living situation should be developed. Greater use of nonreactive measures, such as participation in institutional programs, closed or open doors to hospital rooms, sick rate, and requests for drugs, also could be used both as validation procedures and as a measurement of change in their own right.

In addition to development of validation tests for the role-play test, similar tests should be evolved for other populations. It would be especially useful to have such a test for parents trained in groups in which they would have to role-play a range of situations requiring the use of reinforcement, time out, rule setting, cueing, and so on.

Two of the most important skills taught in the behavioral groups are problem-solving and negotiation. As yet no adequate behavioral test exists for evaluating client ability in these areas. A role-play test could be developed in which clients are to negotiate a set of differences between them and significant others. Criteria would need to be evolved for evaluating the degree of success of the participant.

In the absence of sufficient subjects, many of the above hypotheses may be scrutinized by means of time-series research designs, with each group being considered an N=1. The accumulation of a large sample of such studies in diverse situations certainly would enhance our limited knowledge in this area. It is one of the major theses of this book that each practitioner should, indeed, view each group he or she leads as such an experiment, that systematic data be collected in each group, and that this data eventually be systematized for wider circulation. Care, however, must be taken to describe both negative and positive results. Some form of data bank or other means of broad dispersal is necessary to publicize results of such N=1 studies, since journals tend to publish primarily positive findings.

In conclusion, a behavioral approach to group therapy is an exciting and promising addition to the repertoire of the therapist. Because of its comprehensive technology, it can be taught and applied readily. Because of its goal orientation and high degree of specificity, it is vulnerable to constant evaluation. Because it undergoes evaluation, it is subject to systematic and continuous correction. Because of its educational orientation, it loses the social stigma often attached to psychotherapy. Because of the enthusiasm and behavioral change it appears to engender in clients, it is highly satisfying to its practitioners.

But major and diverse problems still remain that have been pointed out throughout this volume. Only extensive clinical practice and concomitant research will begin to resolve these problems and bring about a further development of group therapy—a behavioral approach.

Bibliography

ABRAHMS, J. L., and G. J. ALLEN, Comparative effectiveness of situational programming, financial payoffs, and group pressure in weight reduction. *Behavior Therapy*, 1974, *5*, 391–400.

AGRAS, W. S., Behavior therapy in the management of chronic schizophrenia. *American Journal of Psychiatry*, 1967, *124*, 240–243.

AIKEN, E. G., Changes in interpersonal descriptions accompanying the operant conditioning of verbal frequency in groups. *Journal of Verbal Learning and Verbal Behavior*, 1965, *4*, 243–247.

ALBERTI, R. E., and M. L. EMMONS, *Your Perfect Right*. (2nd ed.) San Louis Obispo, Cal.: Impact Press, 1974.

ALLYON, T., and N. H. AZRIN, *The Token Economy: A Motivational System for Therapy and Rehabilitation*. Englewood Cliffs, N. J.: Prentice-Hall, Inc., 1968.

AZRIN, N. H., T. FLORES, and S. J. KAPLAN, Job finding club: a group assisted program for obtaining employment. *Behaviour Research and Therapy*, 1975, *13*, 17–28.

AZRIN, N. H., B. J. NASTER, and R. JONES, Reciprocity counseling: a rapid learning-based procedure for marital counseling. *Behaviour Research and Therapy*, 1973, *11*, 365–382.

BALES, R. F., Interaction process analysis, in D. Sills, ed., *International Encyclopedia of the Social Sciences*. New York: Macmillan, 1968.

BANDURA, A., *Principles of Behavior Modification.* New York: Holt, Rinehart, and Winston, 1969.

———, *Psychological Modeling.* New York: Lieber-Atherton, 1974.

———, Psychotherapy based on modeling principles, in A. E. Bergin and S. L. Garfield, eds., *Handbook of Psychotherapy and Behavior Change.* New York: John Wiley, 1971.

BANNISTER, D., The genesis of schizophrenic thought disorder: a serial invalidation hypothesis. *British Journal of Psychiatry,* 1963, *109,* 680–689.

BARRY, W. A., Marriage research and conflict: an integrated review. *Psychological Bulletin,* 1970, *73,* 41–54.

BAUM, J., and J. GARFINKEL, Parent training in groups: a token economy approach, unpublished manuscript. Madison: University of Wisconsin, School of Social Work, 1974.

BAVELAS, A., A. H. HASTORF, A. E. GROSS, and W. R. KITE, Experiments on the alteration of group structure. *Journal of Experimental Social Psychology,* 1965, *1,* 55–70.

BEAN, H. B., *The effects of a role-model and instructions on group interpersonal openness and cohesiveness,* unpublished doctoral dissertation. Morgantown: West Virginia University, 1971.

BECK, D. F., and M. A. JONES, *Progress on Family Problems.* New York: Family Service Association of America, 1973.

BECKER, W. C., *Parents are Teachers.* Champaign, Ill.: Research Press, 1971.

BEISSER, A. R., and N. GLASSER, The precipitating stress leading to psychiatric hospitalization. *Comprehensive Psychiatry,* 1968, *9,* 50–61.

BENNETT, P. S., and R. F. MALEY, Modification of interactive behaviors in chronic mental patients. *Journal of Applied Behavior Analysis,* 1973, *6,* 609–620.

BERGER, R., *A comparison of assertion training and behavioral discussion with older persons,* unpublished doctoral dissertation. Madison: University of Wisconsin, 1976.

BIENVENU, M. J., Sr., Measurement of marital communication. *Family Coordinator,* 1970, *1,* 26–33.

BIRCHLER, G. R., R. L. WEISS, and J. P. VINCENT, Multimethod analysis of social reinforcement exchange between maritally distressed and nondistressed spouse and stranger dyads. *Journal of Personality and Social Psychology,* 1975, *31,* 349–360.

BLOOMFIELD, H., Assertive training in an outpatient group of chronic schizophrenics: a preliminary report. *Behavior Therapy,* 1973, *4,* 277–281.

BOOCOCK, S. S., The life career game. *Personnel and Guidance Journal,* 1967, *46,* 328–334.

BRINKMAN, W., W. KOOMEN, P. POELSTRA, and K. SWART, *Verslag van een groeps-therapie op gedragstherapeutiese grondsiaag* (Report on group therapy based on behavior therapy principles), Psychologisch Laboratorium. Amsterdam, Holland: University of Amsterdam, 1973.

BROCKWAY, B. S., *Assertive training with professional women.* Paper presented at the meeting of the Association for Advancement of Behavior Therapy, San Francisco, December 1975.

BROCKWAY, B. S., F. W. BROWN, D. J. McCORMICK, and H. RESNECK, *Assertive training in the group context,* unpublished manuscript. Madison: University of Wisconsin, 1972.

BURR, W. R., *Theory Construction and the Sociology of the Family.* New York: John Wiley, 1973.

BUTTERFIELD, W. H., and R. PARSON, Modeling and shaping by parents to develop chewing behavior in their retarded child. *Journal of Behavior Therapy and Experimental Psychiatry,* 1973, *4,* 285–287.

CAHALAN, D., I. H. CISIN, and H. M. CROSSLEY, *American Drinking Practices* (Rutgers Center of Alcohol Studies, Monograph No. 6). New Brunswick, N.J.: Rutgers Center of Alcohol Studies, 1969.

CAMPBELL, D. T., Reforms as experiments. *American Psychologist,* 1969, *24,* 409–424.

CAMPBELL, D. T., and J. C. STANLEY, *Experimental and Quasi-Experimental Designs for Research.* Chicago: Rand McNally, 1963.

CARTWRIGHT, D., and A. ZANDER, eds., *Group Dynamics: Research and Theory.* New York: Harper and Row, 1968.

CAUTELA, J. R., A behavior therapy approach to pervasive anxiety. *Behaviour Research and Therapy,* 1966, *4,* 99–109.

————, Covert extinction. *Behavior Therapy,* 1971, *2,* 192–200.

CAUTELA, J. R., R. B. FLANNERY, JR., and S. HANLEY, Covert modeling: an experimental test. *Behavior Therapy,* 1974, *5,* 494–502.

CAUTELA, J. R., and R. A. KASTENBAUM, A reinforcement survey schedule for use in therapy, training, and research. *Psychological Reports,* 1967, *20,* 115–130.

CHURCHILL, S. R., and P. H. GLASSER, Small groups in the mental hospital, in Glasser, Sarri, and Vinter, eds., *Individual Change Through Small Groups.* New York: The Free Press, 1974.

COHEN, R. The effects of group interaction and progressive hierarchy presentation on desensitization of test anxiety. *Behaviour Research and Therapy,* 1969, *7,* 15–26.

CONE, J. D., and E. W. SLOOP, Parents as agents of change, in A. Jacobs and W. Spradlin, eds., *The Group As Agent of Change.* New York: Behavioral Publications, 1974.

CURRAN, J. P., Social skills training and systematic desensitization in reducing dating anxiety. *Behaviour Research and Therapy,* 1975, *13,* 65–68.

DANCE, F. E. X., The "concept" of communication. *Journal of Communication,* 1970, *20,* 201–210.

DELANGE, J., *Effectiveness of systematic desensitization and assertive training with women,* doctoral dissertation. Madison: University of Wisconsin, School of Social Work, 1977.

DILORETO, A. O., *Comparative Psychotherapy: An Experimental Analysis.* Chicago: Aldine-Atherton, 1971.

DINOFF, M., R. F. HORNER, B. S. KURPIEWSKI, H. C. RICKARD, and E. O. TIMMONS, Conditioning verbal behavior of a psychiatric population in a group therapylike situation. *Journal of Clinical Psychology,* 1960, *16,* 371–372.

DITTMEN, A. T., *Interpersonal Messages of Emotion.* New York: Springer Publishing Company, Inc., 1972.

DUBLIN, L. I., Benefits of reducing. *American Journal of Public Health,* 1953, *43,* 993–996.

D'ZURILLA, T. J., and M. R. GOLDFRIED, Problem solving and behavior modification, *Journal of Abnormal Psychology,* 1971, *78,* 107–126.

EDWARDS, N., Case conference assertive training in a case of homosexual pedophilia. *Journal of Behavior Therapy and Experimental Psychiatry,* 1972, *3,* 55–63.

EISLER, R. M., M. HERSEN, and W. S. AGRAS, Effects of videotape and instructional feedback on nonverbal marital interactions: an analogue study. *Behavior Therapy,* 1973, *5,* 551–558.

———, Videotape: a method for the controlled observation of nonverbal interpersonal behavior. *Behavior Therapy,* 1973, *4,* 420–425.

EISLER, R. M., M. HERSEN, and P. M. MILLER, Effects of modeling on components of assertive behavior. *Journal of Behavior Therapy and Experimental Psychiatry,* 1973a, *4,* 1–6.

EISLER, R. M., P. M. MILLER, and M. HERSEN, Components of assertive behavior. *Journal of Clinical Psychology,* 1973b, *29,* 295–299.

EISLER, R. M., P. M. MILLER, M. HERSEN, and H. ALFORD, Effects of assertive training on marital interaction. *Archives of General Psychiatry,* 1974, *30,* 643–649.

ELLIS. A., *Growth Through Reason.* Palo Alto, Cal.: Science and Behavior Books, 1971.

———, *Reason and Emotion in Psychotherapy.* New York: Lyle Stuart, 1962.

ENDLER, N. S., The effects of verbal reinforcement on conformity and deviant behavior. *Journal of Social Psychology,* 1965, *66,* 147–154.

ENDLER, N. S., and E. HOY, Conformity as related to reinforcement and social pressure. *Journal of Personality and Social Psychology,* 1967, *7,* 197–202.

ENDLER, N. S., J. McV. HUNT, and A. J. ROSENSTEIN, An S-R Inventory of Anxiousness. *Psychological Monographs,* 1962, *76* (17, Whole No. 536).

ENDLER, N. S., and M. OKADA, A multidimensional measure of trait anxiety: The S-R Inventory of General Trait Anxiousness. *Journal of Consulting and Clinical Psychology,* 1975, *43,* 319–329.

FAIRWEATHER, G. W., ed., *Social Psychology in Treating Mental Illness: An Experimental Approach.* New York: John Wiley, 1964.

FENSTERHEIM, H., Assertive methods and marital problems, in R. D. Rubin, H. Fensterheim, J. D. Henderson, and L. P. Ullman, eds., *Advances in Behavior Therapy.* New York: Academic Press, 1972a.

FENSTERHEIM, H., Behavior therapy: assertive training in groups, in C. J. Sager and H. S. Kaplan, eds., *Progress in Group and Family Therapy.* New York: Brunner/Mazel, 1972b.

FENSTERHEIM, H., and J. BAER, *Don't Say Yes When You Want To Say No.* New York: Dell Publishing Co., 1975.

FERSTER, C. B., J. I. NURNBERGER, and E. B. LEVITT, The control of eating. *Journal of Mathetics,* 1962, *1,* 87–110.

FERSTER, C. B., and B. F. SKINNER, *Schedules of Reinforcement.* Englewood Cliffs, N.J.: Prentice-Hall, Inc., 1957.

FESTINGER, L., Behavioral support for opinion change. *Public Opinion Quarterly,* 1964, *28,* 404–417.

FISKE, D. W., H. F. HUNT, L. LUBORSKY, M. T. ORNE, M. B. PARLOFF, M. F. REISER, and A. H. TUMA, Planning of research on effectiveness of psychotherapy. *Archives of General Psychiatry,* 1970, *22,* 22–32.

FLANDERS, J. P., A review of research on imitative behavior. *Psychological Bulletin,* 1968, *69,* 316–337.

FRANK, P. W., *Behavioral approach to the treatment of social skills of chronic mental patients in a group setting,* unpublished manuscript. Madison: University of Wisconsin, 1974.

FRANKS, C. M., *Behavior Therapy, Appraisal, and Status.* New York: McGraw-Hill, Inc., 1969.

FREEDMAN, B. J., *An analysis of social behavioral skill deficits in delinquent and undelinquent adolescent boys,* doctoral dissertation. Madison: University of Wisconsin, 1974.

FRIEDMAN, P. H., The effects of modeling and role-playing on assertive behavior, in R. D. Rubin, H. Fensterheim, A. A. Lazarus, and C. M. Franks, eds., *Advances in Behavior Therapy.* New York: Academic Press, 1971.

GALASSI, J. P., and M. D. GALASSI, Validity of a measure of assertiveness. *Journal of Counseling Psychology,* 1974, *21,* 248–250.

GALASSI, J. P., M. P. KOSTKA, and M. D. GALASSI, Assertive training: a one year follow-up. *Journal of Counseling Psychology*, 1975, *22*, 451–452.

GAMBRILL, E. D., and C. A. RICHEY, An assertion inventory for use in assessment and research. *Behavior Therapy*, 1975, *6*, 550–561.

GENTILE, J. R., A. H. RODEN, and R. D. KLEIN, An analysis of variance model for intrasubject replication design. *Journal of Applied Behavior Analysis*, 1972, *5*, 193–198.

GERARD, D. L., and G. SAENGER, *Outpatient Treatment of Alcoholism*, Monograph No. 4. Toronto: University of Toronto Press, 1966.

GERBNER, G., On defining communication: still another view. *Journal of Communication*, 1966, *16*, 99–100.

GITTLEMAN, M., Behavior rehearsal as a technique in child treatment. *Journal of Child Psychology and Psychiatry*, 1965, *6*, 251–255.

GLASS, G. V., V. L. WILLSON, and J. M. GOTTMAN, *Design and Analysis of Time-Series Experiments.* Boulder, Colorado: Associated University Press, 1975.

GOLDFRIED, M. R. and T. J. D'ZURILLA, A behavioral-analytic model for assessing competence. In C. D. Spielberger, ed., *Current topics in clinical and community psychology*, Vol. I. New York: Academic Press, 1969.

GOLDSMITH, J. B., and R. M. McFALL, Development and evaluation of an interpersonal skill training program for psychiatric inpatients. *Journal of Abnormal Psychology*, 1975, *84*, 51–58.

GOLDSTEIN, A. P., K. HELLER, and L. B. SECHREST, *Psychotherapy and the Psychology of Behavior Change.* New York: John Wiley, 1966.

GOLDSTEIN, A. P., H. J. MARTENS, H. A. VAN BELLE, W. SCHAAF, H. WIERSMA, and A. GOEDHART, The use of modeling to increase independent behavior. *Behaviour Research and Therapy*, 1973, *11*, 31–42.

GOODRICH, W., R. RYDER, and H. RAUSH, Patterns of newlywed marriage. *Journal of Marriage and Family*, 1968, *30*, 597–602.

GOTTMAN, J. M., N-of-one and N-of-two research in psychotherapy. *Psychological Bulletin*, 1973, *80*, 93–105.

GOTTMAN, J. M., *The topography of marital conflict*, unpublished paper. Bloomington, Indiana: University of Indiana, 1975.

GOTTMAN, J. M., and S. R. LEIBLUM, *How To Do Psychotherapy and How To Evaluate It.* New York: Holt, Rinehart, and Winston, 1974.

GOTTMAN, J. M., R. M. McFALL, and J. T. BARNETT, Design and analysis of research using time series. *Psychological Bulletin*, 1969, *72*, 299–306.

GOUGH, H. G., *Manual for the California Psychological Inventory.* California: Counseling Press, 1967.

GOUGH, H. G., and A. B. HEILBRUN, Jr., *The Adjective Checklist Manual.* Palo Alto, Cal.: Consulting Psychologists Press, 1965.

GREENE, B. L., *A Clinical Approach to Mental Problems: Evaluation and Management.* Springfield, Ill.: C. C. Thomas, 1970.

GRIFFITHS, R. D., and M. JOY, The prediction of phobic behavior. *Behaviour Research and Therapy,* 1971, *9,* 109–118.

GUTRIDE, M., A. P. GOLDSTEIN, and G. F. HUNTER, *The use of modeling and role-playing to increase social interaction among schizophrenia patients,* unpublished manuscript. Syracuse, N.Y.: Syracuse University, 1972.

HAGEN, R. L., Group therapy versus bibliotherapy in weight reduction. *Behavior Therapy,* 1974, *5,* 222–234.

HALEY, J., Marriage therapy. *Archives of General Psychiatry,* 1963, *8,* 213–234.

HARMATZ, M. G., and P. LAPUC, Behavior modification of overeating in a psychiatric population. *Journal of Consulting and Clinical Psychology,* 1968, *32,* 583–587.

HARTMAN, F. R., A behavioristic approach to communication: a selective review of learning theory and a derivation of postulates. *A. V. Communication Review,* 1963, *11,* 155–190.

HARTMANN, D. P., and C. ATKINSON, Having Your Cake and Eating It Too: a note on some apparent contradictions between therapeutic achievements and design requirements in N-1 studies, *Behavior Therapy,* 1973, *4,* 589–591.

HATHAWAY, S. R., Some considerations relative to nondirective psychotherapy counseling as therapy. *Journal of Clinical Psychology,* 1948, *4,* 226–231.

HAUSERMAN, N., S. ZWEBACK, and A. PLOTKIN, Use of concrete reinforcement to facilitate verbal initiation in adolescent group therapy. *Journal of Consulting and Clinical Psychology,* 1972, *38,* 90–96.

HECKEL, R. B., S. L. WIGGENS, and H. C. SALZBERG, Conditioning against silences in group therapy. *Journal of Clinical Psychology,* 1962, *8,* 216–217.

HEDQUIST, F. J., and B. K. WEINHOLD, Behavioral group counseling with socially anxious and unassertive college students. *Counseling Psychologist,* 1970, *17,* 237–242.

HERSEN, M., and A. S. BELLACK, Social skills training for chronic psychiatric patients: rationale, research findings, and future directions. *Comprehensive Psychiatry,* in press.

HERSEN, M., R. M. EISLER, and P. M. MILLER, Development of assertive responses: clinical, measurement, and research considerations. *Behavior Research and Therapy,* 1973, *11,* 505–521.

————, An experimental analysis of generalization in assertive training. *Behaviour Research and Therapy,* 1974, *12,* 295–310.

HERSEN, M., R. M. EISLER, P. M. MILLER, M. B. JOHNSON, and S. G. PINKSTON, Effects of practice, instructions, and modeling on components of assertive behavior. *Behaviour Research and Therapy,* 1973, *11,* 443–451.

HERSEN, M., S. M. TURNER, B. A. EDELSTEIN, and S. G. PINKSTON, Effects of phenothiazines and social skills training in a withdrawn schizophrenic. *Journal of Clinical Psychology,* 1975, *31,* 588–594.

HICKS, M. W., and M. PLATT, Marital happiness and stability: A review of the research in the sixties, in C. B. Broderick, ed., *A Decade of Family Research and Action,* National Council on Family Relations, 1971, 59–78.

HOLLANDER, E. P., J. W. JULIAN, and G. A. HAALAND, Conformity process and prior group support. *Journal of Personality and Social Psychology,* 1965, *2,* 852–858.

HOMME, L. E., A. P. CSANYI, M. A. GONZALES, and J. R. RECHS, *How to Use Contingency Contracting in the Classroom.* Champaign, Ill.: Research Press, 1969.

HOPS, H., WILLS, T. A., PATTERSON, G. R., and WEISS, R. L., The Marital Interaction Coding System, unpublished manuscript, University of Oregon and Oregon Research Institute, 1972.

IHLI, K. L., and W. K. GARLINGTON, A comparison of groups versus individual desensitization of test anxiety. *Behaviour Research and Therapy,* 1969, *7,* 207–210.

JACOBSON, E., *Progressive Relaxation.* Chicago: University of Chicago Press, 1938.

JAKUBOWSKI-SPECTOR, P., Facilitating the growth of women through assertive training. *The Counseling Psychologist,* 1973, *4,* 75–86.

JOHNSON, T., V. TYLER, R. THOMPSON, and F. JONES, Systematic desensitization and assertive training in the treatment of speech anxiety in middle school students. *Psychology in the Schools,* 1971, *8,* 263–267.

JULIAN, J. W., D. W. BISHOP, and F. E. FIEDLER, Quasi-therapeutic effects of intergroup competition. *Journal of Personality and Social Psychology,* 1966, *3,* 321–327.

KAHN, M., Nonverbal communication and marital satisfaction. *Family Process,* 1970, *9,* 449–456.

KANFER, F. H., and J. S. PHILLIPS, *Learning Foundations of Behavior Therapy,* New York: John Wiley, 1970.

KANFER, F. H., and G. SASLOW, Behavioral diagnosis, in C. M. Franks, ed., *Behavior Therapy: Appraisal and Status.* New York: McGraw-Hill, Inc., 1969.

KASS, D. J., F. M. SILVERS, and G. M. ABROMS, Behavioral group treatment of hysteria. *Archives of General Psychiatry,* 1972, *26,* 42–50.

KATAHN, M., S. STRENGER, and N. CHERRY, Group counseling and behavior therapy with test-anxious college students. *Journal of Consulting Psychology,* 1966, *30,* 544–549.

KATZ, D., and R. KAHN, Open system theory, in J. G. Maurer, ed., *Readings In Organizational Theory: Open System Approaches.* New York: Random House, 1971.

KAZDIN, A. E., Covert modeling, imagery assessment, and assertive behavior. *Journal of Consulting and Clinical Psychology,* 1975, *43,* 716–724.

————, Covert modeling, model similarity, and reduction of avoidance behavior. *Behavior Therapy,* 1974a, *5,* 325–340.

————, The effect of response cost and aversive stimulation in suppressing punished and nonpunished speech disfluencies. *Behavior Therapy,* 1973, *4,* 73–82.

————, Effects of covert modeling and model reinforcement on assertive behavior. *Journal of Abnormal Psychology,* 1974, *83,* 240–252.

————, The effects of model, identity, and fear-relevant similarity on covert modeling. *Behavior Therapy,* 1974b, *5,* 624–635.

KELLY, G. A., *The Psychology of Personal Constructs.* New York: W. W. Norton & Company, 1955.

KERLINGER, F. N., *Foundations of Behavioral Research.* (2nd ed.) New York: Holt, Rinehart and Winston, Inc., 1973.

KILLIAN, D. H., The effects of instructions and social reinforcement on selected categories of behavior emitted by depressed persons in a small group setting. *Dissertation Abstracts International,* 1971, *36*(6–B), 3640.

KIMMEL, P. R., and J. W. HAVENS, Game theory vs. mutual identification: two criteria for assessing marital relationship. *Journal of Marriage and Family,* 1966, *28,* 460–465.

KIND, J., The relationship of communication efficiency to marital happiness and an evaluation of short-term training in interpersonal communication. *Dissertation Abstracts International,* 1968, *29,* 1173–B.

KNOX, D., *Marriage Happiness,* Champaign, Ill.: Research Press, 1972.

KONDAS, O., Reduction of examination anxiety and stage fright by group desensitization and relaxation. *Behaviour Research and Therapy,* 1967, *5,* 275–282.

LANDIS, J. T., Social correlates of divorce or nondivorce among the unhappily married. *Marriage and Family Living,* 1963, *25,* 178–180.

LANG, P. J., D. LAZOVIK, and D. J. REYNOLDS, Desensitization suggestibility and pseudotherapy, in G. E. Stollark, B. G. Guerney, and M. Rothberg, eds., *Psychotherapy Research.* Chicago: Rand McNally, 1966.

LAWRENCE, H., and M. SUNDEL, Behavior modification in adult groups. *Social Work,* 1972, *17,* 34–43.

LAWS, D. R., and M. SERBER, Measurement and evaluation of assertive training with sexual offenders, in R. E. Hosford and C. S. Moss, eds., *The Crumbling Walls: Treatment and Counseling of Prisoners.* Champaign, Ill.: University of Illinois Press, 1975.

LAZARUS, A. A., *Behavior Therapy and Beyond.* New York: McGraw-Hill, Inc., 1971.

———, Behavior therapy in groups, in G. M. Gazda, ed., *Basic Approaches to Group Psychotherapy and Group Counseling.* Springfield, Ill.: C. C. Thomas, 1968, 149–175.

———, Behavior rehearsal vs. nondirective therapy vs. advice in effecting behavior change. *Behaviour Research and Therapy,* 1966, *4,* 209–212.

———, Group therapy of phobic disorders by systematic desensitization. *Journal of Abnormal and Social Psychology,* 1961, *63,* 505–510.

LEDERER, W. J., and D. D. JACKSON, *The Mirages of Marriage.* New York: W. W. Norton & Company, 1968.

LEITENBERG, H., The use of single-case methodology in psychotherapy research. *Journal of Abnormal Psychology,* 1973, *82,* 87–101.

LEVINGER, G., and D. J. SENN, Disclosure of feelings in marriage. *Merrill-Palmer Quarterly,* 1967, *1,* 237–249.

LEWINSOHN, P. M., M. S. WEINSTEIN, and T. ALPER, A behavioral approach to the group treatment of depressed persons: a methodological contribution. *Journal of Clinical Psychology,* 1970, *26,* 525–532.

LIBERMAN, R., A behavioral approach to group dynamics: reinforcement and prompting of cohesiveness in group therapy. *Behavior Therapy,* 1970, *1,* 141–175.

LINDSEY, G., and D. BYRNE, Measurement of social choice and interpersonal attractiveness, in G. Lindsey and E. Aronson, eds., *The Handbook of Social Psychology* (2nd ed.). Reading, Mass.: Addison-Wesley, 1968, pp. 452–525.

LINSK, N., M. W. HOWE, and E. M. PINKSTON, Behavioral group work in a home for the aged. *Social Work,* 1975, *20,* 454–463.

LOBITZ, W. C., and J. LoPICCOLO, New methods in the behavioral treatment of sexual dysfunctions. *Journal of Behavior Therapy and Experimental Psychiatry,* 1972, *3,* 265–271.

LOCKE, H. J., *Predicting Adjustment in Marriage.* New York: Holt, Rinehart, and Winston, 1951.

LOMONT, J. F., F. H. GILNER, N. J. SPECTOR, and K. K. SKINNER, Group assertion training and group insight therapies. *Psychological Reports,* 1969, *25,* 463–470.

LOTT, A.J., and B. E. LOTT, Group cohesiveness, communication level, and conformity. *Journal of Abnormal and Social Psychology,* 1961, *62,* 408–412.

MACDONALD, M. L., C. U. LINDQUIST, J. A. KRAMER, R. A. MCGRATH, and L. L. RHYNE, Social skills training: the effects of behavior rehearsal in groups on dating skills. *Journal of Counseling Psychology,* 1975, *22,* 224–230.

MCFALL, R. M., and D. B. LILLESAND, Behavior rehearsal with modeling and coaching in assertion training. *Journal of Abnormal Psychology,* 1971, *77,* 313–323.

MCFALL, R. M., and A. R. MARSTON, An experimental investigation of behavior rehearsal in assertive training. *Journal of Abnormal Psychology,* 1970, *2,* 295–303.

MCFALL, R. M., and C. T. TWENTYMAN, Four experiments on the relative contributions of rehearsal, modeling, and coaching to assertion training. *Journal of Abnormal Psychology,* 1973, *81,* 199–218.

MACPHERSON, E. L. R., Selective operant conditioning and deconditioning of assertive modes of behavior. *Journal of Behavior Therapy and Experimental Psychiatry,* 1972, *3,* 99–102.

MAGER, R. F., *Preparing Instructional Objectives.* Palo Alto, Cal.: Fearon Publishers, 1972.

MAHONEY, M. J., *Cognition and Behavior Modification.* Cambridge, Mass.: Ballinger Publishing Co., 1974.

MALEY, R. F., Group methods and interpersonal learning on a token economy ward, in A. Jacobs and W. Spradlin, eds., *The Group as Agent of Change.* New York: Behavioral Publications, 1974.

MARRONE, R. L., M. A. MERKSAMER, and P. M. SALZBERG, A short duration group treatment of smoking behavior by stimulus saturation. *Behavior Research and Therapy,* 1970, *8,* 347–352.

MASH, E. J., R. LAZERE, L. TERDAL, and A. GARNER, *Modification of mother-child interactions: a modeling approach for groups,* unpublished manuscript. Portland: University of Oregon Medical School, 1970.

MASTERS, W. H., and V. E. JOHNSON, *Human Sexual Inadequacy.* Boston: Little, Brown and Co., 1970.

MEHRABIAN, A., and H. REED, Some determinants of communication accuracy. *Psychological Bulletin,* 1968, *70,* 365–381.

MELNICK, J., Comparison of replication technique in the modification of minimal dating behavior. *Journal of Abnormal Psychology,* 1973, *81,* 51–59.

MENDELSON, L. A., Communication patterns in high and low marital adjustment. *Dissertation Abstracts International,* 1970, *31,* 4919–A.

MILLER, G. R., On defining communication: another stab. *Journal of Communication,* 1966, *16,* 88–98.

MILLER, H. R., and M. M. NAWAS, Control of aversive stimulus termination in systematic desensitization. *Behaviour Research and Therapy*, 1970, *8*, 57–61.

MINTER, R. L., A denotative and connotative study in communication. *Journal of Communication*, 1968, *18*, 26–36.

MISCHEL, W., *Personality and Assessment*, New York: John Wiley, 1968.

MOWRER, O. H., The behavior therapies with special reference to modeling and imitation. *American Journal of Psychotherapy*, 1966, *20*, 429–461.

MURPHY, D. C., and L. A. MENDELSON, Communication and adjustment in marriage: investigating the relationship. *Family Process*, 1973, *12*, 317–326.

MYERS, A. E., Team competition, success, and adjustment of group members. *Journal of Abnormal and Social Psychology*, 1962, *65*, 325–332.

NAVRAN, L., Communication and adjustment in marriage. *Family Process*, 1967, *6*, 173–184.

NYDEGGER, R. V., The elimination of hallucinatory and delusional behavior by verbal conditioning and assertive training. *Journal of Behavior Therapy and Experimental Psychiatry*, 1972, *3*, 225–227.

OAKES, W. F., Reinforcement of Bales categories in group discussion. *Psychological Reports*, 1962, *11*, 425–535.

OAKES, W. F., A. E. DROGE, and B. AUGUST, Reinforcement effects on conclusions reached in group discussion. *Psychological Reports*, 1961, *9*, 27–34.

O'LEARY, K. D., W. C. BECKER, M. B. EVANS, and R. A. SAUDARGAS, A token reinforcement program in a public school: a replication and systematic analysis. *Journal of Applied Behavior Analysis*, 1969, *2*, 3–13.

OLSON, R. P., and D. J. GREENBERG, Effects of contingency-contracting and decision-making groups with chronic mental patients. *Journal of Consulting and Clinical Psychology*, 1972, *38*, 376–383.

OSBORN, S. M., and G. G. HARRIS, *Assertive Training for Women*. Springfield, Ill.: C. C. Thomas, 1975.

PACE, R. W., and R. R. BOREN, *The Human Transaction*. Glenview, Ill.: Scott Foresman & Company, 1972.

PATTERSON, G. R., and J. A. COBB, A dyadic analysis of "aggressive" behaviors: an additional step toward a theory of aggression, in J. P. Hill, ed., *Minnesota Symposia on Child Psychology*, Vol. 5. Minn.: University of Minnesota Press, 1971.

PATTERSON, G. R., and H. HOPS, Coercion, a game for two: intervention techniques for marital conflict, in R. E. Ulrich and P. Mountjay, eds., *The Experimental Analysis of Social Behavior*. Englewood Cliffs, N.J.: Prentice-Hall, Inc., 1972.

PATTERSON, G. R., and J. B. REID, Reciprocity and coercion: two facets of social systems, in C. Neuringer and J. Michael, eds., *Behavior Modification in Clinical Psychology.* Englewood Cliffs, N.J.: Prentice-Hall, Inc., 1970, pp. 1–177.

PAUL, G. L., *Insight vs. Desensitization in Psychotherapy: An Experiment in Anxiety Reduction.* Stanford, Calif.: Stanford University Press, 1966.

PAUL, G. L., and D. T. Shannon, Treatment of anxiety through systematic desensitization in therapy groups. *Journal of Abnormal Psychology,* 1966, 71, 124–135.

PEAL, J., *Responsibility of Administration to Group Therapy Programs.* State of Michigan, Department of Mental Health, Lansing, mimeographed, 1965.

PECKHAM, P. D., G. V. GLASS, and K. D. HOPKINS, The experimental unit in statistical analysis. Journal of Special Education, 1969, 3, 337–349.

PENICK, S. B., R. FILION, S. FOX, and A. J. STUNKARD, Behavior modification in the treatment of obesity. *Psychosomatic Medicine,* 1971, 33, 49–55.

PERCELL, L. P., P. T. BERWICK, and A. BEIGEL, The effects of assertive training on self-concept and anxiety. *Archives of General Psychiatry,* 1974, 31, 502–504.

PERROW, C., Hospitals, technology, structure and goals, in J. G. March ed., *Handbook of Organizations.* Chicago: Rand McNally, 1965.

PHELPS, S., and N. AUSTIN, *The Assertive Woman.* San Luis Obispo, Cal.: Impact Press, 1975.

PIERCE, R. M., and J. DRASGOW, Teaching facilitative interpersonal functioning to neuropsychiatric inpatients. *Journal of Counseling Psychology,* 1969, 16, 295–298.

RAPPAPORT, A. F., and J. HARRELL, A behavioral exchange model for marital counseling. *The Family Coordinator,* 1972, 21, 202–212.

RATHUS, S. A., An experimental investigation of assertive training in a group setting. *Journal of Behavioral Therapy and Experimental Psychiatry,* 1972, 3, 81–86.

———, Instigation of assertive behavior through video tape-mediated assertive models and directed practice. *Behaviour Research and Therapy,* 1973a, 11, 57–65.

———, A 30-item schedule for assessing assertive behavior. *Behavior Therapy,* 1973b, 4, 398–406.

RAUSH, H. L., W. A. BARRY, R. K. HERTEL, and M. A. SWAIN, *Communication, Conflict and Marriage.* San Francisco: Jossey-Bass, 1974.

REID, J. B., Reliability assessment of observation data: a possible methodological problem. *Child Development,* 1971, 41, 1143–1150.

RENNE, K. S., Correlates of dissatisfaction in marriage. *Journal of Marriage and the Family,* 1970, *32,* 54–67.

RICHEY, C., *Increased Female Assertiveness through Self-Reinforcement,* unpublished doctoral dissertation. Berkeley: University of California, 1974.

RIMM, D. C., and D. C. MADEIROS, The role of muscle relaxation in participant modeling. *Behaviour Research and Therapy,* 1970, *8,* 127–132.

RIMM, D. C., and M. J. MALONEY, The application of reinforcement and participant modeling procedures in the treatment of snake-phobic behavior. *Behaviour Research and Therapy,* 1969, *7,* 369–376.

RIMM, D. C., and J. C. MASTERS, *Behavior Therapy: Techniques and Empirical Findings.* New York: Academic Press, 1974.

RITTER, B., The group desensitization of children's snake phobia, using vicarious and contact desensitization procedures. *Behaviour Research and Therapy,* 1968, *6,* 1–6.

ROBINSON, M., and A. JACOBS, The effect of focussed videotape feedback in group psychotherapy with mental hospital patients. *Psychotherapy: Theory, Research and Practice,* 1970, *7,* 169–172.

ROSE, S. D., A behavioral approach to the group treatment of parents. *Social Work,* 1969, *14,* 21–29.

———, Group training of parents as behavior modifiers. *Social Work,* 1974, 156–162.

———, In pursuit of social competence. *Social Work,* 1975, *20,* 33–40.

———, Training parents in groups as behavior modifiers of their mentally retarded children. *Journal of Behavior Therapy and Experimental Psychiatry,* 1974, *5,* 135–140.

———, *Treating Children in Groups.* San Francisco: Jossey-Bass, 1972.

ROSE, S. D., C. COLES, J. FLANAGAN, B. FLANIGAN, and J. SHERMAN, *Behavioral Treatment of Smokers and Weight Watchers in Groups.* Madison: University of Wisconsin, School of Social Work, 1970.

ROSE, S. D., J. L. EDLESON, and J. J. CAYNER, *Interpersonal skill training for social workers,* Social Work, 1976, in press.

ROSE, S. D., J. FLANAGAN, and D. BRIERTON, Counseling in a correctional institution: a social learning approach, paper presented at the National Conference on Social Welfare, Dallas, 1971.

RUTTER, M., *Maternal Deprivation Reassessed.* Baltimore, Md.: Penguin Books, 1972.

RYDER, R., and D. GOODRICH, Married couples responses to disagreements. *Family Process,* 1966, *5,* 18–25.

SATIR, V., *Conjoint Family Therapy.* Palo Alto, Cal.: Science and Behavior Books, Inc., 1964.

————, *Peoplemaking.* Palo Alto, Cal.: Science and Behavior Books, Inc., 1972.

SCHACHTER, S., N. ELLERSTON, D. MCBRIDE, and D. GREGORY, An experimental study of cohesiveness and productivity, in D. Cartwright and A. Zander, eds., *Group Dynamics.* New York: Harper and Row, 1968, pp. 192–198.

SCHAEFER, H. H., M. B. SOBELL, and K. C. MILLS, Baseline drinking behaviors in alcoholics and social drinkers kinds of drinks and sip magnitude. *Behaviour Research and Therapy,* 1971, *9,* 23–28.

SCHINKE, S. P., and S. D. ROSE, Interpersonal skill training in groups. *Journal of Counseling Psychology,* 1976, *23,* 442–448.

SCHWARTZ, A. N., and H. L. HAWKINS, *Patient Models and Affect Statements in Group Therapy.* Proceedings of the 73rd Annual Convention of the American Psychological Association, 1965.

SELLTIZ, C., M. JAHODA, M. DEUTSCH, and S. W. COOK, *Research Methods in Social Research.* New York: Holt, Rinehart and Winston, 1959.

SERBER, M., Teaching the nonverbal components of assertive training. *Journal of Behavior Therapy and Experimental Psychiatry,* 1972, *3,* 179–184.

SHERMAN, T. M., *An examination of the relationship between student behavior change and teacher mode of response,* unpublished doctoral dissertation. Knoxville, Tenn.: University of Tennessee, 1971.

SHERMAN, T. M., and W. H. CORMIER, The use of subjective scales for measuring interpersonal reactions. *Journal of Behavior Therapy and Experimental Psychiatry,* 1972, *3,* 279–280.

SHOEMAKER, M. E., and T. L. PAULSON, Group assertive training for mothers: a family intervention strategy, in E. J. Mash, ed., *Parenting: The Change, Maintenance, and Direction of Healthy Family Behaviors.* New York: Brunner/Mazel, 1976.

SIDMAN, M., *Tactics of Scientific Research.* New York: Basic Books, 1960.

SISTLER, A., *Interpersonal skill training with older persons,* unpublished manuscript. Madison: University of Wisconsin, School of Social Work, 1975.

SKINNER, B. F., *Verbal Behavior.* Englewood Cliffs, N.J.: Prentice-Hall, Inc., 1957.

SLAVIN, D. R., Behavior ratings as an accelerator for retardates in a halfway house, in R. D. Rubin and others, eds., *Advances in Behavior Therapy.* New York: Academic Press, 1972.

SPIVACK, G., and J. SPOTTS, *Devereux Child Behavior (DCB) Rating Scale.* Devon, Penn.: Devereux Foundation Institute for Research and Training, 1966.

STAATS, A. W., Language behavior therapy: a derivative of social behaviorism. *Behavior Therapy,* 1972, *2,* 165–192.

STAATS, A. W., and C. K. STAATS, *Complex Human Behavior: A Systematic Extension of Learning Principles.* New York: Holt, Rinehart and Winston, 1963.

STEVENSON, I., and J. WOLPE, Recovery from sexual deviations through overcoming of nonsexual neurotic responses. *American Journal of Psychiatry,* 1960, *116,* 737–742.

STUART, R. B., Behavioral remedies for marital ills: a guide to the use of operant-interpersonal techniques, in A. S. Gurman and D. G. Rice, eds., *Couples in Conflict: New Directions in Marital Therapy.* New York: Aronson, 1974.

———, Operant-interpersonal treatment for marital discord. *Journal of Consulting and Clinical Psychology,* 1969, *32,* 675–682.

———, A three-dimensional program for the treatment of obesity. *Behavior Research and Therapy,* 1971, *9,* 177–186.

STUART, R. B., and B. DAVIS, *Slim Chance in a Fat World: Behavioral Control of Obesity,* Champaign, Ill.: Research Press, 1972.

TAIT, C. D., and E. T. HODGES, *Delinquents: Their Families and the Community.* Springfield, Ill.: C. C. Thomas, 1962.

THAYER, L. O., On theory building in communication: some conceptual problems. *Journal of Communication,* 1963, *13,* 217–235.

THOMAS, E. S., C. L. WALTER, and K. O'FLAHERTY, A verbal problem checklist for use in assessing family verbal behavior. *Behavior Therapy,* 1974, *5,* 235–246.

THORESON, E. C., and B. POTTER, Behavioral group counseling, in G. M. Gazda, ed., *Basic Approaches to Group Psychotherapy and Group Counseling.* Springfield, Ill.: C. C. Thomas, 1973.

TOLMAN, C. W., and R. H. BARNSLEY, Effects of verbal reinforcement on conformity and deviant behavior: replication report. *Psychological Reports,* 1966, *19,* 910–916.

TRUAX, C. B., and R. R. CARKHUFF, *Toward Effective Counseling and Psychotherapy: Training and Practice.* Chicago: Aldine, 1967.

TRUAX, C. B., and D. G. WARGO, Effects of vicarious therapy pretraining and alternate sessions on outcome in group psychotherapy with outpatients. *Journal of Consulting and Clinical Psychology,* 1969, *33,* 440–447.

TRUAX, C. B., D. G. WARGO, R. R. CARKHUFF, F. KODMAN, Jr., and E. A. MOLES, Changes in self-concepts during group psychotherapy as a function of alternate sessions and vicarious therapy pretaining in institutionalized mental patients and juvenile delinquents. *Journal of Consulting Psychology,* 1966, *30,* 309–314.

TWENTYMAN, C. T., and R. M. McFALL, Behavioral training of social skills in shy males. *Journal of Consulting and Clinical Psychology,* 1975, *43,* 384–395.

UDRY, R. J., *The Social Context of Marriage* (2nd ed.). Philadelphia: Lippincott, 1971.

UDRY, J. R., H. A. NELSON, and R. NELSON, An empirical investigation of some widely held beliefs about marital interaction. *Journal of Marriage and Family Living,* 1961, *23,* 388–390.

UNDERWOOD, B. J., and R. W. SCHULTZ, *Meaningfulness and Verbal Learning.* Philadelphia: Lippincott, 1960.

VEST, L., *Transitional activity group: increasing involvement of deaf clients in community activities through use of contingency contracting of behavioral assignments, role-play, and behavioral rehearsal,* unpublished manuscript. Madison: University of Wisconsin, 1974.

WAGNER, M., Reinforcement of verbal productivity in group therapy. *Psychological Reports,* 1966, *19,* 1217–1218.

WAGNER, M. K., Reinforcement of the expression of anger through role-planning. *Behaviour Research and Therapy,* 1968, *6,* 91–94.

WALKER, H. M., *Walker Problem Behavior Identification Checklist (WPBIC).* Western Psychological Services, 1970.

WALKER, H. M., and J. LEV, *Statistical Inferences.* New York: Holt, Rinehart and Winston, 1953, 284–287.

WALKER, H. M., R. H. MATTSON, and N. K. BUCKLEY, Special class placement as a treatment alternative for deviant behavior in children, in F. A. M. Benson, ed., *Modifying Deviant Social Behavior in Various Classroom Settings,* (Monograph Series 1). Eugene: University of Oregon, Department of Special Education, 1969.

WATSON, D. L., and R. G. THARP, *Self-Directed Behavior: Self-Modification for Personal Adjustment.* Belmont, Cal.: Brooks-Cole Publishing, 1972.

WATZLAWICK, P., J. BEAVIN, and D. D. JACKSON, *Pragmatics of Human Communications.* New York: W. W. Norton & Company, 1967.

WEBB, E. J., D. T. CAMPBELL, R. D. SCHWARTZ, and L. SECHREST, *Unobtrusive Measures: Nonreactive Research in the Social Sciences.* Chicago: Rand McNally, 1966.

WEINMAN, B., P. GELBART, M. WALLACE, and M. POST, Inducing assertive behavior in chronic schizophrenics: a comparison of socioenvironmental, desensitization, and relaxation therapies. *Journal of Consulting and Clinical Psychology,* 1972, *39,* 246–252.

WEISS, R. L., G. R. BIRCHLER, and J. P. VINCENT, Contractual models for negotiation training in marital dyads. *Journal of Marriage and Family Living,* 1974, *36,* 321–330.

WEISS, R. L., H. HOPS, and G. R. PATTERSON, A framework for conceptualizing marital conflict: a technology for altering it, some data for evaluating it, in L. A. Hamerlynck, L. C. Handy, and E. J. Mash, eds., *Behavior Change: Methodology, Concepts, and Practice.* Champaign, Ill.: Research Press, 1973.

WHALEN, D., Effects of a model and instructions on group verbal behavior. *Journal of Consulting and Clinical Psychology,* 1969, *3,* 509–521.

WIEMAN, R. J., D. I. SHOULDERS, and J. H. FARR, Reciprocal reinforcement in marital therapy. *Journal of Behavior Therapy and Experimental Psychology,* 1974, *5,* 291–295.

WILKINS, W., Desensitization: social and cognitive factors underlying the effectiveness of Wolpe's procedures. *Psychological Bulletin,* 1971, *76,* 311–317.

WILLIAMS, R. I., and R. L. BLANTON, Verbal conditioning in a psychotherapeutic situation. *Behaviour Research and Therapy,* 1968, *6,* 97–103.

WILLS, T., R. L. WEISS, and G. R. PATTERSON, A behavioral analysis of the determinants of marital satisfaction. *Journal of Consulting and Clinical Psychology,* 1974, *42,* 802–811.

WINER, B. J., *Statistical Principles in Experimental Design* (2nd ed.). New York: McGraw-Hill, Inc., 1971.

WITKIN, S., and J. Smits, *Group assertive training: Clinical study II,* unpublished manuscript. Madison: University of Wisconsin, School of Social Work, 1974.

WODARSKI, J. S., R. A. FELDMAN, and N. FLAX, Social learning theory and group work practice with antisocial children. *Clinical Social Work Journal,* 1973, *1,* 78–93.

WODARSKI, J. S., R. L. HAMBLIN, D. R. BUCKHOLDT, and D. E. FERRITOR, *The effects of different reinforcement contingencies on cooperative behaviors exhibited,* paper presented at the fifth annual meeting of the Association for the Advancement of Behavior Therapy, Washington, D.C., September 1971.

WOLLERSHEIM, J. P., Effectiveness of group therapy based upon learning principles in the treatment of overweight women. *Journal of Abnormal Psychology,* 1970, *76,* 462–474.

WOLPE, J., *The Practice of Behavior Therapy* (2nd ed.). New York: Pergamon Press, Inc., 1973.

WRIGHT, J. C., The relative efficacy of systematic desensitization and behavior training in the modification of university quiz section participation difficulties. *Dissertation Abstracts International,* 1973, 33, 3328B–3329B.

YOUNG, E. R., D. C. RIMM, and T. D. KENNEDY, An experimental investigation of modeling and verbal reinforcement in the modification of assertive behavior. *Behaviour Research and Therapy,* 1973, *11,* 317–319.

ZANDER, T., *Group assertive training for single women,* unpublished manuscript. Madison: University of Wisconsin, School of Social Work, 1974.

Name Index

Subject Index